JEW

Key Words in Jewish Studies

Series Editors
Deborah Dash Moore, University of Michigan
MacDonald Moore, Vassar College
Andrew Bush, Vassar College

JEW

CYNTHIA M. BAKER

RUTGERS UNIVERSITY PRESS
New Brunswick, New Jersey, and London

Library of Congress Cataloging-in-Publication Data

Names: Baker, Cynthia M., author.

Title: Jew / Cynthia M. Baker.

Description: New Brunswick, New Jersey : Rutgers University Press, [2016] | Series: Key words in Jewish studies ; 8 | Includes bibliographical references and index.

Identifiers: LCCN 2016015517| ISBN 9780813563039 (hardcover : alk. paper) | ISBN 9780813563022 (pbk. : alk. paper) | ISBN 9780813563046 (e-book (web pdf)) | ISBN 9780813573861 (e-book (epub))

Subjects: LCSH: Jews—Identity. | Antisemitism.

Classification: LCC DS143 .B25 2016 | DDC 305.892/4—dc23

LC record available at https://lccn.loc.gov/2016015517

A British Cataloging-in-Publication record for this book is available from the British Library.

Visit our website: http://rutgerspress.rutgers.edu

For Daniel ~ from whom I have learned so much
And to the memory of Marvin Mirsky ~ who first challenged me to
consider the proposition that "religion is ethnicity"

Contents

Foreword

The Rutgers book series Key Words in Jewish Studies seeks to introduce students and scholars alike to vigorous developments in the field by exploring its terms. These words and phrases reference important concepts, issues, practices, events, and circumstances. But terms also refer to standards, even to preconditions; they patrol the boundaries of the field of Jewish studies. This series aims to transform outsiders into insiders and let insiders gain new perspectives on usages, some of which shift even as we apply them.

Key words mutate through repetition, suppression, amplification, and competitive sharing. Jewish studies finds itself attending to such processes in the context of an academic milieu where terms are frequently repurposed. Diaspora offers an example of an ancient word, one with a specific Jewish resonance, which has traveled into new regions and usage. Such terms migrate from the religious milieu of Jewish learning to the secular environment of universities, from Jewish community discussion to arenas of academic discourse, from political debates to intellectual arguments and back again. As these key words travel, they acquire additional meanings even as they occasionally shed long-established connotations. On occasion, key words can become so politicized that they serve as accusations. The sociopolitical concept of assimilation, for example, when turned into a term—assimilationist—describing an advocate of the process among Jews, became an epithet hurled by political opponents struggling for the mantle of authority in Jewish communities.

When approached dispassionately, key words provide analytical leverage to expand debate in Jewish studies. Some key words will be familiar from long use, and yet they may have gained new valences, attracting or repelling other terms in contemporary discussion. But there are prominent terms in Jewish culture whose key lies in a particular understanding of prior usage. Terms of the past may bolster claims to continuity in the present while newly minted language sometimes disguises deep connections reaching back into history. Attention must be paid as well to the transmigration of key words among Jewish languages—especially Hebrew, Yiddish, and Ladino—and among languages used by Jews, knitting connections even while highlighting distinctions.

An exploration of the current state of Jewish studies through its key words highlights some interconnections often only glimpsed and holds out the prospect of a reorganization of Jewish knowledge. Key words act as magnets and attract a nexus of ideas and arguments as well as related terms into their orbits. This series plunges into several of these intersecting constellations, providing a path from past to present.

The volumes in the series share a common organization. They open with a first section, Terms of Debate, which defines the key word as it developed over the course of Jewish history. Allied concepts and traditional terms appear here as well. The second section, State of the Question, analyzes contemporary debates in scholarship and popular venues, especially for those key words that have crossed over into popular culture. The final section, In a New Key, explicitly addresses contemporary culture and future possibilities for understanding the key word.

To decipher key words is to learn the varied languages of Jewish studies at points of intersection between academic disciplines and wider spheres of culture. The series, then, does not seek to consolidate and narrow a particular critical lexicon. Its purpose is to question, not to canonize, and to invite readers to sample the debate and ferment of an exciting field of study.

Andrew Bush
Deborah Dash Moore
MacDonald Moore
Series Co-Editors

Acknowledgments

When the editors of the Key Words in Jewish Studies series contacted me to ask if there was a term or phrase in the broad field of Jewish studies about which I could imagine writing an entire book, I took some time to ponder the prospect. Then, surprised by my own audacity, yet throwing all caution to the wind, I gave in to intellectual curiosity and wrote back with the query "How about *Jew?*" I knew that the proposition was both utterly apt (it is, after all, as "key" a term as one could wish) and utterly absurd (given that it represents one of those proverbial conceptual seas in which one could easily drown). But, most of all, I knew that it promised a challenging and enlightening adventure.

Writing this book has, indeed, been such an adventure, involving forays into fields as diverse as Yiddish studies and genome mapping, postwar Continental philosophy and American art and ethnography, nineteenth-century British literature and race science, and Bible and medieval history, with far-flung expeditions into a dizzying array of associated fields. At every step along the way, I have been accompanied by friends and colleagues generous with both their time and their expertise. Without these guides and companions, I could not have dared the journey whose result is the present volume.

My heartfelt thanks, in this regard, are due, first of all, to Andrew Bush, who sent me my first-ever "fan letter" in response to my book *Rebuilding the House of Israel*; who later invited me to contribute to this series; and who offered invaluable feedback and encouragement throughout the long writing process that ensued. I am deeply grateful to the National Endowment for the Humanities for having funded my participation in a summer seminar on the Jews of Venice, and for subsequently having awarded me a full-year fellowship for this book project. I am likewise deeply grateful to Bates College for generous funding and research time contributed toward the completion of the book; to the Bates Ladd Library staff for help in acquiring research materials; and to my Bates faculty colleagues—in particular, John Strong, Thomas Tracy, Lisa Maurizio, Margaret Imber, Thomas Hayward, Senem Aslan (for help with the Turkish materials), Laura Balladur (for help with French linguistics), and Donald Dearborn (for help with the genetics materials).

Many friends, colleagues, and students have contributed to my greater understanding of elements of this capacious subject and to the refinement of my ability to convey that understanding. Some of these have gifted me with brief or extended conversations by e-mail or in person, some by commenting on drafts of chapters or parts of chapters, some by inviting me to deliver papers or presentations, some by inviting me to advise their undergraduate theses, and some in less tangible fashion. Among these, I would like especially to acknowledge Catherine Bell, mentor and friend, of fond memory and Daniel Boyarin, whose scholarly insights enrich every chapter of this book; along with Howard Adelman, Shaul Bassi, Murray Baumgarten, Julia Watts Belser, Ellen Birnbaum, Nathaniel Bowe, Ross Brann, Adina Brin, Denise Buell, Elizabeth Castelli, Steven Fine, Charlotte Elisheva Fonrobert, Katharina Galor, Maxine Grossman, Susannah Heschel, Teresia Hinga, Steven Pavlos Holmes and Carlene Holmes Pavlos, Stefanie Hoss, Tal Ilan, Tamar Kamionkowski, Eliza Kaplan, Gil Klein, Ross Kraemer, Michal Kravel, Hayim Lapin, Jon Lewis, Susan Marks, Catherine Murphy, David Nirenberg, Donald Polaski, Adele Reinhartz, Samantha Rothberg, Natalie Schriebman, Elisabeth Schüssler Fiorenza, Seth Schwartz, Naomi Seidman, Deepti Shenoy, Lawrence Wills, and various anonymous manuscript readers. I ask indulgence from others whose names belong on this list but do not appear, as a result of my oversight. Thank you to the series editors, Deborah Dash Moore, MacDonald Moore, and Andrew Bush, whose sensitive readings and wise comments have helped to improve parts of the manuscript, and to Marlie Wasserman, of Rutgers University Press, whose patience and judicious nudging have enabled it to come to fruition in the course of time.

Finally, I am, as always, indebted to my beloved partner and in-house editor extraordinaire, Seth Mirsky, and to my wonderful extended family, whose perplexity over my scholarly work has never for a moment diminished their sustaining love and support for me.

Jew or *Jew*? A Note on Orthography

Throughout this book I have chosen to italicize the noun *Jew*. *Jew* in italics may be read as signifying a word, figure, person, allegory, metaphor, phantasm, caricature, synecdoche, image, stereotype, identity, persona, and the like. To what may be the consternation of many readers, I do not employ italics (or "scare quotes"), as opposed to roman type, to distinguish between real *Jews*—or "real" *Jews*—and *Jew(s)* as figment or figure, nor between *Jew* as self and *Jew* as other. It serves the critical aims of this study to keep all dimensions of the word *Jew* in provocative and, I hope, productive tension with one another. The same aim conditions the occasional merging of the singular (*Jew*) and plural (*Jews*) through the use of the parenthetical (*s*)—as in *Jew(s)*. The word *Jewish* is rarely italicized here, however, as it seems often to carry a far more circumscribed charge than does the noun form. I address this distinction further, below.

In italicizing every occurrence of the term *Jew* (apart from those that appear in quotations by other authors), I invite the reader always to read the term with the complex depth and dimensionality it harbors, and to maintain the sense of heightened attentiveness to it that italics tend to evoke. To this end, as well, I often treat the collective form of the word— *Jews* or *the Jews*—grammatically as a singular, rather than plural, noun. Again, this choice is intended to interrupt the equivalency reflexively assumed between word and material object / subject, and to replace that unselfconscious equivalency with the critical tensions and questions associated with the *word* as a cultural artifact. This is to say, even when the word *Jews* is used to designate a group of people who self-identify or are identified by others by the term, a far larger—or, at times, far more partial—world of meanings and questions inevitably attends such usage. To the best of my ability, I avoid treating the word as though it bore a single or self-evident definition. Rather, the word *Jew(s)* and its worlds and ways of meaning are precisely the objects and subject matter of this study.

JEW

Introduction

A good friend in college once told me a story about his parents' search for an apartment while his father was stationed at an army base in Louisiana during World War II. After much looking and many dead ends, the young couple found the perfect place and were wrapping up a congenial conversation with the prospective landlady when she came out with her final question: "You're not *Jews*, are you? I don't rent to *Jews*." Without missing a beat, my friend's father, so I am told, replied, "We're Hebrews," a response that apparently satisfied the landlady. A few days after having signed the long-term lease and moved in, the young couple were startled by a loud banging on their front door. They opened it to find the landlady, quite beside herself, fuming and sputtering in furious agitation. "A Hebrew is a *Jew*! You're *Jews*!" she spat. Again, without missing a beat, my friend's father nodded and replied, "Yeah, how 'bout that?" as he closed the door in the landlady's face.

Another, more bemusing, anecdote: A number of years ago, in an undergraduate course I was teaching on Jewish ethics at a university in California, a Jewish student born and raised in Israel, whose parents were Israeli expatriates, insisted in class—unequivocally and unselfconsciously—that *Jew* is a derogatory term. The assertion was challenged by another Jewish student—this one American born and bred—who countered that *Jew* is a "neutral" descriptor, like *Buddhist* or *Canadian*, and that she, for one, was proud to call herself a *Jew*. Unmoved, the young Israeli held his ground, insisting that *Jew*, like every other ethnic slur, is never merely descriptive but always demeaning.

So who decides what the word *Jew* means and connotes? Who gets to "own" it? We tend to think that bigotry ought not determine the meaning or content of identity terms; that those who identify by a particular name should, instead, be able to establish its meaning—or at least have the final say in determining its primary connotations. But can this ever be the case for the name *Jew*? Has it ever been so?

Jew is no simple ethnic slur—in fact, it need not, in itself, be a slur at all, despite its ready and recognizable uses as such. As the above anecdotes illustrate, *Jew*, for some, is a term of deep pride or desire; for others, it is a term of deep loathing. Is it ever "neutral," in the way that my American student presumed *Canadian* or *Buddhist* to be? Were one to see *Jew* spray-painted on a wall almost anywhere in the world, in almost any language, would its impact not be measurably different from the same treatment of these other terms? And yet the words *Jew* and *Jews* are also stock-in-trade in the mundane world of academic Jewish studies, where they regularly serve as descriptors whose meaning is often treated as self-evident. Context, although key, is not everything when it comes to the word *Jew.*

To further parse the classroom exchange described above: The young Israeli's assertion is entirely comprehensible within the context of a strain of Zionism that, from early on, drew on images of *Jews* "in Diaspora" as degraded and unhealthy in order to encourage immigration by those who might, in their own nation-state, become wholesome, muscular "Hebrews" and, later, "Israelis" settling, working on, and defending the Homeland.[1] Stereotypes of unwholesome and corrupt *Jews* came ready-made from the nationalist narratives, related folklores, and racialized "science" of emerging modern Europe and were put to use by both Jewish nationalists and Jewish Communists. It would be far too simplistic, then, and not terribly enlightening, to label people on one or another side of these campaigns as "self-hating," just as it would be far too facile to characterize the fraughtness of the word *Jew* as purely a "Gentile issue," or a function of Jewish assimilation (or of a lack of Jewish assimilation), or in the terms of any of a number of superficial, reductive analyses proffered by various scholars and cultural critics over the years.

What is it about this particular identity term—*Jew*—such that it can be made to convey so broad a range of often diametrically opposed meanings? *Jew* has served as a cipher for materialism *and* intellectualism, socialism *and* capitalism, worldly cosmopolitanism *and* clannish parochialism, eternal chosenness *and* unending curse—and the list goes on. What is the fascination and phobia of *Jew*, and whence does the word derive such persistent malleability and power throughout history and across continents—even to the modern "Far East"? In *Chinese Perceptions of the 'Jews' and Judaism*, Zhou Xun recites a litany of opposites very similar to the above, of "definitions of 'Jew' [*Youtai*] in modern China." She concludes with the wry observation that "anything which is not Chinese is Jewish, at the same time anything which is Chinese is also Jewish; anything which the Chinese aspire to is Jewish, at the same time anything which the Chinese despise is Jewish."[2]

This book seeks to offer a coherent and sustained study of this key word, *Jew*, that lies not only at the heart of Jewish experience and Jewish studies but, indeed, at the heart of Western civilization and beyond. No attempt is made here to survey and catalogue all the many ways in which the term has been and is used, nor the full variety of meanings assigned it in the myriad contexts, languages, locales, and time periods in which it appears, for that would be an impossible undertaking. In any case, many excellent studies of the meanings and images associated with *Jew* in various historical contexts are already available. David Nirenberg's *Anti-Judaism: The Western Tradition*, for example, has recently sought to proffer a kind of global "history of thinking about [and 'with'] 'Judaism'" from ancient Egypt to Nazi Europe.[3] Neither do I directly engage the "who is a *Jew?*" question, except to reflect on the phenomenon as a way to illuminate some of the cultural dynamics out of which the question arises and to which it gives shape. Rather, the project of this book is to explore the significance and implications of a single key insight regarding the word *Jew*.

Owning the Word

Those identified as *Jews* have not, in fact, owned the word *Jew* or controlled the discourse about it—or even much used the term—for most of the past two thousand years. There is a striking paucity of *Jew* as a *self-designation* from the second century CE to the cusp of the modern era.[4] *Jew* does not feature in the traditional service of the *siddur* (Jewish daily prayers) or *machzor* (Jewish Holy Day liturgies). It rarely appears in midrash or Talmud (the classical postbiblical Jewish canon). In the vast majority of writing by *Jews* before the modern period—a body of literature largely comprising commentary on the biblical and classical texts, liturgical poetry, sermons, and responsa (ethical and legal deliberations)—one is hard pressed to find much use of the name *Jew*. There are, of course, exceptions to this generalization. Most significant is the Yiddish word *yid* (or *yeed*), a word whose functions in Yiddish vernaculars can be strikingly different from those of *Jew*—much less "Yid"—in dominant Western languages (see chapter 2). Instead, *yisrael* or *b'nei yisrael* (*bar yisroel* in Yiddish, from talmudic Aramaic)—"sons/son of Israel"—was the common self-referential identity term, a name that is now more or less confined to liturgical or Orthodox use, while *Israeli* names a citizen of a modern nation-state who might or might not identify as a *Jew*. Even for much of the past few centuries of Jewish usage, the term *Jew* has often been strategically exchanged for "Hebrew." Such exchange appears in the above account of the angry landlady or, more familiarly, in the names of such public institutions as the YMHA and YWHA (founded in 1854 and 1888, respectively), the Jewish (or "Hebrew") counterparts to the "Christian" YMCA and YWCA. "Israelite" has often functioned similarly, as in the French organization Alliance Israélite Universelle, whose 1860 founding charter juxtaposes *"israélites idéalistes et militants"* to *"juifs ou tous ceux qui sont victims de préjugés"* in a fashion not unrelated to the Zionist usages described above.[5]

By contrast, for most of two long millennia, the word *Jew* has been predominantly defined and delimited as a term for *not-self*. It has often signified an absolute *other*, the very antithesis of the Western Christian *self*. Almost all modern Western forms of the word—*Jew, Jude, juif, Judío, giudeo, jood, Zsidó*, etc. (and even the Yiddish word *yid*)—came into being in decidedly Christian-dominant societies and geopolitical contexts, and, with the exception of *yid*, they seem often to have taken their earliest written form in commentaries, translations, and sermons on the New Testament by Christians for Christians. In fact, the word *Jew(s)* appears with far greater frequency in the Christian New Testament and bears far greater significance there than it does in the Hebrew Bible / Old Testament, where it is rare.

The most persistent meanings and force of the term *Jew(s)* derive, then, from an antique Christian worldview in which *the Jews* functions foundationally as a kind of originary and constitutional alterity, or otherness. *The Jews* serves as the alpha to the Christian omega; the "Old" to the Christian "New"; the "particular" to the Christian "universal"; grounded and bound materialism to visionary, redeemed spirituality; deicide to self-sacrificial love—at best, the sainted or moribund "ancestor"; at worst, the evil "spawn of Satan" to a godly, good, and triumphantly immortal Christianity. *The Jews*, in other words, serves instrumentally to name the key *other* out of which *and* over against which the Christian *self* was and is constituted. *Jew* is Christian cultures' signifier for the fraught, debased, material primordiality *out of which* spiritual and moral stature must *arise, from which* it may *free itself*, and *back to which* it is always in danger of *falling* (a threat or condition commonly labeled "Judaizing"). Hence, *Jew(s)* becomes a key element in formulations of Christian identity through narratives of origin, aspiration, and liberation, as well as of abjection, rejection, and otherness.

Part of what this means is that *Jew(s)*—signifier and signified, word and connotations—has become a constant element not only in the historical formation and formulation of Western (Christian and post-Christian) identities but also of the categories by which the contours of identity are articulated. Some key examples may serve to illustrate this observation.

To begin with, Saint Augustine, in his biblical commentaries, sermons, and letters, is among the most significant articulators of Christian uses and meanings of *Jew*. "*Jew, Jewish, Judaism, synagogue, Israel*: These words and their cognates appear countless times in Augustine's writings, as in the writings of most patristic authors," notes Paula Fredriksen in *Augustine and the Jews*.[6] That these earliest formulators of Christian doctrine made such heavy use of *Jew(s)* and related words speaks volumes about the words' centrality to the historical creation of Christian identity and worldview. For Augustine, as for many Christian theologians before and since, *the Jews* names "a miserable enslavement of the spirit" that manifests an inability "to lift the eye of the mind above what is corporeal and created, that it may drink in eternal light."[7] Mortal and moral blindness characterizes both the condition of all humanity before the coming of Christ and the subsequent affliction of all those who remain unenlightened by Christian virtue and proper biblical interpretation. "Pagans" might be converted, enlightened, and assimilated into the "us" of the universal Christian community. Errant "flesh" might be tamed and disciplined to give way to the higher aspirations of an eternal "spirit." *Jew*, by contrast, represents an affliction unsusceptible to remedy and, hence, like flesh to spirit, an ongoing danger to the spiritually striving "we."

Developed to combat the wide diversity of belief and practice *among Christians* of his, and prior, centuries, Augustine's formulations about *Jews* were not clearly directed toward persons identified by that name. Rather, they were directed at his own Christian ecclesiastical colleagues and opponents and served to delineate, in his terms, *what it meant to be a proper Christian.*

In a doctrine that came to have profound effect on subsequent generations of Christian theologians and heads of state, Augustine insisted that *Jews*, as afflicted affliction, as self-perpetuating "miserable enslavement," as inherent other, *must be sustained* in service to orthodox Christianity as emblem and assurance of the truth of the Church's theological claims. *Jews* names eternal "signposts" along the historical path that leads to Christian Truth; indeed, it names the very "desk" upon which those Christian Truths are recorded, read, and studied. *Jews* signifies simultaneously the chosenness and antiquity to which emerging orthodox Christianity laid claim and the visible abjection, degradation, and suffering to which all enemies of God and Truth are eternally condemned. *Jews* signifies all this and more to Augustine, his colleagues, and his heirs. In this sense, *Jews* becomes the very substrate upon which the towering edifice of Christendom is founded.

Later on, *Jew* as foundational mirror-opposite is strikingly distilled in the images of Synagoga and her twin, Ecclesia, that appear in medieval art throughout Europe. In one of the better-known examples of the genre, on the western portal of the thirteenth-century Cathedral of Notre Dame in Paris, the two figures flank the central, enthroned Christ in perfect symmetry: Ecclesia (Church) at the right hand of Christ, Synagoga on the sinister (left) side. Ecclesia wears a crown; Synagoga's lies fallen at her feet. Ecclesia looks forward; Synagoga bends under the weight of abjection, the Edenic serpent wound about her head rendering her blind. Ecclesia bears an upright Eucharistic chalice and cross-surmounted standard with wind-filled pennant; Synagoga's lance-shaped standard is broken, her pennant furled, and the upside-down tablets of the "Old Law" dangle in her limp grasp. From Ecclesia's full waist hangs a pilgrim's flask; Synagoga's emaciated midsection is cinched by an ever-tightening belt. The number and placement of such twin figures—upon the portals, windows, and altarpieces of Europe's cathedrals, as well as in the ornamentation of Christian holy books from as early as the ninth century—bespeak the vital role of haunted reflection or counterpart assigned to *the Jews* throughout millennia of Christian self-representation.

The modern rise of secularism and the nominal separation of church and state saw no diminution of appeals to *Jew(s)* as an antithetical key to the formulation of Western cultural identities. Although the "final solution" of the Nazi Reich is the most obvious and shattering modern instance of such appeal, rhetoric from the French Revolution provides earlier examples, including the following, composed in a somewhat different key.

On December 23, 1789, Stanislas Clermont-Tonnerre famously proposed to the Revolutionary French National Assembly: "We must refuse everything to the Jews as a nation and accord everything to Jews as individuals."[8] The declaration is emblematic for the way in which it invokes *(the) Jews* to grapple with larger fundamental questions regarding the relationship between collectives and individuals in a modern democracy. *The Jews* is here identified as "a nation," but the larger speech in which this declaration occurs also refers to the collective as a "religion" or "creed"; a "people," "organization," or "association." "They should not be allowed to form in the state either a political body or an order," concludes Clermont-Tonnerre in a statement that points to—and beyond— *Jews*. "They must be citizens individually. It is repugnant to have in the state an association of non-citizens and a nation within the nation."[9]

Clermont-Tonnerre's speech is notable, as well, for the way in which *the Jews* stands as "they" in opposition to the presumptive "we" of French democracy and nation; the seemingly particular exception to an otherwise universal humanity and the declaration of individual rights made in its name. *Jews* becomes the key *other* whose relationship to the collective French *self* will determine the authenticity of the Revolution's democratic claims. "Few people treated the debate on the Jews as concerning only 'a part of society,'" observes Gary Kates, who continues: "Non-Jews chose to address this issue because the emancipation debate was not really about the Jews at all. Since there were so few Jews in France, and since they played little role in the Revolution, they were easily turned into symbols of something else. . . . The debate over Jewish emancipation was . . . a debate over what it meant to be a French citizen."[10] The French revolutionary debate about *Jews* was a debate about the constitution of the Western democratic subject or self. The Dreyfus affair a century later might be characterized in a similar fashion.[11] The ability of *Jew(s)* to serve this function on the modern European political stage owes no small debt to Augustine's much earlier utilization of *Jew(s)* in constituting his primordial Christian subject in the Roman imperial era.

A crucial element of the modern emancipation debates—one that will be explored in greater detail in chapter 1—concerns what have become, in our era, two of the chief categories by which Western identities are formulated: ethnicity and religion. The two are opposed in Clermont-Tonnerre's speech, which contrasts nation/people to religion/creed as divisible, self-evidently discrete, and mutable attributes of individual identity. Here again, *Jew(s)* serves as the axis around which this particular distinction takes shape (a shape that emerges long before the European Enlightenment, as we shall see). The discrete and opposing nature of these categories has since that time become a given in the articulation of late modern and postmodern identities—especially *Jewish* ones: "I am a *Jew* by ethnicity," goes a familiar assertion, "but I don't practice the religion."

The question of what *Jew* signifies, then, is embedded in very particular ways in the construction and negotiation of foundational categories and concerns of Western identities and cultures. In part this is because *Jew* also comes to signify the confusion or insufficiency of emerging or established categories. One of the more pointed readings of this dynamic is offered by Zygmunt Bauman, who coins the term "allosemitism" to describe what he perceives as a Western cultural gestalt that goes beyond the simple dichotomy of antisemitism versus philosemitism. (*Semite* is a peculiar modern euphemism for *Jew*.)[12] Allosemitism, for Bauman, names "a radically ambivalent attitude" associated with *Jew*, a kind of "apprehension and vexation related not to something or someone disquieting through otherness and unfamiliarity, but to something or someone that does not fit the structure of the orderly world, does not fall easily into any of the established categories . . . [but] tend[s] to sit astride all the usual divides and elide all the criteria normally deployed to draw them."[13]

An unexpected illustration of this singular quality associated with *Jew* may be found in twenty-first-century Turkey, where the term is applied to people who would not self-identify as *Jews*. In the first decade of this century, according to Mesut Yeğen, the doubled name "*Jew* Kurds" (*Yahudi Kürtler*) began to appear in Turkish popular media, along with all manner of reports about the crypto-Jewishness of Muslim Kurds, their suppressed genetically Jewish ancestry, and their purported ties to Israel.[14] The phrase "*Jew* Kurds" appears to belong to a complex Turkish nationalist narrative that figures all Kurds as unassimilable, transnational, internal aliens in modern Turkey and Iraq who "do not fit the structure of the orderly world" (a world of recognized nation-states, of Turkish republican values, of "mainstream" Islam, of enlightened modernity, etc.), which they thereby disrupt, destabilize, and call into question. Although *Kurd*, alone, would appear to function, in this context, in a fashion that resonates with Bauman's claims about *Jew*, the wedding of the two names in Turkish nationalist discourse evokes much larger frames and claims than the regionally specific *Kurd* could evoke on its own.

An ironic counterpoint to this phenomenon is found in the international frenzy over an opinion essay published in a Turkish newspaper in 2008 by the former director of the Essen Center for Turkish Studies in Germany, Faruk Şen. In what Şen understood to be a gesture of solidarity with Turkish *Jews* and, in particular, with Turkish Jewish businessman İshak Alaton, who had publicly criticized what he had identified as Turkish state-sponsored antisemitism, Şen reportedly wrote: "Five million two hundred thousand Turks live in Europe, which once attempted to rid itself of Jews through acts of extreme horror. They [Turks] have become the new Jews of Europe . . . they suffer discrimination and exclusion just as the Jews did—though to a different degree and with different outward appearances."[15] He concluded the essay: "We, as European Turks, know your value to our country. As Europe's new Jews, your 5.2 million comrades in Europe understand you the best. Don't allow the anti-Semitic attitudes of certain groups in Turkey to upset you, we, as the Turkish nation and Europe's new Jews[,] are behind you."[16] When Şen's words were translated from Turkish to German and reported in the *Frankfurter Allgemeine Zeitung*, his German executive board forced his resignation from the institute he had helped to found and had overseen for twenty-three years. The board reportedly accused Şen of inciting "racial friction" and suspended him despite pleas from Alaton and the general secretary of the Central Council of Jews in Germany, Stephan Kramer, who insisted that "he is neither a Holocaust relativizer nor an anti-Semite," but he "had always been a friend to the Jewish community."[17] Comments in the German press at the time, according to Şen, asserted that "Jews *were being insulted in the article.*"[18] In referring to Turks as "*Europe's new Jews,*" Şen was hardly introducing a novel formulation. He was, in fact, participating in a popular discourse that had begun to emerge years before and that continues to this day. In chapter 3, I explore this discourse, and others, built around conceptions of *new Jews.*

Jew often functions, then, on the one hand, as a malleable tool for constructing, testing, clarifying, and challenging ever-changing and ever-evolving cultural forms and analyses and, on the other, as a bedeviling and anxiety-provoking violation of all such forms, boundaries, and classifications. *Jew*, in Western vernaculars, has long been a name for the internal and constitutive other, as well as the persistent fly in the ointment of grand cultural projects and narratives. What it has *not* long been is a name for the (collective or individual) self. The historically recent appropriation of *Jew*, in dominant Western vernaculars, as a term of self-identification is the result of a centuries-long process. It is one that is inescapably (and intriguingly) fraught, not only because of the term's history, but because even now—perhaps especially now—the name *Jew* defies all claims to proper possession or exclusive ownership.

A case in point is the popular maxim that, "after Auschwitz, we are all *Jews.*" In John Biguenet's short story "I Am Not a Jew," for example, the lead character's wife insists: "After Hitler . . . what choice do we have? We have to be Jews, all of us."[19] This impassioned assertion follows on the American tourist-protagonist's run-in with German neo-Nazi skinheads who address him as *Judenschwein*—to which he replies, sincerely, if ungrammatically, "*Ich bin nicht Juden.*" Not so, his wife insists, for when "they split the world into Jews and Nazis," not choosing to be a *Jew* means winding up "on the wrong side."[20]

That's all very well and good, others would contend, but such people are not *real Jews*, and for those of us who are *born Jews*, it is not a choice. Yet Shawn Landres, cofounder and CEO of Jumpstart, "a thinkubator for sustainable Jewish innovation," would seem to disagree.[21] "Today," he says, "we [who identify as *Jews*] are all Jews by choice because we have the opportunity to choose something other than Judaism [or Jewishness] every day."[22]

The foregoing varied and contradictory assertions highlight a key aspect of modern appropriations and arbitrations of claims to *Jew* as a name for self: namely, a veritable explosion in modifiers. "Real" *Jews*, for example, are presumably distinguishable from "imaginary" or "figural" or "pseudo" *Jews.*[23] And yet, when the title character of Woody Allen's film *Annie Hall* tells her suitor Alvy Singer, "You're what Grammy Hall would call a 'real Jew,'" the utility of the modifier "real" for clarifying or distinguishing much of anything is shown to be illusory, at best.[24] Allen pushes the point further when Alvy joins Annie and her family for an Easter dinner of ham with all the trimmings and finds himself imagining Annie's Grammy Hall picturing him in the seventeenth-century garb and barbering of an Eastern European Hasid—Alvy's vision of a "real" *Jew.* This example may illustrate why—at least, in scholarly writing—"real" (as well as *Jew*) frequently appears in quotation marks, signaling a recognition that reality has many dimensions, aspects, and interrelations, not all of which manifest on the same order but which all have measurable effect in the perceptible world.

Jew "by birth" is frequently juxtaposed with Jew "by choice" or "by religion." But, again, the genealogical modifier can carry radically different meanings and implications in different contexts (medical versus halachic versus nationalist or racist, for example), at least as much as do the phrases "by choice" or "by religion," to which it is commonly set in opposition. Moreover, "according to the [Reform Judaism] movement's decision on patrilineal descent, the supposition of Jewishness conferred by birth must be authenticated by the individual's commitment to Judaism. Thus the born-Jew also becomes a Jew by choice."[25] "New Jews," a phrase that, as previously noted, has been employed in a variety of contexts at the turn of the newest millennium (and only sometimes as a label for recent converts to Judaism), carries a startling echo to the phrase "New Christians" coined centuries ago to describe Christianized Jews, as well as their generations of descendants in a Europe marked by state-enforced conversions and a conformity to Christianity policed by the Inquisition. The multiplication of modifiers for Jew is itself an intriguing modern phenomenon inviting exploration and analysis, and one that I take up at various points throughout this book.

In offering the above handful of examples of Jew(s) in modern discourse, I intend merely to observe that the use of the term (and its variations) in each and every such statement conveys understandable meaning laced with complex, historically and ideologically laden connotations. Each appropriation of the name as a self-designation—collective and individual, with and without modifiers—may be subject to contention and contestation while explicitly serving as an act of identity construction and empowerment. There are, certainly, institutionalized arbiters of who and what count(s) as Jew(s) in many different contexts—Jewish Federations, day schools, and synagogues are among such arbiters, as were the Nazi Reich and its erstwhile neo-Nazi spawn; as are the legislature and courts of Israel and many other nation-states; as is Halacha (rabbinic jurisprudence), variously determined; as is the Oxford English Dictionary, among others. Yet, ultimately, no one person, group of people, or institution has, or can have, a lock on this deceptively simple but powerful key word, Jew.

Tracking the term Jew through diverse eras, contexts, and genres, it turns out, can provide a way of seeing—with depth and nuance—the ongoing construction and negotiation of "the West" and of the westernized self in a wide array of registers.

Jews, Jew, the Jews, the Jew, Jewish, Jewess

If you recently used Google to search for the word "Jew," you may have seen results that were very disturbing. . . . If you use Google to search for "Judaism," "Jewish" or "Jewish people," the results are informative and relevant. So why is a search for "Jew" different? One reason is that the word "Jew" is often used in an anti-Semitic context. Jewish organizations are more likely to use the word "Jewish" when talking about members of their faith.[26]

This "explanation of our search results" appeared prominently for years (although no longer) on the first results page when one searched the word "Jew" using Google's Internet search engine. The explanation continued, "Someone searching for information on Jewish people would be more likely to enter terms like 'Judaism,' 'Jewish people,' or 'Jews' than the single word 'Jew.'"

Assuming these assertions to be true—and Google's search algorithms presumably bore them out—why is it the case that "Jewish organizations" and genuinely inquisitive people "would be more likely" to avoid the singular noun *Jew* in favor of the adjective *Jewish*, or even the plural *Jews*, whereas "anti-Semites" would be more likely to gravitate to the singular *Jew*? What accounts for these patterns—patterns that go well beyond the particulars of Google searches or broader Internet practices and might be found throughout popular culture and common usage? No similar disparities between singular and plural or noun and adjective seem to obtain, for example, for terms like "Christian(s)" or "Swede/Swedish"—either as Internet search terms or as general identity labels. Nor have such predilections regarding the grammar of *Jew* always been in evidence.

For the writer of the Gospel of John, as for later theologians like Augustine and Martin Luther, *the Jews*, definite plural, names a problem and an evil seldom condensed or essentialized into the singular. An individual *Jew* like Jesus, Peter, Paul, or Mary can even escape all association with the ills attributed to the collective category. That said, the character of the betrayer in the Christian Gospel narratives, *Judas*, bears the name from which the noun *Jew* itself derives. The identification of this singular *Judas* with *Jew* persists as a trope through centuries of Christian anti-Jewish art and literature.[27]

By the time Christopher Marlowe writes *The Jew of Malta* (featuring a character named Barabbas, after the criminally militant foil to the imprisoned Jesus in the Gospel narratives) and Shakespeare creates, in *The Merchant of Venice*, his Shylock, "*the Jew*" (shadow double to the Christian "Merchant," for whom *the Jew* is both life's blood and death threat), the singular noun has come fully to stand for a potent distillation of the collective. The exemplum- or specimen-like nature of such a *Jew* receives further emphasis through application of the definite article: *the Jew*, in particular, becomes the facilitating device for a host of ideological projects. *The Jew* takes its place among other iconic figures and tropes (the witch, the devil, the fool, the king, etc.) that populate medieval and modern morality plays, fables, folktales, and other phantasmic productions. It is largely from this *Jew*, especially in its guises as "moneylender," "peddler," or "-monger," that the verb "to jew"—defined along the lines of "to cheat or overreach . . . to drive a hard bargain . . . to haggle"—derives.²⁸ Deadly renderings of *the Jew* by the likes of Henry Ford (*The International Jew*, 1920–1922) and Joseph Goebbels (*Der Jude*, 1929, and compare the 1940 Nazi propaganda film *Der Ewige Jude*, "The Eternal Jew") are well known and continue to be widely disseminated. Thus, *the Jew* as a longstanding popular signifier for the contemptible goes some way toward explaining the persistent discomfort of many with the grammatically singular *Jew*, its particular appeal to bigots, and hence some "very disturbing" Google search results.

The Jews, like *the Jew*, can and does function in a similar fashion, as described above, most often in polemical contexts. But unlike *"The Jew of Malta,"* plural phrases like *"the Jews* of Malta," *"the Jews* in antiquity," *"the Jews* under Ottoman rule," or *"Cultures of the Jews"* tend to appear less burdened by the essentialism that prevails in the absence of such accompanying, qualifying prepositions.²⁹ Such appearances, however, are deceiving. As Andrew Bush observes about the latter phrase, *"Cultures of the Jews,"* the title of a multivolume project hailed at the time of its publication for its innovative approach to historiography of *Jews*, "Biale [the editor] rewrites 'the culture' as the plural 'cultures' in his title, but it will require a new key in Jewish Studies to learn to eliminate the 'the' that so frequently universalizes some Jews as 'the Jews.'"³⁰

Whereas many now use the term *Jew* casually, unpointedly, and without a second thought, *Jew* is nonetheless often avoided in day-to-day speech by others who perceive that avoidance to be a gesture of politeness or social sensitivity. "Hebrew" or "Israelite," as previously noted, have sometimes been substituted for *Jew* in English, and *Evrei* is now widely used this way in Russian, having replaced the abused and abusive *Zhid*. *Ebreo* is now standard in Italian. *Musevi* (from Musa—that is, Moses; hence, "Mosaist") serves the same "neutralizing" impulse in Turkish, where it can take the place of the often derogated *Yahudi* (from the Arabic). Yet such avoidance can clearly have the effect of reinforcing the sense that there is something inherently distasteful or despicable in the identification *Jew*. In other words, avoidance can let bigotry have the final say. This dynamic is perhaps most complicated in places like contemporary Germany, where *Jew—Jude—*bears a particularly heavy burden. In common parlance there, one might hear, instead, *Israelitische*, or the careful circumlocutions *Deutsche mosaischen Glaubens* ("a German of Mosaic faith") or *unsere jüdischen Mitbürger* ("our Jewish fellow citizen").[31] English-to-German dictionaries commonly offer a different translation for *Jew*: *Person jüdischer Abstammung* ("a person of Jewish descent")—a phrase that likewise avoids the noun but introduces a host of sticky assumptions and resonances regarding genealogy.

The phrase "of Jewish descent" (or "extraction" or "ancestry"), among other things, would seem to provide a polite distance allowing a person thus characterized the freedom either to claim as meaningful a heritage associated with that "descent" or to disregard it as irrelevant. Such politesse, though, seems often to be employed when the heritage in question is perceived to be somehow problematic, a "background" from which one may wish to "extract" oneself.

The adjectival form *Jewish*, by itself, is another matter. As a personal identifier—"I am Jewish; she is Jewish"—the word presumes a larger collective in which the designee's membership is acknowledged: persons or citizens, for example—forms of status at times withheld from those labeled *Jews*. The German phrase *unsere jüdischen Mitbürger*, cited above, surrounds the adjective *Jewish* with both another adjective ("our") and a noun ("fellow citizen") associated with belonging, while *Person jüdischer Abstammung* anchors the adjective *Jewish* to the respected and respectful noun *person*. "The Jewish community" similarly names one of a number of imaginable (if essentialized) communities that thereby are understood to share some commonalities with one another. That relative inclusiveness, it seems, can serve to "soften" or dissipate many of the sharper associations and exclusions that haunt the noun form *Jew(s)*. It is also somewhat more difficult to essentialize a singular adjective: "the Jewish man of Malta" is no murderously demonic fiend, and Shylock "the Jewish *person*" would hardly need to ask, "If you tickle us do we not laugh?" Nonetheless, as a form of the word *Jew*, the adjective *Jewish* also remains susceptible to use as a term of opprobrium and is no more stable than the noun.

Tellingly, in some of its earliest historical appearances in the singular form, the word translated as *Jew*—*yehudi*—functions as a kind of adjective. It is found in the appellation *ish yehudi*, "a Jewish man" (or "a man [who is] a *Jew*"), a phrase appearing in Zechariah 8:23 to describe a prophetic vision and again in Esther 2:5 to describe Mordecai, advisor to King Ahasuerus and kinsman to Queen Esther. The singular noun, *yehudi*, and the collective form, *yehudim*, appear multiple times in this latter book, as well, and even a verb form—*mityahadim*—"to act as, or become [like] *Jews*"—appears once. The book of Esther is among the small handful of books in the Hebrew Bible/Old Testament in which these words are found at all. Only in the late, postexilic books of Esther, Ezra-Nehemiah, and Daniel (and the deuterocanonical Maccabees) is *Jew(s)* found with any frequency.

In the book that bears her name, Mordecai's kinswoman Esther shares his Jewish identifications and loyalties, but she, herself, is never termed *isha yehudit*, the feminine form of the appellation that describes Mordecai. In English, as well, one does not tend to call Esther a *Jewess*—at least, not anymore. Many English-language dictionaries will advise that that term is always, often, or usually "offensive" (without explaining why this should be so—although the diminutive, derivative, and zoological associations of the suffix -*ess* might provide some clues).[32] Online search results at the time of this writing consist principally of such dictionary definitions, along with blogs and zines reclaiming or exploiting the word.[33] Nevertheless, in contrast to *Jew*, to my knowledge, no apologia has ever appeared for "very disturbing" search results for *Jewess*. *Jewess* is different from *Jew* in more ways than this. It has its own intriguing attributes related to, yet not entirely congruent with, those of *Jew*. Although I touch on some of these, briefly, later in this book, *Jewess* calls for a book of its own.

Outline of This Book

The present volume, like other volumes in the Key Words in Jewish Studies series, is divided into three major parts: "Terms of Debate," "State of the Question," and "In a New Key." Chapter 1, "Terms of Debate," engages current scholarly debates about the origins of *Jew(s)* and how best to understand and represent what the term signifies in its pre-Christian and Christian-era appearances. These debates are particularly informative in highlighting, on the one hand, the extent to which the earliest *Jew(s)* are both products and vital components of modern identities and imagined communities and, on the other, the extent to which our modern identity categories and conceits are, themselves, still quite beholden to antique discourses about *Jew(s)*. Chapter 2, "State of the (*Jew*[ish]) Question," takes as its framework the complex challenges and potentialities inherent in appropriating the term *Jew*—a term that for so long, and so virulently, signified abject otherness—as a term for self. It explores a rich tapestry of discourses about *Jew(s)* whose common threads include multilayered reflections about owning and belonging, unity and difference, memory and loss. Chapter 3, "In a New Key: New *Jews*" considers some of the newer genealogics of *Jew* in an age of Internet cultures, genetic sequencing, precarious nationalisms, and proliferating identities.

One final word on *Jew*: there is, of course, no final word on *Jew*—much less is one to be found in the pages of this book. This volume is a decidedly partial and intentionally slender one. What I do not know or have not said here about *Jew* (including about those aspects I have engaged) could obviously fill numberless volumes (and, indeed, has done and will do so). But if I contribute any useful formulations or insights, or if my work provokes any questions about this key word, *Jew*, that others take up and fruitfully pursue, then I will have done here what I set out to do.

1 Terms of Debate

"Ethnicity": memory, response, attitude, mood,
coded into the soul, transmitted through generations. Defined this broadly, I suspect, ethnicity is only a public metaphor, like sexuality or
age, for a knowledge that bewilders us.

Richard Rodriguez, "An American Writer"

Race is religion. The evidence lies in the Semites.

Gil Anidjar, *Semites: Race, Religion, Literature*

Once upon a time we knew who was a Jew. . . .
Now we are not so sure.

Shaye J. D. Cohen, *Beginnings of Jewishness:*
Boundaries, Varieties, Uncertainties

A decision regarding the juridical status of *Jews* in the Austro-Hungarian
Empire, handed down by the Imperial Court in Vienna in 1909, based on
legislation from 1867, states:

> Notwithstanding the views and aspirations of the Jews in Galicia and
> Bucovina concerning their juridical status in the state, the entire histori-
> cal development of Austrian legislation with reference to their juridical
> status is that they are regarded and treated not as an ethnic group
> [*Nationalität*] but as Sons of the Mosaic Faith, a religious community
> [*Religionsgesellschaft*].[1]

The plaintiffs in the case argued that, as *Jews* (*Juden*), their distinctiveness
and relation to the state ought to be legally construed as that of a
Nationalität or *Volksstämmer*—a "nationality" or "ethnic group"—a standard bureaucratic category in the multinational empire. In dismissing this
claim, the judiciary brought to bear "the entire historical development"
of the legal tradition in maintaining that *Jew* names *instead* a "Son of the

Mosaic Faith."² To categorize *Jew* otherwise, the court implied, would be to innovate.³

In addition to highlighting and historicizing the juxtaposition of "ethnicity" to "religion" in the naming and positioning of *Jew* in the modern West, the Austro-Hungarian ruling underscores the ways in which narratives of "historical development" are frequently called upon to adjudicate claims of later ages. In this sense, debates about original meanings and the historical development of terms are never merely academic or theoretical. The terms of these debates and their outcomes both are shaped by the larger sociopolitical contexts in which they occur and in turn help to shape those larger contexts. A close examination of current, ongoing debates about the origins of *Jew(s)* precisely illuminates these dynamics. It reveals the extent to which the earliest *Jew(s)* become mirrors of modern identities and aspirations and, as well, the ways in which our modern understandings and attributions are themselves a function of ancient discourses about *Jew(s)*.

Specifically, this chapter explores the formation and formulation of— as well as debates over—the key sociological categories currently employed to define *Jew(s)*. Chief among these categories are "ethnicity/ race" (commonly presumed to name "secular" phenomena) and "religion" (a much-contested concept, commonly presumed to describe phenomena distinguishable from the "secular" that represent a universal human impulse expressed through particular systems of belief and practice labeled "religions"). *Jew* plays an essential part in the historical development of these (theological/sociological) categories such that meanings attributed to *Jew* are inextricably bound up with these categories and the various manners and contexts in which they are combined or juxtaposed. Such categories as "ethnicity/race" and "religion" shape current knowledge about the origin of *Jew(s)* in ways that can obscure and exclude as much as they illuminate.

First *Jews*

The word *Jew*, like its cognates in other medieval and modern languages, derives from the ancient Greek *Ioudaios* and the Latin *Iudaeus*, which, in turn, are related to the Hebrew *yehudi* and Aramaic *yehuda'i*. Although this derivation is clear, well established, and uncontested, there is ongoing scholarly debate over whether the word *Jew* is, in fact, the appropriate or best translation of these ancient terms in the earliest writings in which they appear. The terms of this debate concern the nature of early identity categories and whether or not the ancient, pre-Christian subject in question (singular or plural) can be fairly and adequately named by much later terms like *Jew, Jude, juif, judío,* and so forth, which arose within explicitly Christian contexts and which remain tightly enmeshed in Christian theological paradigms. *Jew(s)*, it is argued, is a "religious" designation and must be reserved for naming members of a "religious" community. A different term and a different narrative must, then, be generated to distinguish this "religious" meaning from a supposedly earlier "ethnic" or "national" one.

Yehudi (pl. *yehudim*) hearkens back to the biblical tribal name Yehudah/Judah, which designates the Israelite tribe whose territory became the bulk of the southern Israelite kingdom, according to the biblical narratives of the First and Second Books of Kings. Following the Assyrian destruction of the northern kingdom (Israel) in the eighth century BCE, Yehudah/Judah became the only remaining Israelite kingdom. *Yehud*, as this territory was subsequently known under the Babylonian and Persian Empires, became the Judaea (Judea) found in ancient Greek and Latin texts.

At first blush, it would appear that the appellation *yehudi* and its ancient derivatives refer, then, simply to an inhabitant of this particular geopolitical locale situated in the far-eastern Mediterranean (or far-western Arabia). *Judaean* is the noun coined to signify this regionally inflected personal identity. Such a straightforward regional signification is complicated, however, by a number of factors. For one thing, in some of their earliest occurrences, the terms *yehuda'i* and *yehudi(m)* refer to persons *outside* that locale, not within it, and often with indication of ancestry elsewhere (e.g., in the Elephantine papyri from fifth-century BCE Egypt, whose *yehuda'i* are, according to Joseph Blenkinsopp, almost certainly from northern Israel and Aramea).[4] In other early occurrences, the terms are employed by a minority elite settled—or resettled—in Yehud under Persian imperial auspices (as in the biblical books of Ezra and Nehemiah). Furthermore, even when applied to persons or groups within the region of Yehud/Judaea, the term is explicitly reserved for only some inhabitants and settlers there, and not others. In fact, oddly, the "people(s) of the land" is a phrase employed in biblical texts expressly to exclude other inhabitants of the land of Yehud/Judaea from among the ranks of the *yehudim* or *yehuda'i*. *Yehudit* (the feminine form that corresponds to the masculine *yehuda* or *yehudi*) is the name of one such "daughter of the land" who marries Jacob's brother Esau, a full generation before Yehudah/Judah, son of Jacob and Leah, becomes the designated, eponymous founder of the "tribe of Judah."[5]

Yehudim appears as a tribal/national designation in II Kings 16:6, and Assyrian Akkadian inscriptions refer to the defeat of the *"iauda'ai* king." Apart from a few such instances, the Hebrew and Aramaic terms of collective identification first begin to appear in measurable numbers in literature and inscriptions related to the Babylonian conquest of the kingdom of Judah (c. 587 BCE) and its aftermath. Elites of that kingdom, according to biblical accounts, were forcibly transferred to cities in the heart of the Babylonian Empire; others fled to Egypt. As a small, displaced minority, these deportees and refugees may have come to identify themselves—or to be identified by those around them—as *yehuda'i*, Aramaic for "those from Yehud." When the Babylonian Empire fell to the Persians in the late sixth century BCE, colonization of the province of Yehud was overseen by the Persian imperial administration and included the apparently voluntary transfer—or repatriation—of a population from Babylonia calling itself the *yehuda'i, yehudim, Yisrael,* and *bene ha-golah* or *bene galuta*—"children of the exiled." Among these colonists were many who asserted descent from the earlier deportees but who denied any association with or relation to those who had remained living in Yehud (much less to those who might have come to reside there after the destruction by the Babylonians).[6] We do not know whether or not these latter also began to—or continued to—call themselves *yehudim* despite apparent claims to exclusive ownership of the term by the "children of the exiled."

According to this reconstruction, the terms *yehudim* (in Hebrew) and *yehuda'i* (in Aramaic) named a population transferred to the heart of Babylonia (or fled to Egypt) as a result of imperial conquest and destruction. The dynamic of displacement and constitution as a minority culture, then, may account for the adoption or attribution of an appellation—*yehudim* or *yehuda'i*—not otherwise utilized outside such a context. Likewise, the displacement of a minority group from Babylonia and its reconstitution in Yehud as local intermediaries with (or colonial representatives of) the Persian imperial government may account for the appropriation of a provincial identity—*yehudim* or *yehuda'i*—by the new arrivals/returnees as an assertion of local standing and legitimacy. Hence, *yehudim* or *yehuda'i* might first have been coined as part of a foundational narrative of kinship, geography, and piety by this settlement (or resettlement) movement at the same time that it might already have been in use by inhabitants of the colonized Persian land called Yehud.

If these earliest Hebrew and Aramaic, and later Greek and Latin, terms were to be translated as *Yehudean/Judaean* rather than as *Jew* (as is becoming widespread practice among those who study antiquity), then *Judaean* would seem to signify any or all of the following: a native or resident of the region of Judaea; an expatriate of that territory; a settler there; a member of an extended tribal group; a member of a religious subculture; a descendant or adherent of any one of these. Yet if *Judaean* is not coterminous with *Jew*, then the question still remains as to who and what constitute the earliest *Jews* and what is the nature of their relationship to *Judaeans, Israelites,* and *Hebrews.*

Answers to these questions vary widely among scholars.[7] Different bodies of scholarship point to different time periods and different sociopolitical forces or events to pinpoint the emergence of *Jews* onto the world stage and to propose a variety of related distinctions and comparisons. The vast majority of studies, however, share quite similar frameworks, analytical terminology, and fundamental assumptions. Three concise formulations by three prominent scholars serve nicely to illustrate both the divergences and the underlying conformity:

> In the Babylonian and Persian periods [sixth to fourth centuries BCE], the term "Judean" added to its former tribal and territorial meanings, the new religious one of "Jew."[8]

> All occurrences of the term *Ioudaios* [as well as *yehudi* and *yehuda'i*] before the middle or end of the second century BCE should be translated not as "Jew," a religious term, but as "Judaean," an ethnic-geographic term. In the second half of the second century BCE the term *Ioudaios* for the first time is applied even to people who are not ethnic or geographic Judaeans but who . . . have come to believe in the God of the Judaeans (i.e., they have become "Jews").[9]

> Some scholars in recent years have asked whether *Ioudaioi* and its counterparts in other ancient languages are better rendered "Jews" or "Judaeans" in English. This essay puts that question in a larger frame, by considering first *Ioudaismos* and then the larger problem of ancient religion. It argues that there was no category of "Judaism" in the Graeco-Roman world, no "religion" too, and that the *Ioudaioi* were understood until late antiquity [approximately the fourth century CE] as an ethnic group comparable to other ethnic groups, with their distinctive laws, traditions, customs, and God. They were indeed Judaeans.[10]

Two things are striking about this series of formulations. First is the fact that the three accounts locate the same watershed phenomenon—the emergence of *Jew(s)*—in three very different eras, several centuries apart: one in the so-called Babylonian and Persian periods of the sixth to fourth centuries BCE, another in the so-called Hellenistic period of the second century BCE, and still another in the so-called late antique or early Christian period of the third and fourth centuries CE.

The second factor worthy of note is an apparent consensus among all three formulations that *Jew* may be made to signify a religious identity in express contradistinction to an ethnic one and, moreover, that a historical progression may be discerned whereby the ethnic entity evolves into a religious one—only the latter of which is properly termed *Jew(s).*[11]

It is difficult to account for this clearly artificial limitation of the semantic range of *Jew* in a world and time (our own) in which millions identify (and are identified) as nonreligious, antireligious, atheist, and secular *Jews*. Likewise, the compulsion to provide two distinct categories and names—"ethnic" *Judaeans* versus "religious" *Jews*—by which to translate identical terms (whether *yehudim, yehuda'i, Ioudaioi,* or *Ieudei*) from ancient linguistic cultures that display no inclination to such bifurcation is a curious one. (It should be noted that this is primarily a preoccupation of English-language scholars that rarely appears to exercise scholars writing in languages other than English.) Indeed, one would be hard pressed to discover another identity term from Mediterranean and Near Eastern antiquity subjected by contemporary historiographers to this same kind of functional partition—with the significant possible exception of *Hellenos*: "Hellene" / "Greek."[12] What is it about *Jew(s)* that has led historians in our day and age to insist on limitations of definition so foreign to current usage and semantic bifurcations so alien to the ancient words and worlds they purport to translate?

A *Jew* Outward or a *Jew* Inward?

Modern scholarship on the terms *yehudim, Ioudaioi,* and their cognates was, from its inception and until very recent generations, the purview of Christian philologists, homilists, and biblicists. In the 1661 edition of *A Complete Christian Dictionary Wherein the Significations and Several Acceptations of All the Words Mentioned in the Holy Scriptures of the Old and New Testament*, the entry on *Jew* is subdivided into three categories: "Naturall" (citing Zechariah 8:23; Nehemiah 2:16; and Acts 10:28), "Outward," and "Inward" (the latter two glossing Romans 2:28–29).[13] The entry is almost entirely devoted to distinguishing between these latter two: a "Jew inward: One, who is a Jew in truth, though he be not so by name or Nation . . . that is to say, one who professeth himself to be one of God's people, and is so indeed, and before God, in spirit and in heart, being faithful and holy," versus a "Jew outward: He that is a Jew by Nation, name and profession only."

The choices and distinctions here are intriguing. Of the scores of texts that the editors might have chosen for this entry, none were chosen from among those that associate the term *Jew* with deicide or the diabolical (from the Gospel of John, for example, where the word appears over seventy times, nearly always with negative connotation), but only those in which *Jew* carries a positive, even admirable, valuation were selected. At the same time, the distinctions provided for three kinds or classes of *Jew* are quite instructive. "Naturall," while unelaborated, are clearly ancestral *Jews*, and of the three (redemption-oriented) passages cited, two highlight the joining by God of Gentiles to such *Jews*, while the Nehemiah verse appears in a narrative of the restoration of Jerusalem. The "inward" and "outward" *Jews* of the bulk of the entry then turn the focus to individual choice: both the "inward" and "outward" *Jews* choose to "profess" themselves to be of God's people, but only one of the two chooses to be so "in truth . . . indeed, and before God, in spirit and in heart being faithful and holy," whereas the other does not. "Profession" is key, as the "Jew in truth" may be "not so by name or Nation."

Notable in this early English lexicon are the (explicitly Pauline-inflected) inclination to define *Jew* according to distinctions between "nation" and "faith"; the claim to ownership of the term *Jew* on the part of pious Christians who are "not so by [nature,] name or Nation"; and the didactic or homiletic tone that leaves no doubt that there remain many false, faithless, and spiritually lacking members of the "nation" that bears the name *Jews*. The choice of the Pauline "inward" and "outward" binary is exemplary, in this *Christian Dictionary*, of the project of formation and edification of the Christian self or subject. As Judith Butler observes in another context,

> What constitutes through division the "inner" and "outer" worlds of the subject is a border and boundary tenuously maintained for the purposes of social regulation and control . . . a mediating boundary that strives for stability. And this stability, this coherence, is determined in large part by cultural orders that sanction the subject and compel its differentiation from the abject. Hence "inner" and "outer" constitute a binary distinction that stabilizes and consolidates the coherent subject.[14]

In the context of this early modern *Christian Dictionary*, then, the invocation of Paul's "inward" and "outward" *Jew* serves didactically to instantiate and fortify the believing Christian subject. *Jew* as both appropriated subject and circumscribed object is fully an instrument of Christian moral formation; *Jew* is *both* the godly self and the faithless other of the Christian subject. It is hardly its own entity.

Fast-forward to the turn of the twenty-first century, to the standard *Greek-English Lexicon of the New Testament and Other Early Christian Literature*,[15] where the entry on *Ioudaios* begins with an extended parenthetical apologia whose difficult grammar and circumlocutions serve to convey a sense of profound unease attached to the word *Jew*:

> (Since the term "Judaism" suggests a monolithic entity that fails to take account of the many varieties of thought and social expression associated with . . . adherents, the calque or loanword "Judean" is used in this and other entries where *Ioudaios* is treated. Complicating the semantic problem is the existence side by side of persons who had genealogy on

their side and those who became proselytes; . . . also of adherents of Moses who recognized Jesus as Messiah . . . and those who did not do so. Incalculable harm has been caused by simply glossing *Ioudaios* with "Jew," for many readers or auditors of Bible translations do not practice the historical judgment necessary to distinguish between circumstances and events of an ancient time and contemporary ethnic-religious-social realities, with the result that anti-Judaism in the modern sense of the term is needlessly fostered through biblical texts).[16]

Thus, several hundred years later, the distinctions found in the 1661 *Christian Dictionary* between "nature" or "nation" (here, "persons who had genealogy on their side") and "profession" (here, "those who became proselytes" and "adherents of Moses") are still foregrounded. The difference between the two categories is no longer characterized as moral, theological truth but rather as a "semantic problem," with those *Ioudaioi* "who recognized Jesus as Messiah" apparently posing this problem in a particularly acute manner. The didactic quality of the earlier iteration is retained here, as well, although in this post-Holocaust era it carries a more hand-wringing and less polemical tone. An attempt to further parse this difficult preamble leads the reader to ascertain the following:

1) that the term *Judaism* misrepresents or fails to describe its referent sufficiently;
2) that *Judaean* is a calque or loanword (which, as it first occurs in English, is calqued or loaned, it seems, from the adjectival to the nominal and not from one language to another) that, in some unspecified way and without itself being defined, ameliorates the misrepresentation (of diversity?) effected by the term *Judaism* or perhaps by the term *Jew*;
3) that *Jew* dangerously misrepresents or fails to translate *Ioudaios* sufficiently;
4) that readers or auditors of Bible translations *ought to* distinguish between past and present with regard to *Jew*, if not with regard to other aspects of Scripture;
5) that many lack "the historical judgment necessary to distinguish between circumstances and events [unspecified] of an ancient time and contemporary ethnic-religious-social realities [also unspecified], with the result that anti-Judaism in the modern sense of the term is needlessly fostered through biblical texts" featuring the word *Ioudaios* (the doubled passive construction leaving the regrettable result without subject or agent);
6) that anti-Judaism also has a premodern sense discontinuous with its modern sense;
7) that "incalculable harm has been caused" by translating ("glossing") *Ioudaios* as *Jew*.

While much remains unclear—with regard to cause, effect, "circum-stances," "realities," and means of amelioration—this preface leads the reader to the conclusion that there now exists a moral imperative no longer to speak or write the word *Jew* in translating ancient Christian biblical and other texts. Instead, as a hedge against modern anti-Judaism, translators and readers should replace *Jew* with *Judaean*.

A subsequent preamble introduces the longest subheading of the same entry, that devoted to the "*Ioudaioi* or 'Judeans' for the most part" in the Gospel of John.[17] Here the definition reads:

> those who are in opposition to Jesus, with special focus on hostility emanating from leaders in Jerusalem, center of Israelite belief and cult; there is no indication that John uses the term in the general ethnic sense suggested in the modern use of the word "Jew," which covers diversities of belief and practice that were not envisaged by biblical writers, who concern themselves with intra-Judean (intra-Israelite) differences and conflicts.[18]

Note that, in contrast to the three scholarly passages cited above on the earliest emergence of *Jews*, wherein *Jews* signifies a religious element added to or superseding an ethnic or ethno-geographic entity termed *Judaean*, here *Jew* is purported to convey a "general ethnic sense," whereas *Judaean* is offered as an alternative designation for the evange-list's "leaders in Jerusalem, center of Israelite belief and cult." In other words, by contrast with the ethnic category *Jews*, *Judaeans* serves here as a regional religious signifier.

But even this distinction seems hopelessly fuzzy as "the modern use of the word 'Jew' . . . covers diversities of belief and practice," while the ancient texts "concern themselves with intra-Judean (intra-Israelite) differences"—including "differences," one must presume, precisely of "belief and practice." Moreover, if *Judaean* here signifies a Jerusalem-centered regionalism, then what could be intended by the apparently synonymous "Israelite"? The entire lexical entry seems hopelessly caught between inarticulate euphemism and ongoing debates about religion versus ethnicity and related terminologies. As Christianity so deeply, so tragically, and for so many centuries largely *owned* the word *Jew*, current public heirs to that legacy, such as the editors of a standard New Testament lexicon or *Wörterbuch*, appear hard pressed to manage the responsibility that has come with that inheritance.

Clearly, the content of the distinction intended between *Judaean* and *Jew* differs widely—even diametrically—from author to author and case to case. So, too, does the stated rationale for introducing the distinction. Steve Mason, a Josephus scholar, for example, asserts that his motive in employing this distinction lies not in problematic New Testament passages and the harms and hostilities that might be fostered through them. Rather, he is motivated by the desire for a mechanism by which he might gain "empathic entry into [the] . . . worlds of discourse" of ancient subjects and their collective self-conceptions:

> Given the theological context of some "Jew-Judaean" debates, especially in relation to the Gospel of John, let me stress at the beginning that my interests are historical and philological: to engage the mindset, values, and category formations of the ancients. How did *they* understand the phenomena their world presented to them, and what do their terms reveal about their values and assumptions?[19]

How, then, do Mason's "philological interests" coincide with the "semantic problem" faced by New Testament lexicographers?

Although content, context, and rationale differ significantly among those who adopt the bifurcated terminology *Judaean/Jew*, what persists, as noted above, is the division between elements that are currently assembled under the rubric *ethnicity* (nation, genealogy, nature, tribe) versus those gathered under *religion* (profession, adherence, faith, belief). Part and parcel of this dualism is the implication or assertion that the former represents a given or inherited condition whereas the latter involves choice and, more than that, aspiration (realizable through fundamental transformation or conversion) to a higher, more developed, and enlightened level of individual and/or collective being. In this respect, ethnicity versus religion shares a great deal with such other dualisms as *outward* versus *inward*, *letter* (or *flesh*) versus *spirit*, *worldly* versus *heavenly*, and *particular/local* versus *universal*, which come to shape Christian rhetoric and worldview.

It appears, then, that our modern sociological/anthropological dualism *ethnic* versus *religious*, which is commonly presented as objective, neutral, and rationally secular description when invoked in social-scientific analyses, may nonetheless be as deeply rooted in a Christian Western worldview as are the more theologically explicit dualisms to which it so closely conforms. Indeed, the patterns of correspondence ethnicity = flesh/particular and religion = spirit/universal are as consistent and striking in recent academic studies of the origins of *Jews* as are historicized narratives of cultural transformation that unselfconsciously replicate Christian supersessionist paradigms.

To return to the three excerpts quoted above, in which current scholars narrate the historical progress of *yehudim/Ioudaioi* from ethnic or tribal *Judaeans* to religious *Jews*: the theological pattern of religion/spirit supplementing or superseding ethnicity/flesh is immediately evident.

Moreover, the sign of *spirit* or the sociological indicator of *religion* that features in such narratives is the quintessentially Christian-inflected one of conversion to a belief. "Belief," as Donald S. Lopez Jr. observes, merely "appears as a universal category because of the universalist claims of the tradition in which it has become most central, Christianity." Christianity's global reach and political power have served to make "belief the measure of what religion is understood to be."[20]

Shaye J. D. Cohen's *The Beginnings of Jewishness* provides only one among many narratives that follow this pattern, but it serves as a key case in point. Early in his preface Cohen asserts that "behind the philological shift from 'Judaean' to 'Jew' is a significant development in the history of Judaism . . . *the progression from ethnicity to religion had advanced* to the point where individual gentiles who came to believe in the God of the Jews were accepted as Jews themselves."[21] In the final sentence of the book's final chapter, Cohen summarizes the matter even more forcefully and theologically: "Religion overcame ethnicity."[22] Joseph Blenkinsopp employs the same paradigm when he holds up Zechariah 8:23 as a text whose invocation of *yehudi* is "clearly religious" and signals "a time when Judaism was accepting proselytes . . . a time when the term *yehudim* had left the topographical-ethnic sense well behind."[23]

Paul's "outward" and "inward" Jews are likewise echoed in such scholarship on the earliest *Jews*. In his definition of *Jew* as "a function of religion," for example, Cohen states that a "*Ioudaios* is someone who believes (or is supposed to believe) certain distinctive tenets, and/or follows (or is supposed to follow) certain distinctive practices; in other words, a *Ioudaios* [in this sense] is a Jew, someone who worships the God whose temple is in Jerusalem and who follows the way of life of the Jews."[24] Aside from the apparent circularity of the final clause, what is most noteworthy about this definition of *Jew* are the dichotomies "believes (or is supposed to believe)" and "follows (or is supposed to follow)." Whether the "supposed" in these formulations is intended as prescription or presumption (or both) is not as clear as the impulse to note a distinction—one that conforms closely to the distinction between the "true faith" of the "inward Jew" and the unmet obligation or expectation of the "outward Jew." After all, who else but the *Ioudaios* by "birth" or "nation" would be "supposed" to believe, follow, and worship in the "certain distinctive" ways intimated?

And yet, for Cohen, this definition of *Ioudaios* as *Jew* serves precisely to frame and introduce (in the sentences immediately following the one quoted) a historical narrative of the invention of "religious conversion to Judaism" during the Hellenistic period. The abrupt jump from "what Jews are supposed to believe and do" to the "conversion of gentiles" might strike some readers as a kind of non sequitur, but the sequence is eminently familiar to close readers of Paul's letters (and the Gospels) and, in particular, to ancient and modern interpreters of Romans 2:28–29.[25] Only "Jews according to the flesh" (to invoke Pauline terminology) could fall short in "supposed belief and practice," whereas anyone in the world (any Gentile) could, in fact, choose, through belief and practice, to join the "sons and heirs," to be "grafted on" to "God's people." Having followed the theological path of sundering the "outward" ("Judaean") from the "inward Jew," Cohen then proceeds, by historiographic fiat, to rejoin them into one: "In the Hellenistic period," he assures his readers, "virtually all 'Judaeans' will have been Jews."[26] Not all are of one flesh, but all can choose to be one in spirit.

The inward/outward binary, however, is supple enough to do double duty with regard to subject formation in relation to the categories "ethnicity" and "religion." For Cohen, as for others, and notwithstanding de rigueur acknowledgments of the social construction of ethnicity, "ethnicity is immutable."[27] It is inborn, inbred, *inward* in the very current sense upheld by adherents of DNA-driven "genetic identities."[28] By contrast, "religion is mutable"—it can be changed like clothing, like a mask, like culture.[29] Hence, the binary of ethnic Judaean/religious Jew is also useful for securing an immutably ethnic "ancestor" to modernity's mutably professing *Jew*. The double binary (ethnic Judaean/religious Jew) doubly binds and thereby doubly stabilizes the otherwise historically contingent subject that it doubly names. The current marking and marketing of ethnicity as an "inward" (in our very DNA!) dimension of the subject along with the concomitant demotion of religion to "outward" (optional, a matter of preference) follows the logic of the Pauline distinction as framed in the *Christian Dictionary* definition of *Jew* cited above. That is, if the true religious profession that constitutes the believing subject requires/creates its opposite—namely, false profession—then it seems inevitable that any and all profession may be suspected of being "merely outward": a suspicion that fueled the centuries-long Inquisition and that has become an article of faith to the aspiring secularism of a post-Enlightenment age.

Jews, Women, Slaves

Regardless of their potentially stabilizing effects on contemporary identity, claims about ancient "ethnicity" versus "religion," or "birth" versus "belief," invoke a rarefied world and worldview in which actors and agents are, for the most part, free and male. Arguments for the heuristic usefulness of identity categories that focus solely on birthright or personal choice are permeated by deep gender and class disparities that enable and sustain the entire discourse. Attention to slaves and the nonmale part of the population profoundly complicates the terms of these debates.

Those born into slavery, for example, often—though not always—had no legally recognized ethnicity in Mediterranean antiquity, while those who became enslaved were often shorn of their ethnicity—including any choice in matters of worship or piety.[30] The biblical commands (reiterated later at Qumran) that compelled male slaves to be circumcised, and that included them in Passover and other "insider" observances, point to the absence of personal choice, the mutability of ethnicity, and the existence of the concept of "conversion of outsiders" centuries before the "shift from immutable ethnicity to mutable religion" that creates *Jews* from *Judaeans* according to the paradigm under scrutiny here.

Likewise, "ethnicity" and "personal choice" as applied to women— regardless of social class—are problematic. As Ross Kraemer observes:

> The daughter of an Israelite is not herself an Israelite, any more than the daughter of an Athenian citizen is herself an Athenian. . . . Ethnicity is thus fundamentally about fathers and sons. More generally, then, ethnicity is an attribute of men that applies secondarily to women by virtue only of their connection to men, so that women can easily, or more easily, lose their ethnicity [or have it altered], for instance through marriage. . . . Women cannot effect the transmission of ethnicity in and of themselves, the later rabbinic definition of a Jew as the child of a Jewish mother notwithstanding.[31]

To the extent that "ethnicity" applies to ancient women at all, even secondarily, it—like "belief" or "religion"—is a fluid category of relationship and as much a matter of choice (often someone else's) or compulsion ("for instance through marriage") as of "birth." If "ethnicity" is not a reliable identity category that meaningfully illuminates the lives and relationships of ancient women (or that does so in ways radically differently than when applied to free men), then what precisely *does* "ethnicity" describe, and how does absorption into an "ethnic group" through marriage or enslavement differ in any measurable sense from "conversion" into a "religious group" by the same means?

Those who hold that "the redefinition of Jewish society in religious (and political) terms, as opposed to tribal or ethnic . . . terms, was a product of the second half of the second century BCE [such that] social conversion became possible then, not before," must disregard or exclude myriad social practices that routinely governed the lives of "free" women and male and female slaves (who, combined, formed a majority of the ancient population) in order to sustain such claims and categories.[32] The same is true of those who retain the paradigm but situate the posited "redefinition of Jewish society" either earlier or later. In fact, Cohen avers that it is not until the first or second century CE that "the idea arose that gentile women (wives) too must convert" in order to become Jews "even if married to a Jewish husband."[33] According to Cohen, the reason women are irrelevant to the ethnicity-to-religion (r)evolution that "redefined Jewish society" is that "as a dutiful wife [a woman] would abandon her ancestral gods and automatically accept the religion of her husband"—at least, in theory.[34]

Daniel R. Schwartz adds the further proposition that Josephus, writing at the end of the first century CE, appears "willing to allow for conversion by men but not yet by women . . . because women were anyway subject to their husbands and so had to do according to the laws that bound them" (again, in theory).[35] Schwartz derives this conclusion by finding that Josephus is more than willing to refer repeatedly to Gentile men "becoming" Jews, while saying no more regarding women in a similar position than that they have "gone over to the Judaic regulation" or are "drawn to the Jewish cult," and the like. That is, such women "do like Jews" without, in Josephus's terms, "becoming" Jews. "This," Schwartz emphasizes, "is a problem about women."[36]

Unsurprisingly, the biblical character Ruth frequently appears as a "problem" addressed by scholars engaged in the "ethnicity" versus "religion," Judaean/Jew debates. The variety of ways in which this female character and her declaration of allegiance to her adopted community are described, in these debates, provides a fascinating and revealing case in point. Recall that Ruth is the "Moabite" widow of a man "of Bethlehem in Judah" who, with his father, mother, and brother, sought refuge from famine for more than ten years in the land of Moab. Following the death of the three men, the three widows depart "to go back to the land of Judah," whereupon the matriarch Naomi orders her daughters-in-law, Ruth and Orpah, to "return each of you to your mother's house." It is at this point that Ruth—who by the end of the story gives birth to the grandfather of the future king David—utters this profoundly moving formula: "Where you go, I will go; where you lodge, I will lodge; your people shall be my people, and your God my God. Where you die, I will die—there will I be buried. May the LORD do thus and so to me, and more as well, if even death parts me from you!"[37] Kraemer appeals to this passage as the "paradigmatic example" of how "the integral relationship between ethnicity and devotion to deities has substantial implication for questions about what is often termed religious conversion."[38] "In such an environment" as that envisioned in the Hebrew Bible, she suggests, "a change of deities entails a change of ethnicity, something that can be effected at least through marriage, and perhaps also through other social mechanisms such as adoption."[39] Ruth's declaration, then, clearly "highlights the connections between ethnicity, ancestry, territory, and veneration of the gods," such that Ruth, in coming to accept the God of Naomi and to be incorporated into Naomi's clan, comes to share her ("Judaean") ethnicity, as well.[40]

Cohen disagrees. He addresses Ruth in a single sentence in a single footnote, asserting that Ruth is never other than "a foreigner whose foreignness remains even after she has attempted to adopt the ways of her surroundings."[41] In the absence of any explanation, readers are left to guess at the meaning of this awkward formulation and the reasoning behind Cohen's assessment.

In explicit agreement with Cohen, Seth Schwartz seeks to provide some of the absent rationale:

> In the fantasy of the storyteller, Ruth left her ancestral gods behind in her father's house and accepted the God of Elimelekh's family exclusively . . . yet always remained a Moabite. But when King Antiochus in 2 Maccabees (9.12–7), and Achior the Ammonite in the book of Judith (14.10) came to recognize the power of the God of Israel (and no such moment is recorded in the case of Ruth), they actually *became ioudaioi*. . . . the idea that someone can become Jewish by accepting the authority of the God of Israel plus some ceremonial acts . . . whereas previously one might similarly adopt Yahweh-worship, enter an enduring relationship with a Judaean family, become in some way part of the *'am* ("nation" or extended clan-group) of the Judaeans, and be the ancestor of Judaeans, without acquiring the ethnicon "Judaean"/*ioudaios*/*yehudi* oneself— does indubitably entail a small but fateful conceptual shift.[42]

Schwartz's argument is intriguing, albeit rather slippery, and it prompts some observations and questions specifically about gender. The three strikes against Ruth outlined by Schwartz are:

1) that she "always remained a Moabite," as the story persists in referring to her as such;
2) that her declaration to Naomi that "your God will be my God" does not "recognize the power of the God of Israel" in such a way that Ruth, like Antiochus and Achior, would "become Jewish by accepting the authority of the God of Israel";
3) that Ruth never "acquir[es] the ethnicon 'Judaean.'"

Each objection involves some sleight of hand and (although worthy of extended response) may be dispatched with brevity—which leaves the larger question as to why such effort is put to the task of disqualifying Ruth in the first place. Regarding the specifics of the objections:

1) Ruth's Moabite origins are indeed a key element of the story's plot and ideology, just as are Achior's Ammonite origins; hence, neither

character ever sheds the ethnonym of origin. Unlike Achior, however, Ruth is repeatedly described in very explicit (and often formally patriarchal) kinship terms, as when Boaz—who is addressed by Ruth as "next of kin" and identifies himself both to her and publicly as such (3:9–13; 4:1–8; the expression is a highly technical one)—pronounces before witnesses: "I have acquired Ruth the Moabite, wife of Mahlon, to be my wife, to maintain the dead man's name on his inheritance, in order that the name of the dead man may not be cut off from his kindred and from the gate of his native place" (4:10). This speech concisely illustrates both Kraemer's point about how women function as a means to the end of male "ethnicity" *and* the sense that Ruth counts neither more nor less than a "native-born" woman as means to this end. For Schwartz this quality makes Ruth "in some way part of the 'am . . . of the Judaeans" but not herself a "Judaean." Would not this same formulation, then, aptly describe "native-born" women, as well? Are they perhaps likewise "part of the 'am" while not being regarded as "Judaeans" in their own right?

2) Antiochus and Achior both "recognize the power of the God of Israel" in the devastating defeat of their respective armies; Ruth pledges herself to the "God of Israel" in an oath that binds her to deity, land, and people, as it binds her to Naomi in life and beyond death. Does the "small but fateful conceptual shift" posited by Schwartz (and Cohen before him) really represent the historical emergence of the concept of "religious conversion" in the stories about the men, in contrast to its absence in the story of the women, or is the shift rather one from a "feminine" language of relationship and connection in the one story to a "masculine" one of (military) "power" and "authority" in the other two?[43]

3) Ruth never "acquir[es] the ethnicon 'Judaean,'" but neither does Achior. Nor do any of the "native" characters in the books of Ruth and Judith bear this particular ethnicon.[44] Antiochus alone of the three offers (unsuccessfully) to "be like" or "become" a *Ioudaios* in II Maccabees, a book in which this ethnicon appears frequently, as it does in the book of Esther, where a terrified populace attempts to become indistinguishable from *yehudim*, as well.

The "problem" of Ruth, it seems, is not that the story historically precedes a conceptual shift that makes possible "conversion" and thus ushers in the phenomenon of Jewish "religion." It is not that Ruth was "born too soon," but rather that the character Ruth is a woman, with the constraints and associations that attend that gender designation throughout antiquity, as well as in current scholarship. To repeat Daniel R. Schwartz's assertion, *this is a problem about women.*

For his part, Schwartz identifies this "women problem" in Josephus's treatment of Ruth, as well:

> Josephus seems to have thought that Gentile men can become Jews via circumcision, but that Gentile women, who cannot be circumcised, cannot become Jews. They can only do like Jews do. It is, apparently, this point of view that explains the striking fact that Josephus, although devoting several pages to the biblical story of Ruth (*A.J.* 5.318–337), ignores the most famous passage in the book: Ruth's declaration at 1:16–17 that "your people shall be my people and your God shall be my God." At *A.J.* 5.322 Josephus simply skips over this declaration. Although Ruth's declaration has typically been taken as a formal statement of conversion, Josephus didn't apparently know what to make of that, and so left it out.[45]

Ruth presents a different problem altogether for the ancient rabbis. In Ruth Rabbah, the book-length midrashic commentary on the biblical story, the rabbis are very clear that Ruth is a convert—the quintessential convert—a proper Jewish mother, a pious devotee of the God of Israel, and an exemplary member of the people to whom she is joined. The key issue that requires resolution for them is the perpetual exclusion of all Moabites from the community of Israelites decreed in Deuteronomy 23:4.[46] How can Ruth the Moabite be counted as one of their own when the Bible expressly forbids it? The rabbinic solution is both ingenious and revealing: it turns out that Ruth is not, after all, a Moabite. According to the rabbinic reading introduced (and reiterated three times) in Ruth Rabbah 4:1, the biblical injunction excludes only "the Ammonite *but not the Ammonitess*, the Moabite *but not the Moabitess*." Problem solved.

The gender distinction drawn by the rabbis in this instance illustrates (yet again) the often easy separability of women from a collective ethnic identity. Here, women are not subject to the ethnic exclusion applied to the men of "their" ethnic group: a "Moabitess" is not a Moabite, nor is an "Ammonitess" to be counted as an Ammonite.[47] And by this same logic, we are led to conclude that a "Jewess" is not a *Jew*, nor is she a *Judaean*; she is something other. But the logic of the rabbis in this regard is hardly theirs alone. The reading that enables Ruth to be counted, in Seth Schwartz's terms, "part of the *'am* . . . of the Judaeans" yet not, herself, one of them, could preclude *any* woman from counting as a *Judaean*. The rabbinic formulation neatly encapsulates an insight about gender that has far-reaching (if routinely disregarded) implications for all scholarship that would put its faith in categories like "ethnicity," "religion," and "conversion" to construct histories and secure identities: namely, that these categories, like *Jew* itself, are and always have been deeply gendered.

The "problems" regarding *Jew* that are expressed in current scholarship on antiquity through distinctions between "ethnic" and "religious" content and connotation—and further by plotting this dualism historiographically as a "progression," "overcoming," or "leaving well behind" the one for the other—are as inconceivable outside an unreflectively patriarchal and androcentric worldview as they are unfathomable outside a Christian theological paradigm. Far from transcending the latter, they in fact replicate it. In these scholarly studies, the triumph of religion over ethnicity is most commonly narrated as the historicized, progressive emergence of a means of (potentially universal) access to group identity through "belief"—further betraying a disregard for the complexities and contradictions of gender and class. Yet what is at play here is not merely a matter of observable parallels and similarities between theological and social-scientific dualisms; rather, the very terms "ethnic" (from the Greek *ethnos*) and "religion" (from the Latin *religio*) are themselves the products of a long history of Christian discourses specifically related to *Jew(s)*.

From *Ethnos* to Ethnicity/Race and Religion

Scholarship on the meaning and uses of the term *ethnos* and on concepts corresponding to "ethnicity" in Greco-Roman antiquity burgeoned at the turn of the third millennium as modern "ethnic studies" joined the ranks of interdisciplinary programs at numerous universities. Similarly, critical examination of *religio, thréskeia, eusebeia,* and related concepts in antiquity has attended renewed explorations of the category of "religion" and its functions in pre- and post-Enlightenment epistemologies. In the fields of Jewish and early Christian studies, analysis of these ancient and modern categories has produced some particularly significant insights.[48]

Ethnos first appears in classical Greek literature as a generic word for "group." As Jonathan Hall observes, the word "designates a class of beings (humans or animals) who share a common identification. While it can be applied to populations that we might today recognize as 'ethnic groups,' it may also be employed to describe groups of birds, bees, boys or girls."[49] With time, the term takes on a more technical resonance in describing group identities associated with narratives of kinship and character that become part of a broad system whereby each such *ethnos* stands in hierarchical relation to others on a spectrum that runs from Hellene (or, later, Roman) *down* to barbarian. These classes of people, or *ethné*, are described as having their own peculiar customs and practices but also as partaking of more and less admirable qualities that set superior *ethné* nearer to, and inferior ones farther from, the Greek or Roman ideal. Similarly, objectionable practices and qualities such as cannibalism and incest, dishonesty and laziness, are attributed to "them" in order to rhetorically construct a valorized ethnic "us." This conceptual system, by which "we" can be distinguished from "they," was never static, uniform, nor entirely consistent in its characterizations or theories regarding, for example, the impact of environment, genealogy, diet, ritual, and governing institutions on the constitution and character of diverse *ethnē*. The system was, however, from its inception, deeply embedded in Greek colonial (and then Roman imperial) projects. Inferior *ethnē* had to be governed by their superiors.

Scholars of antiquity debate the extent to which this conceptual system relied on assertions of fixity or immutability versus to what extent a sense of fluidity or mutability might always have been in play.[50] Could an inferior *ethnos* evolve "better" character traits or outgrow "undesirable" ones (or vice versa), and could an individual member of one *ethnos* become a member of another in toto, in combination, or as a hybrid?[51] Although there is variation across time and from one ancient author to another, the conceptual web spun around the term *ethnos* (and related terms like *genos, laos,* and *phylos*) is expansive and pliant enough to serve a variety of rhetorical ends. Hence, a particular *ethnos* (or *gens*) might, in some accounts, be irretrievably destined to military defeat and enslavement or hopelessly barbaric while, in others, it or its members might be susceptible to the civilizing influences of a superior people (or vice versa). Some, like the *Ioudaioi* (*Jews/Judaeans*), might represent a consternating mixture of venerable antiquity and philosophical ancestry, on the one hand, combined with barbaric practices like genital mutilation, pig taboos, and parochial superstitions, on the other. Regarding *Ioudaioi*, a disgusted Seneca (according to Augustine) complains that "the custom of this most wicked *gens* has so prevailed it is now adopted in all the world. *The vanquished have given laws to their victors*" (*victi victoribus leges dederunt*).[52]

Ethnos and *genos*, then, come to signify rhetorical and juridical constructs that functioned within broad ideological contexts (military, colonial, imperial—including resistance and accommodation to these) throughout the Greco-Roman world.[53] These framed "an exceptionally robust taxonomy for classifying" and characterizing one's own allegiances, values, qualities, and associations in relation and opposition to those attributed to others, whether the classifier identified as a member of a superordinate people or of a subordinated one.[54] To expand on the example of the *Ioudaioi* summarized above: while some, like Seneca, would characterize their barbaric practice of genital mutilation as unworthy even of slaves, others, like Philo of Alexandria, could praise it as the embodiment of a noble integrity and self-control through excision of lust, and still others, like Paul of Tarsus, could bemoan it as an emblem of unenlightened submission to law and letter in place of enlightened acceptance of grace and spirit.[55] The fundamental calculus embodied in the category *ethnos* formed part of a shared discourse employed variously in different contexts to assert the relative esteem owed to one's own group versus the other group(s) thus described.

From at least the fourth century BCE, some writers began to propose that *ethné* were a function of processes of enculturation; that is, that individuals were socialized into an *ethnos*—whether born into association with it or not—through the assimilation of essential characteristics. Of course, for the vast majority of these writers, the only *ethnos* worth being socialized into was the Hellenic one. In an oft-quoted passage from the *Panegyricus*, for example, the Greek rhetorician Isokrates asserts that "the name Hellene seems not to refer to *genos* [birth, race] but rather to *dianoia* [thought, understanding], so that those who share our *paideia* [education, enculturation] are said to be Hellenes more so than those who share our *physis* [nature]."[56] Scholars have long argued that statements like this, and the spread of enculturating institutions embodying this philosophy, indicate that Hellene early on ceased to be an *ethnos* and became something else.[57] Perhaps. Or perhaps such dissociation of *ethnos* from *physis* merely masks and reinscribes the colonial and imperial dynamics that *ethnos, genos,* and related categories came to serve, while reifying and privileging the universalization of Hellene as a "supra" entity beyond the top of the hierarchy of *ethné*. Regardless, later Roman and Christian discourses readily enough demote and particularize Hellene as an identity category in promoting their own claims to cultural primacy and universalism.[58]

By the second century BCE, a chronicler of a resistance movement among *Ioudaioi* in Judaea appropriated the "Hellenistic" colonial conceptual apparatus to coin a new pair of words—*ioudaismos* and *hellenismos*—as a way to characterize competing alignments and valuations of collective character. "Judaizing" and "Hellenizing" in the narrative of II Maccabees name strategies explicitly attributed to *Ioudaioi*—all petty colonial elites, all engaged in attempts to formulate and propagate the essential character and qualities of their own people in terms created within the reigning geopolitical discourse.[59] In a mirroring gesture, the Hebrew writer of I Maccabees produced a diplomatic letter asserting an ancient kinship between the *yehudim* and their noble cousins the Spartans, both peoples "of the family of Abraham."[60] Narratives of common ancestry were standard tools of diplomacy, and Abraham, like Hellen, was seen as the ancestor of many *ethné*. Little more than a century later, Philo of Alexandria avers to his Greek-reading audience that *Ioudaioi* represent the epitome of all the *ethné*: "If a fresh start should be made to brighter prospects . . . I believe that each nation would abandon its peculiar ways, and, throwing overboard their ancestral customs, turn to honouring our laws alone."[61] To Philo, it seems, the ways of the *Ioudaioi* embody in highest form the attributes universally valued by enlightened people, and those ways would be embraced by all such people if a "fresh start" could be made. Paul, a younger contemporary of Philo, goes on to envision a similar fresh start in which all other *ethné* (that is, not of the same rootstock) would become grafted onto the family tree of *Ioudaioi* as welcome—if wild—branches of God's prime cultivar.[62]

A longstanding tradition in Jewish studies (and early-Christianity studies) has sought to marginalize these latter narratives by mapping the Maccabean *ioudaismos/hellenismos* dualism onto a series of other reified ideological dichotomies: homeland/diaspora, Semitic/Greek, integrity/syncretism, resistance/assimilation, and even, oddly, Israelite/*Jew*. Such dichotomies have been used to create distinctions or oppositions between a "more authentic" or "native" (sometimes *particularist*) Jewishness or Judaism attributed to Hebrew/Aramaic speakers in the homeland and a "less authentic," "assimilated," or "compromised" (sometimes *universalist*) version of Jewishness or Judaism attributed to Greek-speaking *Ioudaioi* in diaspora. Although these characterizations have been largely discredited as too simplistic and obviously apologetic, they continue to exert influence. As scholars grapple with the complex dynamics of rhetoric and self-representation; of colonialism, domination, and resistance, these dichotomies still constitute current terms of debate.

A number of proto- and early-Christian writers, in turn, employed the language of *ethnos/genos/phylos/laos* to name the nature of the group to which they belonged. Like those who had employed this conceptual system before them, Christians claimed to stand both at the top of the hierarchy and at the roots of their family tree. They were the "original" and "most human" *ethnos/genos* and at the same time a "new *genos*" or "new *ethnos*"—a new race or birth—one into which all people(s) must become enculturated or "born again" in order to be saved. Denise Buell quotes Clement of Alexandria as a prime articulator of this perspective: "Clement attributes to the Christian people [*laos*] two key attributes: superiority as the 'one saved *genos*' and accessibility via 'faith.'" She elaborates that, inasmuch as

> ethnicity is understood as mutable, then it is possible to argue not only that one can change ethnicity but that one should [i.e., one can and should be "born again"]. Some Christians equate the Christian *genos* with the human race as a whole, rendering it a potentially universal category. For Clement, transformation in the direction of Hellene or

Jew to Christian is privileged. . . . The universalizing potential of the category "Christian" . . . implicitly positions Hellene and Jew as finite and inferior.[63]

For Clement, Jews, Christians, and Hellenes are each an *ethnos*/*genos*— an "ethnicity" or "race"—and they are the only ones that ultimately matter.

During these same early Christian centuries, other key concepts like *religio*—a Latin word originally associated with local civic and familial obligations of piety and propriety—also came to frame more expansive imperial practices. As Buell puts it, "*religio* is one of the building blocks for the construction, display, and negotiation of Romanness [*humanitas*]."[64] Under the banner of *humanitas*, broader regional and ruler-worshiping cults were advanced throughout the Roman Empire that harnessed *religio* to an imperial vision of a "universal order" with the emperor and/as God over all.[65] *Religio* in imperial adaptation thus added a powerful dimension to the universalizing discourses of *hellenismos*. Furthermore, in positioning itself as carrying forth the civilizing project begun by the Hellenes (now characterized as having become degenerate), Rome framed its program of universal conquest within a narrative of inheritance, mission, and unfolding human progress.[66]

The Christian appropriation of this narrative finds expression by numerous writers throughout late antiquity, but few, perhaps, are more robust in this endeavor than Eusebius, the early fourth-century "bishop of Caesarea and self-appointed spokesperson for the new Christian dynasty of Constantine."[67] In his *Ecclesiastical History*, Eusebius envisions a universe that revolves around three kinds of people(s), each defined by its ascribed object of piety and its concomitant part in the unfolding drama of human enlightenment: *Jews* (defunct, monotheistic nonbelievers in Christ), Hellenes (including Phoenicians and Egyptians, as well as Greeks—all degenerate pagans devoted to false gods),[68] and Christians, "the culmination and supersession of the previous two groups, the new people chosen by God to spread the truth toward which all of time and civilization had been leading."[69] These peoples embody distinct beliefs and practices of devotion (*thréskeia* or *eusebeia*), of which there are also exactly three: Christianism, writes Eusebius, is the "third form of religion midway between Judaism and Hellenism, which I have already deduced as the most ancient and venerable of all religions, and which has been preached of late to all nations."[70] Eusebius, then, narrates a worldview organized around *hellenismos, ioudaismos,* and *christianismos,* three systems of belief subsuming all *ethné.* Among these, the oldest, newest, and truest—like Clement's *genos*—is also the only one guaranteeing salvation, a salvation that is now unfolding in history.[71]

As the Roman and Byzantine worlds became ever more structured around Christian-centered attributions of belief and devotional practice, *Jew* came to signify an adherent of what Christian theology construed as a system of belief and practice, labeled "Judaism." This latter term, "used as the name of the Jewish religion only by writers who do not identify themselves with and by that name, until well into the nineteenth century," served as a kind of "foreign currency" to those to whom it was attributed.[72] As a Christian theological construct, Judaism as a "religion of the *Jews*" is one that is superseded and defunct at the very moment that it is crystallized and named as such.[73] In fact, in Eusebius's narrative, *Jews* and their Judaism "arose as a corrupted form of the Hebrew *ethnos*" whose corruption was "a result of Egyptianization [!] before the exodus of the people under Moses."[74] *Jews* as a corrupted line of descent sets the stage for Eusebius's genealogical construal of Christians as the true heirs and descendants of the most ancient and laudable *Hebrews* and Christianity as an uncorrupted *Hebrew* legacy—a rhetorical move that simultaneously dissolves any relation between earliest Christianity and its abject others, the *Jews*.

Many early Christian writers employed the language of *hairesis* or *heresia*—literally, "choice"; hence, "school of thought and practice"—to further refine this schema. *Hairesis*, the term used by Josephus in the late first century CE to describe a variety of voluntary associations among *Ioudaioi* (Pharisees, Sadducees, Essenes), came to be used by Church writers of subsequent centuries to describe what was now framed as a choice between the absolutes of truth and falsehood, good and evil. In the emerging hegemony of the orthodox Christian Church, adherence to any voluntary school of thought other than that of the true and triumphant faith was considered adherence to false belief. Thus, *heresia* came to signify, exclusively, "false belief"—that is, *heresy* in the current theological sense. And many such *heresias* involved wanton "mixing" of beliefs and philosophies of the *Jews* and others with the pure Christianity that *heresiology* attempted to construct.

Within this worldview, *Jew* is always a *chosen* identity—the result of a choice of falsehood over truth—but it is no less an *ethnicized* identity for all that (see below). This element of choice is further reflected in Christian use of a verbal form of *Jew*, *ioudaïzein*—Greek, "to Judaize"—which is employed *not* to name what *Jews* do, but rather to label as unseemly and inappropriate certain "heretical" *Christian* behavior; acts of theological miscegenation, as it were. *Judaizers*, in orthodox Christian usage, are corruptors of a pure, virginal Christianity; heretics whose evil choices give birth to monstrous groups of misbelievers.

In his massive heresiological catalog *Panarion*, Epiphanius of Salamis (c. 315–403) works to enact, among other things, the transubstantiation of what had been *ethné* (to Josephus and Strabo, for example) into historical epochs, each characterized by its submission to one of a succession of heresies. Of this transmutation, Andrew Jacobs (quoting the *Panarion*) observes:

> To the extent that "heresy" defines the un-Christian, Epiphanius the heresiologist can expand notions of Christian truth across all time and space . . . "from Adam until Noah there was barbarism; from Noah until the tower [that is, of Babel], and until Serug, two generations after the tower, came the Scythian superstition; after that . . . until Abraham, Hellenism. From Abraham on, a fear of God ascribed to Abraham: Judaism."[75]

Daniel Boyarin glosses: "For him [Epiphanius], not only 'Hellenism' and 'Judaism' but also 'Scythianism' and even 'Barbarianism' are no longer the names of ethnic entities but of 'heresies,' that is religions other than orthodox Christianity . . . by which he means groups divided and constituted by religious differences fully disembedded from ethnicities."[76] In characterizing Epiphanius's use of ethnic nomenclature for varieties of "belief," or "-isms," plotted along a historical evolutionary continuum, Boyarin provocatively overstates the rubric as one of "religious differences fully disembedded from ethnicities."[77] But rather than fully disembedding belief/religion from ethnicity, Epiphanius explicitly *recapitulates* the colonial/imperial hierarchical taxonomy of *ethné* as a rubric for "divid[ing] and constitut[ing]" collective (in this case, Christian) "selves" and their (non-Christian) "others"—albeit with a virtually exclusive focus on the increasingly salient (for Christians) element of attributed *belief.* It is important to recognize that Epiphanius persists in employing here what Buell has termed "ethnic reasoning."[78] "Barbarian" still names a race of uncouth primitives (or degenerates), as benighted in the age of Christ as they were in the doomed generation of Noah; "superstition" still serves to describe the beliefs of unredeemed peoples and not merely those of the primordial "Scythians"; and "Judaism" (like the superstition of the Scythians) is named after a people, *the Jews,* and *not* after an object of professed belief or devotion, a "ruler of the universe" (as in *christianismos*/"Christianity"). The fact that assessments of peoples' place in salvation history and their fitness for salvation have been joined to the more familiar qualities of fitness to govern, civilize (missionize), and manage, on the one hand, or to be conquered and governed or enslaved (or superseded), on the other, does not mean that "ethnicity" or "ethnic reasoning" has given way to something fully or ontologically distinct.

For Clement of Alexandria in the second century, "rebirth" into the new race of Christians does not represent "a movement from one religious identity to another nor one from an ethno-racial identity to a religious one. 'Religion' and 'ethnicity' or 'race' are mutually constituting."[79] Indeed, for the early Christian theologian Origen, what is most pathetic about *the Jews* after the destruction of the Jerusalem Temple is their survival as an *ethnos* deprived of its cult and hence irreparably deformed.[80] Over the first several centuries of Christianity, the colonial/imperial discourse classifying and ranking people(s) according to *ethnos/genos* is merged with a similarly totalizing discourse classifying all people(s) in relation to "correct" or "supposed" belief and worship and fitting them into "a massive historico-theological . . . [and] comprehensive view of Christian truth . . . plotted along lines of historical progression."[81]

"The *Ioudaioi* were understood until late antiquity as an ethnic group comparable to other ethnic groups, with their distinctive laws, traditions, customs, and God," asserts Steve Mason.[82] Only later did *the Ioudaioi* come to be understood to constitute a "religion." But what changed for *Ioudaioi* was *not* the narratives of shared history and kinship, laws, traditions, customs, and God (although these never have been static phenomena, and so are always plural, in the process of being developed, transformed, adapted, and negotiated). Throughout late antiquity and subsequent centuries, *Ioudaioi/Iudei/yehudim/Jews* continued to be understood to have "distinctive laws, traditions, customs, and [conceptions of] God"—in other words, to retain all those elements earlier associated with *Jews* as an *ethnos*. What did shift was the naming of these attributes by an increasingly empowered and hegemonic Christian orthodoxy, which more and more chose to describe them as a moribund religion (Judaism) of a (mis)believing people, a religion that both preceded and fell far short of "true" religion. Indeed, the English word *religion*, in its earliest and most frequently attested meanings, stands at a far remove from the ancient Latin *religio* and is far more in keeping with this postclassical derivation in signifying institutions, doctrines, and behaviors expressly belonging to orthodox Christianity.[83]

What had been imagined as a collective *ethnos* within a colonial/imperial system of many *ethné* became "particularized" within Christian theology as the particular other to a universal Christianity. In this way *the Jews* became a kind of universal symbol or signifier, one that henceforth could and would be molded to countless (always problematic, and often lethal) cultural projects. Modern scholars who narrate a historicized evolution of *yehudim* or *Ioudaioi* from *ethnos* to *religion*, then, not only reinscribe and reify the ancient Christian, dualistic hierarchies of particular/universal, birth/faith, flesh/spirit, and the like; ironically, they also assert an ontological difference between ethnicity and religion that masks the very ways in which Christian "ethnic reasoning" both outlined a divine imperial mission and theologically constructed *Judaism* and its adherents, *the Jews*, as necessary (but obsolete) elements of Christian salvation history.

Until the nineteenth century, the word *ethnic*, in English as in other European languages, referred exclusively to non-Christians and non-Jews. Like the *ethné* of pre-Christian Greek colonialism, Western Christianity's *ethnikes* are "lesser" peoples, unenlightened and insufficiently cultured (and, importantly, unredeemed) peoples—peoples who, by and large, ought to be ruled and educated by their "betters." *Ethnic* retains this meaning throughout Western history right up to—and including—its appropriation in the mid-nineteenth century as a social-scientific term closely allied to discourses of racialism and nationalism.[84] In practice, this left *the Jews* as the only non-Christian non-ethnics (until the sometime inclusion of Muslims into that category), further marking it as a unique and ambiguous classification between (or beneath) believers and non-believers. In 1728, the Christian Joseph Morgan could report in his *Complete History of Algiers* that the local Muslims "look upon them [*the Jews*] as several degrees beneath . . . Heathens, Ethnicks, Pagans, and Idolaters."[85] It is particularly striking, then, that by the mid-twentieth century, social-scientific discourse often styled *Jews* the quintessential "ethnics"—when it did not cite *Jew* as the odd exception that did not quite fit available categories.

As this brief (and admittedly schematic) survey suggests, not only do the terms "ethnicity" and "religion" come down to us through the prism of early Christian discourse about *the Jews*, but the narrative of progress from ethnicity to religion itself resembles an explicitly Christian historiography—one that morally subordinates ethnicity (as primitive and particular) to religion (as universal aspiration), much as it morally subordinates Judaism and *Jew* (as limited and superseded) to Christianity and Christian (as universal apex of human attainment). This paradigm, not surprisingly, persists in Enlightenment-era classifications of religions as objects of study: "There is no more marked distinction among religions," insists W. D. Whitney in 1881, "than the one we are called upon to make between a race religion . . . the unconscious growth of generations—and a religion proceeding from an individual founder." In this schema, Judaism, not surprisingly, is one such "unconscious growth of generations" (note the ethno-racial and naturalist language here, as well as the disregard of the Abraham- or Moses-as-founder mythos), whereas Christianity is revealed (by a "great man," Jesus) as a religion "growing out of one that was limited to race."[86] Such limited and limiting "ancient faiths," according to Whitney's contemporary Cornelius Petrus Tiele, "where they still survive in some parts of the world and do not reform themselves after the model of the superior religion, draw nearer and nearer to extinction."[87] (Note, again, the naturalist/evolutionary language of "survival"—of the fittest?—and "extinction.")

The emerging scholarly convention of distinguishing between *Jews* and *Judaeans* in antiquity is, as noted above, both a reflection of and, at times, a calculated response to this difficult legacy. *Judaean* is hailed by some as a theologically neutral term suitable for signifying an "ethnic group" that historically preexisted the invention of "religions" and of *Jews* as a class of believers. But the foregoing examination of the history of the categories "ethnic" and "religion," and of their use by both ancient theologians and modern scholars, suggests that, rather than displacing theological and imperialist paradigms with neutral social-scientific descriptors, *Judaean* as "earlier ethnic group" paired with *Jew* as "later adherent of a religion" (or "ethno-religion" or "race religion") only serves to reinscribe these paradigms still more firmly and subtly while obscuring their association with anti-Jewish discourses. Nor is *Judaean*, then, any less theologically determined and embedded than *Jew*.

If "secular" historiography now determines that "religion" ultimately rendered *Judaeans* defunct, to be replaced by theologically constituted *Jews*, then Christian historiography and its current secular iterations have, in fact, effected a supersession far beyond what triumphalist ecclesiology was ever able to accomplish, and *Jews*—at base, at least in part—is/are a Christian construct.[88] In many important respects this is, indeed, the case, and this book is devoted, in part, to examining this construct. But adopting terminological distinctions that map directly onto ancient Christian imperial categories merely serves to collapse any potential for critical distance between Christian theology and non-Christian historiography. Furthermore, as the entries in the turn-of-the-twenty-first-century edition of the *Greek-English Lexicon of the New Testament and Other Early Christian Literature* attest, the practice of segregating *Judaeans* from *Jews* often serves the paradoxical purpose of rendering substantial times, places, and events in historical narratives perplexingly *judenrein*.

Those like Cohen, Blenkinsopp, Morton Smith, and others who narrate an evolution from "ethnicity" to "(ethno-)religion" earlier than the advent of Christianity do little more than resituate the later paradigm farther back along a historical timeline—reconceiving history, in the footsteps of Eusebius, in such a way as to imagine *Jews* and Judaism according to a Roman Christian paradigm long before that paradigm arose. To be sure, adapting a narrative of cultural development and resituating it in an age of Judaean power and relative sovereignty, as Cohen does, is an act of appropriation that can feel genuinely empowering. And certainly universal visions, professions of belief, and various modes of adoption or assimilation of outsider adherents or converts are clearly discernible in the traditions and narratives regarding *yehudim* and *Ioudaioi* from their earliest appearances onward. But the juxtaposition of "ethnicity/birth/ nation" to "religion/belief/conversion," and the plotting of a concomitant historical evolution of "ethnics" toward "religious" enlightenment, hews closely to what is, at base, a pervasive, demonstrably Christian theological paradigm.

Of course, "ethnics" have long since ceased to be merely the "pagans" and "heathens" of Christian classifications and have come to be the bearers of modern racialist and nationalist "identities."[89] In fact, since the eighteenth century (if not much earlier, with the advent of Castilian "blood purity" ideology), "it is clear that the terms 'Jew' and 'Christian' may take on racial as well as religious significance," such that even distinguishing between these two significations often becomes impracticable.[90] Or, as Gil Anidjar puts it, "Religion and race are *contemporary*, indeed, coextensive and, moreover, co-concealing categories."[91]

Judaean as primordial ethnic ancestor now serves, quite literally, to "ground" *Jew* (and, needless to say, the national homeland of the modern Jewish state) in pre- and post-diasporic territoriality. The toponym *Judaean* roots the wandering *Jew* (that target of nationalist—including Zionist—opprobrium) in a territorialized, ancestral ethno-nation and marks *yehudim* as the very "people of the land" from whom biblical writers worked to distinguish them. This aspect of *Judaean* is perhaps most easily illustrated by the name of one of the earliest and largest Zionist youth organizations, "Young Judaea" (Yehudah Ha-zair), founded in 1909 and still active today.

Primordial ethnicity, too, serves to provide a kind of antiquity and genealogy to *Jew* as a modern "secular" identity. *Judaean* nicely complicates, yet resonates with, an Enlightenment narrative of progress from (benighted, parochial, hegemonic) "religion" to the post-Christian reassertion of (secular, progressive, pluralistic) "ethnicities"—a narrative that obviously mirrors the schema of "progress from ethnicity to religion," and similarly masks the deep interdependence and inter-embeddedness of "religion" and "ethnicity/race," as well as their continuing colonial/ imperial legacy. It is a modern narrative well suited to an age that strives to frame and claim science, democracy, and self-determination as secular universal ideals. As such, it would hold strong appeal to those, like the plaintiffs from Galicia and Bucovina with whom this chapter began, for whom the category of "religion" or "Mosaic Faith" felt alien and alienating, while that of "ethnicity" seemed useful, safe, and strategically sufficient for self-naming.

That Austro-Hungarian case highlights yet another aspect of contingency and contrivance in appeals to "ethnicity/race" or "religion" for classifying *Jew*. In its classification of the plaintiffs as belonging to a "religion," the Imperial Court of Austria-Hungary effectively denied them the right to protection of their traditional language (in this case, Yiddish) and associated educational/cultural institutions, such as was granted to entities legally classified instead as "ethnic groups" or, in the juridical language of that context, "nationalities." By contrast, the cousins of these plaintiffs who found their way to the United States in the same period

> arrived in a country that was more tolerant of religious division than ethnic separatism. . . . It's acceptable in America for Catholics to have parochial schools, but separate schools for Italian Americans would be illegitimate. As a result, American Jews switched categories: They identify as a religion but often behave more as an ethnic group. For many, synagogue membership really means belonging to an ethnic club.[92]

In a very real sense, then, classifying *Jew* as one or another *kind* of entity—as naming a member of a race, ethnicity, religion (or ethnoreligion), class, or nation (or even gender)—is a matter of changing fashion and context that reveals more about reigning paradigms and the concerns of those doing the classifying than about the "nature" or "substance" of the object/subject thus labeled.

In Israel, for example, *Jew* is, among other things, a multidimensional legal status that conveys significant and differential rights, privileges, and disabilities. Establishing that status in various contexts requires meeting very different standards and criteria depending upon whether one is a citizen, a resident, or an immigrant to the country—and these criteria have changed and continue to change over time.

Israel's Law of Return, enacted in 1950, which offers immediate Israeli citizenship and other substantial privileges to *Jews* worldwide, was famously tested by the "Brother Daniel" case in which Shmuel Oswald Rufeisen, a Zionist, Holocaust survivor, rescuer of hundreds, and a Catholic priest, was determined by Israel's Supreme Court in 1962 to be a *Jew* by "religious" standards (Halacha) but not a *Jew* by "secular" standards—and, therefore, ineligible for immediate citizenship under the law.[93] The Law of Return was amended in 1970 to extend "the rights of a Jew under this Law" to "a child and grandchild of a Jew, the spouse of a Jew, the spouse of a child of a Jew and the spouse of a grandchild of a Jew, except for a person who has been a Jew and has voluntarily changed his/her religion."[94]

Religion-based restrictions on marriage in Israel (which has no civil marriage) can be far more constraining for those bearing the legal status *Jew* (and those unable to establish their legal identity as *Jew* by "religion") than for others—but these restrictions do not disqualify marriages performed outside the country. Currently, *Jew* or *Jewish* is both a registered "ethnic" or "national" identity in Israel (while "Israeli" is not—except on passports—and "Hebrew" has been, but is no longer) and a separately registered "religious" identity, as is "no religion"—a designation increasingly popular among some of "Jewish ethnic nationality."[95]

A 2013 Pew Research Center survey of "Jewish Americans" determined its qualifying participants on the basis of phone surveys leading to the identification of subjects who were either "Jews by religion" or "Jews of no religion."[96] This latter category, according to survey findings, accounts for 22 percent of all American *Jews*.[97]

A parsing and analysis of each of the preceding examples, although worthwhile and intriguing in its own right, would require venturing too far beyond this chapter's topic of "origins" to pursue in the present context.[98] For now, it must suffice to observe that categories and classifications applied to *Jew* vary significantly over time and among contexts; that they are laden with histories of power and prejudice; and that they serve as much—if not more so—to prescribe as to describe, to delineate and limit as to reveal.

Historiography—the writing of history—has always played a part in (a) people's self-fashioning and aspiration. The historiography of *Jews* long stood within the purview of cultures and institutions for which *Jew* served as counterimage and "less than": less than redeemed, civilized, enlightened; even, at times, less than fully human. In the current era, the historiography of *Jews* has expanded to encompass narratives that ground the claims, self-understandings, and aspirations of many who self-identify as *Jew* (as well as many institutions that claim to represent them) while still employing paradigms and categories deriving from these earlier, often antithetical, discourses.

It would be an understatement to say that there are many debates about *Jew*. Not a few such debates concern meanings and origins. *Religion or Ethnicity?* reads the title of a volume of essays whose subject matter ranges from the Hellenistic Mediterranean in antiquity to "Secular Jewishness . . . Today" and whose subtitle, *Jewish Identities in Evolution*, is redolent of the early-modern naturalist and racialist discourses that first classified the "religion" of *Jews* as both primitive and bound for extinction.[99] Sometimes the stakes in these debates are quite limited. At other times they are—or seem—very high: life and death, survival or extinction. And yet, the higher the stakes are perceived to be, the less compelling, perhaps, the distinctions become. After all, as the terrors and annihilations visited upon those identified as *Jews* in the name of racial/cultural/national purity or eugenics, on the one hand, and in the name of salvation, faith, and the kingdom of heaven, on the other, suggest, "ethnicity/race" and "religion" are *both* woefully inadequate as "public metaphor[s]" (in the words of Richard Rodriguez, quoted above) for naming the differences signified by *Jew.*

2 State of the (Jew[ish]) Question

> The Jew, you know, what does he have that
> properly belongs to him, that wasn't borrowed,
> lent, and never returned?
>
> Paul Celan, "Conversation in the Mountains"

> The expectation of self-determination that self-
> naming arouses is paradoxically contested by
> the historicity of the name itself: by the history
> of the usages that one never controlled, but that
> constrain the very usage that now emblematizes
> autonomy; by the future efforts to deploy the
> term against the grain of the current ones, and
> that will exceed the control of those who seek
> to set the course of the terms in the present.
>
> Judith Butler, *Bodies That Matter*

> Am I that name, Iago?
>
> William Shakespeare, *Othello*

A well-known scene in Woody Allen's film *Annie Hall* finds Allen's char-acter, Alvy Singer, complaining to a friend (who addresses him as "Max") about a recent conversation with some "guys from NBC." Alvy recounts the troubling exchange: To his own innocent question "Did you eat yet, or what?" he hears the reply, as he puts it: "'No; didjoo?' Not, did you, didjoo eat? Jew? No, not did you eat, but Jew eat? Jew? You get it? Jew eat?" "Max," replies his friend, "you see conspiracies in everything."[1]

To Allen's character, the queries "Did you?" and "Jew?" are identical, indistinguishable. "*Jew?*" / "*Did you?*" as query carries the not-quite-veiled charge of unspecified but threatening accusation. *Jew?* is an interrogation, an inquisition, a question explicitly about identity and association—one that often has been received (as it is by Alvy) as a kind of psychic blow. And it can function this way regardless of who is asking the question and of whom it is asked. Franz Kafka, in one of his letters to Milena Jesenska, written from Meran in 1920, describes just this sensation:

> Now I will again say something dumb on the same subject, it's dumb of me to say something I think is correct when I know it will hurt me. . . . And on top of that, Milena is still going on about anxiety, striking my chest and asking: *jste žid?* which in Czech has the same movement and sound. Don't you see how the fist is pulled back in the word *jste*, so as to gain muscle power? And then the word *žid* the happy blow, flying unerringly forward?[2]

Kafka is infatuated with Milena, and their long-distance correspondence is a kind of lovers' play. The "anxiety" (or "neurosis") that first became a symptom of and synonym for *Jew* in nineteenth-century Europe—and that is exploited to such comic effect by Woody Allen—is a prominent thread in many of Kafka's letters to Milena and is the subject of extended meditation in more than one of them. Kafka does not accuse Milena of harming him with her question (in fact, he assures her that any harm to him in this exchange will be self-inflicted). Nonetheless, Kafka's characterization of the word *Jew* as a well-directed blow—albeit a "happy" or "cheerful" one delivered by his beloved—is, so to speak, striking.[3]

Jacques Derrida likewise describes receiving the word *Jew*—in his first recollected encounter with it—as a blow and, even more, a barb. It is intended as such, although not, in this case, as an interrogative. Derrida being Derrida, however, the word comes to *invite* interrogation as a name/noun assigned to and thence embodied by him, a perplexing but increasingly significant element of a contingent sense of self:

> As for the word *jew*, I do not believe I heard it first in my family, nor ever as neutral designation meant to classify, even less to identify a belonging to a social, ethnic, or religious community. I believe I heard it at school in El Biar, already charged with what, in Latin, one could call an insult [*injure*], *Injuria*, in English, *injury*, both an insult, a wound, and an injustice, a denial of right rather than the right to belong to a legitimate group. Before understanding any of it, I received this word like a blow, a denunciation, a de-legitimation prior to any right, prior to any legality. A blow struck [*un coup porté*] against me, but a blow that I would henceforth have to carry and incorporate [*porter, comporter*] forever in the very essence of my most singularly signed and assigned . . . *comportment*. It is as if I had to countersign the blow thus struck prior

even to any possible memory. This word, this performative address . . . this apostrophe was, remains, and carries, older than the claim [*constat*], more archaic than any constative, the figure of a wounding arrow, of a weapon or a projectile that has sunk into your body, once and for all and without the possibility of ever uprooting it. It adheres to your body and pulls it toward itself from within. . . . One can, afterward, assume this word, treat it in a thousand different ways, think it honorable to subscribe to it, to sign and countersign it. But, for me at least, it guards and keeps the mark of this assignation, of this unveiling that denounces, even of this originary accusation, this guilt or responsibility, *granted* dissymmetrically prior to any fault or act.[4]

To young Jacques (as to my young Israeli student), the word *Jew* is neither familiar nor familial. It is not heard in everyday parlance as a term for self, nor for voluntary or commonplace association. Instead, *Jew* is an injurious blow that arrives from outside his home and family and outside himself but comes to lodge so deeply within that it becomes an inalienable—and inherently alienating—part of him. Derrida's account of his experience (an experience shared and recounted by many members of his and other generations and places)[5] instantiates the profoundly ambivalent modern project of translating *Jew* from accusative object to nominative subject. The "Jewish question" that haunts the modern era is, in some measure, a question about the possibility and means of turning this name for *other*, a name that denies, *de*legitimates, and *de*nounces, into a name for *self*, a *pro*nouncement about identity, connection, and the contours of "legitimate" difference.

For much of the past two thousand years, those whom historians and theologians term *Jews* have often not referred to themselves as *Jews*. In many times and places, of course, it has simply not been safe to do so. But there is far more to this phenomenon than mere avoidance. Halachically, liturgically, and literarily, the self-designation was most often *yisrael*—"Israel" or "Israelite," a biblical Hebrew name rich with tradition and honor. Socially and politically, self-identification was often by birthplace or homeland: Alexandrian or Galilean or Judaean in antiquity, for example; Litvak or Galitzianer, American or Israeli more recently. Some, like the descendants of forced converts from the Iberian Peninsula, even appropriated for themselves coded anti-Jewish nomenclature. These latter, for instance, knew each other simply as "(men of) the nation."[6] *Jew* or *Jewish*, as widespread terms of self-designation or intra-group identification, have, by comparison, a far more limited and thorny history.

In the two millennia leading up to the late twentieth century, the term *Jew(s)* was most frequently and forcefully used to denote an other—a "religious" and/or "ethnic" and/or "racial" other; in particular (as discussed in chapter 1), a constitutively necessary other to Christianity and to Christian and post-Christian European cultures. The term clearly retains this connotation to the present day. Prior to the advent of modernity, creation of knowledge about *Jew(s)* was, likewise, primarily a non-Jewish (and often an anti-Jewish) enterprise. Formulating meaning and content for the category *Jew(s)* had everything to do with constructing and sustaining collective identities that were "not that" (whatever "that" was construed to be). This long history of *Jew* as not-self, as dross to be purged in the refinement of (collective and individual) self, reached its devastating apogee in the twentieth century's Nazi war against *the Jew(s)*.

In the present era, by contrast, *Jew* has come more and more to be appropriated as a self-identification, a term by which "we *Jews*" speak about and represent "ourselves" in the common languages of "our" many homelands.[7] Concomitantly, the last century, in particular, has also witnessed an explosion in the number of self-identified *Jews* contributing to discourses about *(the) Jew(s)*. Needless to say, these contributions have emerged within—and are of a piece with—cultural environments shaped by the Enlightenment and Emancipation/Haskalah;[8] by the rise of modern nationalisms, secularism, and sciences; by mass migrations and mobility; and by technologically enhanced mechanisms of production, distribution, and destruction. Moreover, these contributions are part and parcel of the construction of *Jew* as self; of a seeking not merely to defuse harms long associated with the name but to control and lay claim to rhetorical, discursive, and even material powers that the name has accrued.

Currently, *Jew* conveys neither a simple sense of abject otherness nor one of secured selfhood, but rather something far more complex and multifarious. *Jew* has become a deeply and actively contested term (as will already be clear from the introduction and chapter 1), and a term whose appropriation as a signifier for self may be even more fraught than is/was its use as a designation for other. In part, this is no doubt due to the fact that the name itself, "despite the expectation of self-determination that self-naming arouses," will always be constrained by the long history of usage of the name *Jew* for *everything but* an "authentic" self. Constructing and sustaining a self (individually and collectively) is an inherently precarious endeavor; fashioning *Jew* as self is, perhaps, only more so.

In this chapter, I explore the state of the (*Jew*[ish]) question, thus understood, through a brief series of particular lenses. This exploration is intended to be suggestive and inviting of reflection, expansion, and nuance from those both within and beyond the disciplines and subject areas invoked.

The chapter is broadly divided into three sections. The first considers *der yid*, the Yiddish term of address that does—and does not—literally translate to "the *Jew*." The second examines the *Jew* both as a subject area within Jewish-studies scholarship and as key to a process of modern subject- or self-formation by means of such scholarship. The third explores a number of contending claims about what *Jew* can and cannot be made to mean, as well as about the ethical and existential implications of claiming *Jew* as a name for self in the late twentieth and early twenty-first centuries.

Before proceeding, it is worth quoting one more writer who gives eloquent voice to the utterly simple and yet impossibly complicated process of wresting a sense of self out of the experience of *Jew* delivered and received "as a blow." In this account, the blow is delivered by a fist, not by an utterance, and its delivery serves to constitute the *Jew* in question as a subject in the full, Foucauldian sense of *assujetissement* or "subjectivation," a word coined to describe "the formation of a subject through embodied subjection," or, in the words of Judith Butler, to describe how "one inhabits the figure of autonomy only by becoming subjected to a power."[9] It shares this dynamic with the blow cited in Derrida's narrative, above. The present account differs radically, however, in that the blow in question is *delivered* (amid many also received) by the *Jew*.

In an essay entitled "On the Necessity and Impossibility of Being a Jew," philosopher and Holocaust survivor Jean Améry describes his moment of "self-realization" in the Auschwitz concentration camp:

> Before me I see the prisoner foreman Juszek, a Polish professional criminal of horrifying vigor. In Auschwitz he once hit me in the face because of a trifle; that is how he was used to dealing with all the Jews under his command. At this moment—I felt it with piercing clarity—it was up to me to go a step further in my prolonged appeals case against society. In open revolt I struck Juszek in the face in turn. My human dignity lay in this punch to his jaw—and that it was in the end I, the physically much weaker man, who succumbed and was woefully thrashed, meant nothing to me. Painfully beaten, I was satisfied with myself. . . . What I later read in Frantz Fanon's *Les damnés de la terre*, in a theoretical analysis of the behavior of colonized peoples, I anticipated back then when I gave concrete social form to my dignity by punching a human face. To be a Jew meant the acceptance of the death sentence imposed by the world as a world verdict. To flee before it by withdrawing into one's self would have been nothing but a disgrace, whereas *acceptance was simultaneously the physical revolt against it. I became a person not by subjectively appealing to my abstract humanity but by discovering*

myself within the given social reality as a rebelling Jew and by realizing myself as one.[10]

Whereas *Jew* as other might be assimilated, accommodated, tolerated, or annihilated within a realm of "abstract humanity," *Jew* as subject or self could be realized only "within the given social reality" of *Jew* as abject other and in response to it (insofar as response was possible at all).[11] Derrida describes this realization and response as a demand "to countersign the blow thus struck"; Améry's countersign is explicitly a counterblow; and Kafka, in describing himself as "the most Westernized Jew of them all," explains that for him, as such, "everything must be earned [or "conquered"], not only the present and the future, but the past as well— something which is, perhaps, given every human being [as a "birthright"]—this too must be earned. . . . If the Earth turns to the right . . . then I would have to turn to the left to make up for the past."[12]

Jew as self, then, is an open question with often confusing, conflicting, and contrary answers. *Jew* is an ongoing engagement with many and diverse interlocutors—some appearing as antagonists or sparring partners, some as arbiters or advocates. *Jew* as "identity" asks, "Identical to what? To whom?" As a name for self or a version of self, it is also a subversion or subversive kind of self as it arises in Western cultures. As "us" or "we" or "I," it is always also "them." Given the apparently irresolvable state of the "*Jewish* question," it is perhaps only fitting to proceed with a question posed in a peculiarly and quintessentially Jewish language that began to emerge early in the second millennium of the Common Era and that flourished toward that millennium's end before being nearly extinguished.[13]

Vos Macht a Yid?

Colloquially, this common Yiddish query translates roughly as "What's up? How's it going?" A literal translation, however, ends up asking instead, "What's a *Jew* doing?" One might rephrase this peculiar and obtuse question, this partial and naive translation, by asking: Is *yid* merely another word for *Jew* (or *Jew* for *yid*)? Does *Jew* properly translate *yid*? What is the relationship between the two terms? Are they equivalents or something else? Dictionaries invariably translate the Yiddish *yid* to the English *Jew* (or the French *juif*, the Spanish *judío*, and so on)—but the asserted equivalence invites far more nuance.

Jew seldom functions in English the way that *yid* functions in Yiddish, and the latter carries decidedly different connotations from "Yid" in English. In his comical follow-up to *The Joys of Yiddish*, Leo Rosten writes in *The Joys of Yinglish* that "Yid" is "an offensive, demeaning, disagreeable way of referring to a Jew—if you pronounce this *Yid*, to rhyme with 'kid,' instead of YEED, to rhyme with 'deed.' Jews say 'Yeed'—unless they want to characterize a Jew as a coarse, vulgar, ill-mannered, greedy, grubby (*et alia*) person."[14] Here in a nutshell, it seems, is *Jew* as self ("Yeed") versus *Jew* as other ("Yid"). But is it that simple? In one sense, yes; in another, no. "Yid" (pronounced to rhyme with "kid"), while clearly appropriated from the Yiddish, may be incorporated into a sentence spoken by anyone in any language (including, in theory, Yiddish—or "Yinglish"), in order to demean a *Jew* qua *Jew*. (And, for that matter, it is not clear that *yid/yeed* could always be distinguished from "Yid" in a sentence spoken in English.) Adding yet another wrinkle to the question, the terms "Yid," "Yiddo," and "Yid Army" have become proud rallying cries for the fans of some European soccer clubs—and of the British Tottenham Hotspur football team, in particular—many of whom otherwise have little use for or identification with the name *Jew* (much less *yid*).[15]

Postcolonial and linguistic theories provide all manner of tools for analyzing and describing such examples of how language may be manipulated and deployed—through slang words and other means—to mark a variety of internal and external boundaries. Some of these tools will be employed below. For now, I wish merely to forestall the assumption of a too-simplistic calculus of who/what constitutes "us" versus "them," or "real" versus "caricature," or "insider" versus "outsider" with regard to *yid*.

It is a particular attribute of spoken Yiddish that, in addressing an adult male speaker of the language—whether stranger, friend, or associate—polite custom involves calling him "*yid*." The practice is most readily illustrated by the phrase introduced above, *Vos macht a yid?* As John Efron observes, this phrase "is a term of affection and familiarity. . . . [It is] considered warmer and more intimate than the mere use of the person's name to ask after their wellbeing."[16] At the same time, *yid*, in Yiddish speech, also represents the most formal manner of addressing a male stranger in public. For example, "*Ikh miz baitn bei daim yeedn er zol zakh avekzetsen*" is a polite means by which to say, "I must request that the gentleman (lit. "the Jew") be seated."[17] *Der yid*, as a polite or intimate term of address, is a peculiarity of Yiddish linguistic culture. "The *Jew*" can never function this way in English, French, German, Russian, Polish, Spanish, Arabic, or Hebrew. "What's up, *Jew*?" could conceivably work in an appropriative, interventionist fashion similar to the African American greeting "What up, Nigga?" but neither of these phrases bears the force of plain civility. "What's up, *Jew*?" inhabits a linguistic universe decidedly different from *Vos macht a yid?* How, then, might one best convey the meaning of the self-referential name *yid* and provide a sense of how it functions in the varied dialects of the language that has come to be called "Yiddish"?

By way of answer—apropos of Yiddish culture—I cite a story of a story: At the start of her scholarly monograph *Faithful Renderings: Jewish-Christian Difference and the Politics of Translation*, Naomi Seidman relates a story her father (a Hasid who earned a Ph.D. in Jewish history and served as archivist to the Jewish community of Warsaw before World War II) told about serving as an "unofficial liaison between the French authorities and the Jewish refugee community in post-war Paris."[18] Having been called one morning to the Gare de l'Est, where an exhausted and upset group of newly arrived refugees "without proper documents" was being held by the French police, Hillel Seidman asked to speak to the group. He proceeded to address them in Yiddish, collectively as *yidn*, and reassured them that "while the French were certainly *goyim*, they weren't Nazis; nobody would be mistreated" during the time it would take the local Jewish community to arrange their release. When one of the police officers asked what he had said to calm the frantic crowd, Monsieur Seidman, "thinking in French," responded, "I quoted to them the words of a great Frenchman: 'Every free man has two homelands—his own, and France.' I assured them that they, who had suffered so much, had arrived at a safe haven, the birthplace of human liberty." "As my father told it," his daughter concludes, "the *gendarmes* wiped away patriotic tears at his speech."[19]

Thinking and speaking in French to representatives of French state authority (an authority with the power to "differentiate between refugees and citizens, foreign aliens and new immigrants"),[20] the "translator" powerfully invokes the universalizing abstractions of "human liberty" and "every free man" promoted by the French Enlightenment. By contrast, thinking and speaking in Yiddish to survivors of the Nazi terror, he instead addresses himself to the implicit danger: *these* authorities are not Nazis (notwithstanding very recent collaboration between the two); you will not be harmed (this time); there are others of us, *yidn* (myself, for instance), in this place with the power to secure your release. The asymmetry of Hillel Seidman's doubled speech clearly resonates with Améry's juxtaposition (above) of the dignity of "abstract humanity" to the "given social reality of the . . . Jew," and it resonates, as well, with what James C. Scott has characterized as a "public transcript, that is, official history as the record of what can be said in the presence of power," versus a "hidden transcript, the secret communication of a subjugated group."[21]

In further parsing the Yiddish version of her father's recounted speech and its effect on the anxious crowd, Naomi Seidman cites a linguistic feature of Yiddish that Max Weinreich, premier historian of Yiddish, refers to as *"lehavdl loshn*, or 'differentiation language': 'There are words applied to Jews (or even neutrally, when no differentiation is intended), and these have a parallel series that has to begin with a derogatory connotation. . . . ' Chief in this parallel series is the word *goy.* . . . My father, then, in using the word *goyim* [instead of the neutral *nit-yidn*], was invoking the entire culture system . . . [that] distinguishes between the realm that is 'ours' and the realm that belongs to 'them.'"[22]

She continues:

> His main purpose . . . was to reassure the group of refugees that his intentions toward them were entirely friendly. If my father mobilized the differentiation resources of Yiddish, it was to signal to the group that he was a real Jew, one of "us" rather than a neutral player on the deracinated urban field. My father's words were thus a speech act, *doing* something with words rather than merely communicating information. . . . Beyond the content of what he was saying, beyond the choice of the word *goyim*, and before the vocative "*Yidn*," my father's Galicianer Yiddish was itself performing his Jewish affiliations, announcing where he came from and where his sympathies could be assumed to lie. . . . Yiddish, in such speech acts, has a metavalue, signifying in itself—in its distinctive sounds rather than in its communicable content. The implications of such an understanding of language are considerable: If the very use of Yiddish is a form of signification, translation becomes manifestly impossible.[23]

It is precisely such "metavalue," such "signifying in itself," that suggests that a translational equivalency between *yid* in Yiddish and *Jew* in the West's "official" languages is, on some level, "manifestly impossible." Put another way, the Yiddish self-referential *yid* performs a very different speech act than does the dominant vernaculars' *Jew.*

Given this manifest disparity and asymmetry, it is important to bear in mind that the *yid* of Yiddish—in fact, the entire multilingual culture of Yiddish itself (if one can speak of such)—is always at least "doubly situated."[24] "Speaking Yiddish," Seidman observes, "has been described as inhabiting a portable Yiddishland, and my father [in his address to the crowd] could be said to be clearing a shared Jewish space—indeed, given the dialectical variation among Yiddish-speakers, *constructing* a shared space—within the public arena of the European metropolis."[25] *Yid/Yidn* inhabits both spaces—European (or other) metropolis *and* "Yiddishland"—simultaneously; one does not cancel out, displace, or give the lie to the other. Our story's "translator," according to his daughter, is only one among countless instances of such a doubly situated *yid*: drawing on a Hasidic upbringing and doctoral studies in French history, what he "said in Yiddish and what he said in French are equally true, equally faithful to who he was, and equally illuminating of the journey he took."[26]

It is in this multilingual space of double-situatedness, this linguistic culture with its built-in *lehavdl loshn*, that the word *yid* becomes a multifaceted name for self, for the subject of all the common, valued attributes and familiar foibles with which "we" and "I" learn to identify. A *yidish harts*, for example, is a heart "full of compassion for the needy and those in distress; it is always ready to help a fellow man, especially when the other is wronged by either man or nature."[27] In any "public transcript" of a dominant Western vernacular, this definition would be far more familiarly assigned to "a Christian heart," whereas "a Jewish heart" would be that attributed to the likes of Shylock or Fagin or Judas (or perhaps, at best, to the likes of Theodore Herzl), but never to one who merely displays uncommon decency and generosity.[28]

But *yid* in its home language has never become a synonym for "good," as *Christian* has often functioned in the dominant discourses of the West. As a direct result of the meanings attributed to *Christian* and *Jew* through most of (Christian) Western history, a *yidisher mazl* spells *bad* luck for *yidn* (which might be survived by one with an astute *yidisher kopf*). In order to experience the opposite of bad luck, one must have, not *mazel tov*, but rather a dose of *goyisher mazl* (a condition taken for granted by one with a *goyisher kopf*).[29] (Needless to say, there are and have been many other ways to name "bad luck," "good luck," and the like in Yiddish. My focus here is on uses of the words *yid, yidn,* and *yidisher,* in particular.)

Yid as a term for self arises in Yiddish from both its Hebrew/Aramaic and its Germanic or Slavic parentages, and, as the foregoing examples suggest, it is a term for an explicitly *subjected* self (however it might come to be "assumed . . . signed and countersigned," to invoke Derrida's metaphors of agency). By no means, however, should this observation be taken as a characterization of Yiddish speakers as servile or "self-hating." After all, clear-eyed recognition and naming of one's subjected status is a prerequisite for resistance and subversion, whereas denial of such imposed status undercuts these possibilities. *Yid* names a self whose subjection is a function of its otherness to all things *goyisher,* but also of a culturally inscribed subordination of Yiddish to the more privileged Hebrew/Aramaic element (*loshn-koydesh,* "holy tongue") within Yiddish culture itself.

Much has been written about the multilingualism of Yiddish culture—both in terms of what has been called "internal" bi- or multilingualism and in terms of "external" bi- or multilingualism.[30] "Ashkenazic Jews," writes Weinreich, "have always had to be bilingual; most members of the Jewish community had to know—some more, some less—besides their Jewish language, the language [or languages] of the coterritorial majority."[31] Such "external" multilingualism is a widely shared phenomenon found especially, though not exclusively, in colonial/postcolonial and imperial contexts, where an official language differs from that of local minorities or even majorities. Those who termed themselves *yidn* would have been fully aware of the word for *Jew(s)* in the dominant or official local vernacular(s) and slangs, along with the connotations it carried in those linguistic cultures.

External Bilingualism

Some among the Jewish intellectual elites of eighteenth- and nineteenth-century Europe sought to "reclaim" this *Jew* (*Jude, juif*) from the negative connotations it held in the dominant linguistic cultures and render it palatable and honorable as a name for self. Their efforts to do so often went hand in hand with the derogation of Yiddish (and of other "Jewish jargons"), as well as with the "othering" of Yiddish speakers (especially those from Eastern Europe), who frequently came to serve as foils in these reclamation projects.

In his book *Jewish Self-Hatred: Anti-Semitism and the Hidden Language of the Jews*, Sander Gilman traces a historical progression from Martin Luther's characterization of Yiddish as "the language of thieves" and thereby "the natural expression of the Jewish spirit,"[32] through Johann Christoph Wagenseil's late seventeenth-century missionary manual's portrayal of "Yiddish as a sinful act committed by the Jews against the German tongue" (in language redolent of Host-desecration legends),[33] to the eighteenth-century "thinkers of the [German] Enlightenment [who] desired the Jews to convert, not to Christianity, but to the new religion of rationalism" and to abandon their "degenerate" and "corrupt" language that fostered superstition, dishonesty, hypocrisy, and irrationality.[34] Onto the historical stage, thus set, stepped the philosopher Moses Mendelssohn, raised in Yiddish and talmudic culture, later educated in German literature and philosophy, for whom the full embrace and articulation of Enlightenment ideals came to demand not conversion of, but reclamation of, both *der Jude* and *der yid*.

Mendelssohn's way was paved in his venture by his good friend Gotthold Ephraim Lessing, whose play *Die Juden* (*The Jews*) featured a protagonist exhibiting all the noble qualities appropriate for an ideal eighteenth-century European hero. Unlike all previous such heroes, however, Lessing's is revealed, at the climax of the play, to be a *Jew*, while the play's villains, presumed by the audience to be *Jews*, are discovered to be Gentiles. Mendelssohn—in his own day and ever since—has been presented by friends, critics, and biographers as the very embodiment of Lessing's fictional protagonist. The hero of Lessing's later, better-known play *Nathan the Wise* is understood, in turn, to be largely modeled on Mendelssohn himself.

But how did Mendelssohn, as an accomplished Enlightenment thinker, understand that self, in relationship to both the newly idealized and the traditionally derogatory images of *Jew* very much at play in unfolding Enlightenment discourse? One key to answering this question is to be found in Mendelssohn's response to the public challenge posed to him in 1769, by Protestant theologian and physiognomist Johann Kaspar Lavater, either to refute current "scientific proofs" of the truth of Christianity or else concede them and convert. Mendelssohn's response is best perceived as taking shape over a number of years, in a number of languages, and along several axes that, woven together, may be understood to constitute Mendelssohn's formulation of the modern *Jew* as self. In the words of Michael A. Meyer, with Mendelssohn, "an experienced consciousness of the self as Jew first finds articulate expression in the language of a larger intellectual milieu."[35]

First and foremost, Mendelssohn may be said to have modeled *Jew* as self through his famously decorous, gracious, and civil comportment in all times and places. That he understood himself to be embodying an exemplary *Jew* (*Jude*) is clear from his remark to Lavater that "I wish to refute the world's contemptuous opinion of the Jew not by writing disputatious essays but by leading an exemplary life."[36] In that same letter he proceeds to outline a number of what he deems admirable qualities of Judaism taught by "our rabbis"—such as universal access to virtue and salvation and a disinterest in seeking converts. In the 1780s, Mendelssohn went on to publish a translation of the Torah entitled *Sefer Netivot Hashalom* (more commonly known as the *Bi'ur*), executed in an elegant German *written in Hebrew* (hence, also Yiddish) *characters* and accompanied by a commentary drawing on a range of medieval rabbinic Torah commentaries. This was followed closely by his *Jerusalem*, a treatise that called for, among other things, freedom of conscience and religion. *Jerusalem* has been called "the work of a man who had achieved a unique and highly personal blend of the rabbinic culture in which he had grown up and continued to feel at home and the European Enlightenment in which he had immersed himself with such dazzling success."[37] Finally, in addition to working directly and indirectly for the amelioration of social and legal disabilities imposed upon *Jews*, Mendelssohn likely supported David Friedländer's founding of the Freyschule für Knaben, the first modern Jewish public school in Berlin.

Mendelssohn refused Lavater's challenge to refute publicly the most recent "proofs" of Christological claims for obvious reasons—namely, that, as in their medieval iterations, the polemical nature of public disputations would inevitably occasion incivility, imply ungraciousness, provide nothing in the way of genuine enlightenment, and imperil *Jews*. As Andrew Bush has observed, "For Mendelssohn, to accept debate on [the terms offered by Lavater] . . . is already to lose. . . . *The terms of debate*

offered by Lavater . . . were designed to silence him as a Jew."[38] By not responding according to those terms but instead formulating his own, Mendelssohn
seizes a kind of agency that enables him to speak and act as subject of his
own agenda and to redefine terms—in particular, the term *Jew*—toward
his own ends.

This he does, not only in his open letter to Lavater, but most importantly in his book *Jerusalem* and in his creation of a "German" translation
of the Torah for Yiddish/Hebrew readers—one that would enable *yidn* to
better master both the dominant language and the "pristine" biblical
writings, whose Yiddish versions tended to be drastically abridged and
altered for the edification of "women and uneducated men" or "simple
people."[39] Looking back at both of these projects, twentieth-century historiographers have often characterized Mendelssohn as navigating a kind
of divided consciousness or psychic split between a *Jew* self and a Western
Enlightenment self. Meyer refers to him as "living in two worlds," where
"Mendelssohn the philosopher confronted Mendelssohn the Jew," and
Alexander Altmann asserts that "to some it appeared that the two sections of *Jerusalem* represented the coexistence of two separate halves of
his personality rather than a unified whole."[40] Gilman, for his part, prefers to understand Mendelssohn's projects within a framework of "Jewish
self-hatred" and anti-Yiddishism and posits a "split that occurs in
Mendelssohn's self-definition as a Jew" by which Mendelssohn's works
position him as a "good Jew" over against the disputatious, Talmud-
immersed, Yiddish-speaking "bad Jews" of the "East."[41] In other words,
Gilman reads Mendelssohn as formulating a rationalist "good *Jew* self" by
concomitantly formulating a "bad *yid* non-self." There is very little in the
writings of the ever-temperate and decorous Mendelssohn, however, to
indicate such derisive and divisive attitudes, whereas his lifelong engagement with talmudic and midrashic literature and his body of Yiddish
correspondence might be read as counterevidence to the charge.

If Gilman's assessment is not easily made to stick to Mendelssohn
himself, it is undoubtedly compelling, however, with regard to others of
Mendelssohn's circle and writers of later decades and centuries who did,
in fact, explicitly derogate Yiddish and the *Ostjuden*—or superstitious,
unenlightened Eastern European *yidn*—over and against whom they
defined their "Western" selves. "Jews such as Ackord and Friedländer,"
writes Gilman, "saw their own distancing of the malevolent qualities of
the Jews living in the East, qualities seen as universal by many of their
Christian contemporaries, as an acceptable means of localizing charges
about the hidden language of the Jews."[42] Such "displacement" of the
dominant culture's standard negative understandings of *Jew* onto *yidn*, on
the part of many who sought to appropriate *Jew* as a name for a virtuous

and honorable self within a Western framework, is well documented for the late eighteenth century and beyond. Evidence is overwhelming, as well, for the ways in which this dynamic ultimately undermined the security of both *Juden* and *yidn*, West and East.

Internal Bilingualism

Of equal significance for understanding *der yid* is the "internal bilingualism" of Yiddish culture. Again, Weinreich is credited with popularizing the notion of what he calls "the symbiosis of Yiddish and Loshn-koydesh throughout the entire history of Ashkenaz."[43] Besides being written in the Hebrew alphabet and incorporating or adapting many Hebrew and Aramaic words, Yiddish, from its inception, has always coexisted with its *loshn-koydesh*. This Yiddish/Hebrew bilingualism—or, better, diglossia— does not take the form of two parallel languages, but rather "involves relations of complementarity, symbiosis, and hierarchy; the two languages divide one linguistic terrain between themselves, as it were, so that one set of concepts derives from Hebrew and another from Yiddish. . . . The lines along which Hebrew and Yiddish split the field of language functions correspond to other social and cultural structures that organize the Ashkenazic community."[44] For example, "correspondences can be drawn between Hebrew-Yiddish relations and such important oppositions as sacred/profane, educated/uneducated . . . writing/speech . . . and the (equally unstable) male/female, masculine/feminine binary opposition."[45]

Hebrew is the sacred language of the Torah; rabbinic Hebrew and Aramaic, the sacred languages of prayer and study. Yiddish, by contrast, is the language of the marketplace and kitchen. Hebrew and Aramaic are central to the education of boys, but only mere rudiments of each are provided, generally speaking, to girls. Yiddish is the language of conversation, the first language of children, the *mame-loshn*. *Loshn-koydesh* is the formal language of legal correspondence and recording.

With regard to the name *yid* as a self-designation, this "internal bilingualism" manifests in a number of different ways. For example, as noted above, the common Hebrew designations *yisrael* and *b'nei yisrael* serve, throughout history and cross-culturally, as the primary self-designations in Jewish liturgical, halachic, and premodern literary contexts—including among Yiddish-speaking populations. For everyday usages, on the more "profane" or "secular" side of this split field, the name *yidn* became the most common collective term, but, even here, "the individual Jew was frequently called *bar-yisroel* (son of Israel)," from talmudic Aramaic, rather than the corresponding singular *yid*.[46] Nonetheless, *"der yid"* and *"reb yid"* became polite, formal modes of address of (male) strangers, while the friendliest of familiar salutations came to be *"Vos macht a yid?"*

There is, on the other hand, no polite way to address a woman using any form of the name *yid*—in fact, many sources emphasize the irredeemably derogatory nature of the feminine *yidene* (and parallels). As Michael Wex's decidedly nonacademic introduction to common Yiddish usage explains, "The only feminine equivalent of *reb yeed* is the word that means 'Mrs.' in the non-Yiddish language of the country in which you happen to find yourself."[47] The word *yid* applied to a man is polite; applied to a woman (in either the "generic" masculine or the specific feminine), it is an insult. Use of a local (dominant-vernacular) term of address marks one as an outsider to Yiddish culture when directed to a man, yet as an insider when directed to a woman. The gendering of the Hebrew-Yiddish divide invites further elaboration in the present context.

Weinreich locates this gendering in the very earliest centuries of the emergence of Yiddish literature:

> The prospective public of the new literature in Yiddish consisted not only of women, but also of the less educated men. But it so came to be that a kind of legal fiction was created: obviously women are not versed in Hebrew books, let them therefore partake of Jewishness by means of Yiddish. The most frequent advertising version found on the title pages and in the introductions of older Yiddish works is "proper and intelligible for women and girls." Meanwhile, since the works were already in existence, uneducated men also came to enjoy them.[48]

Weinreich's unselfconscious assertion that "obviously women are not versed in Hebrew books" derives from a long and strong tradition (not without faint countertraditions) of the exclusion of women from Hebrew and talmudic study—a tradition that goes as far back as the early rabbinic movement in the first centuries of the Common Era. Torah/Talmud study, as many have noted, "defined the ideal male, indeed defined maleness itself" in the cultures in which it was (is) embraced.[49]

This hierarchical "internal bilingualism" that genders Hebrew as "masculine" and Yiddish as "feminine" has profound implications for an understanding of the contingencies and negotiations that give shape to *yid* as a term for self. "The 'femininity' of Yiddish was a problem, above all, for men and masculinity," observes Naomi Seidman, one that became even more urgent with the growth and flourishing of a modern secular Hebrew literature in addition to traditional rabbinic Hebrew/Aramaic forms. "The choice between Yiddish and Hebrew, for bilingual writers or the bilingual community, often pitted 'masculinity' against 'femininity' within the individual man or male community, rather than men against women. This was especially true in the modern period, with the foregrounding of the notion of writing as individual expression" and reading as an individual experience.[50] Reading and writing as a means of constructing, expressing, and sustaining a sense of individual and/or collective self is as fraught and gender-laden an enterprise within Yiddish culture as is writing a Jewish self in other early-modern European linguistic cultures. And transposing between a Yiddish self and a Jewish self, if not "manifestly impossible," can be, at best, "an ambivalent operation of self-translation."[51]

The stakes of the gendered Yiddish/Hebrew binary rise exponentially and shift dramatically with the emergence and triumph of Zionism in the late nineteenth and twentieth centuries. In assimilating and reproducing European models of militarized, nationalistic masculinity, statist Zionism tended to deride both the talmudic quietism of rabbinic tradition and the secularist internationalism of Yiddish culture as equally "feminine" and deplorable symptoms of *galut*—"exile" or "dispersion" from the biblical homeland. "[Theodore Herzl's] attitude, shared by most early Zionists, was *an internal and external disavowal* of the anti-Semitic stereotype of Jewish men as unmanly, and it affirmed the European-wide equation of manliness and rightful membership in the nation."[52]

In their attempts to formulate a collective Zionist identity, early Zionist writers pursued a range of strategies for either "reclaiming" or rejecting *Jew(s)*. Among those who prevailed, regardless of their position on *Juden*, all seem united in their derision and rejection of *yidn*—a derision that carried over, decades later, to *yidn* as victims and survivors of Nazi concentration camps—in contrast to heroic "ghetto fighters," "rebels," and "partisans."[53] Max Nordau famously proposed to rehabilitate *Juden* and *yidn* through a program of *"Muskeljudentum"* that would take these despised effeminate men and turn them into Zionist "muscle Jews."[54] Herzl, for his part, adopted the name *"Mauschel,"* a derogatory German slang for *Jew*—in particular, for those who spoke Yiddish or spoke German with a Yiddish accent—to deride opponents of his Zionism. For Herzl, *Mauschel* is the wretched doppelgänger to *der Jude*:

> As a type, my dear friends, *Mauschel* has always been the dreadful companion of the Jew and so inseparable from him that they were always confused. The Jew is a man like all others, no better, no worse . . . but *Mauschel* is a distortion of human character, unspeakably mean and repellent. Where the Jew experiences pain or pride, *Mauschel* only feels miserable fear, or faces you with a sneering grin . . . impudent and arrogant. The Jew aspires to higher levels of culture, *Mauschel* pursues only his own dirty business.[55]

For Herzl, *Jew* (*Jude*) is a name for self, and that *Jew* is Zionist. An anti-Zionist is, then, not a *Jew* but rather is *Mauschel*, a despicable *yid*. Finally, in his obituary for Herzl in 1905, a young Vladimir Jabotinsky determined that neither *yid* nor *Jew* could serve the Zionist as a name for self. In fact, "the typical Yid" is the very *opposite* of Jabotinsky's admirable "Hebrew," just as it is of the Nazis' glorious "Aryan":

> Our starting point is to take the typical Yid of today and to imagine his diametrical opposite. . . . Because the Yid is ugly, sickly, and lacks decorum, we shall endow the ideal image of the Hebrew with masculine beauty. The Yid is trodden upon and easily frightened and, therefore, the Hebrew ought to be proud and independent. The Yid is despised by all and, therefore, the Hebrew ought to charm all. The Yid has accepted submission and, therefore, the Hebrew ought to learn to command. The Yid wants to conceal his identity from strangers and, therefore, the Hebrew should look the world straight in the eye and declare: "I am a Hebrew."[56]

Yid(n) functions, throughout the long history of Yiddish usage, as a term for self—for "I," "we," "us"; as a name for home and family, memory and aspiration, voice and frame. *Jew, Jude, juif,* and the like were only much later adapted to these uses, and, as with the modern Israeli Hebrew *yehudi(m)*, that adaptation often has been accomplished (to the extent that it has been so) over and against *der yid*. (I leave it to others to parse that fascinating Israeli *yehudi[m]* as I have begun to do for *yid*.) But *yid*, a name for a richly imagined self in an explicitly Jewish (Yiddish) linguistic culture, has never granted its owners (even the Zionists among them) the illusion of autonomy, never provided them a pretense of free self-determination, never pretended to name an ideal—universal or particular—as so many other names for self in other linguistic cultures have purported to do. Even prior to the disparagements of recent centuries, *yid*, although a name for self, always also named an other—both to those who determined the "public transcripts" of dominant culture and to the *bar* and *b'nei yisroel* of its own holy traditions.

Der Yid *Today*

So, *vos macht a yid?* How fares *der yid* in the twenty-first century?

"*Der Yid*" survives today as the name of a Satmar Hasidic, anti-Zionist, Yiddish-language weekly newspaper founded in New York City in 1953 and currently read by tens of thousands of "ultra-Orthodox" Yiddish speakers around the world. Yiddish remains an everyday language almost exclusively among ultra-Orthodox Hasidic or *haredi* communities committed to premodern Yiddish culture's absolute valorization of traditional study of Talmud and Torah. In these deeply sectarian communities, Yiddish serves as a countercultural force opposing select aspects of modern, secularist culture and values and as a mechanism for maintaining a premodern ideal of *yidn* and *b'nei yisroel* epitomized by the "passive, pale, gentle, and physically weak *Yeshiva-Bokhur.*"[57] The anti-Zionism of these communities is of a piece with their sense of themselves as *yidn.*

Feminist talmudist Daniel Boyarin has, in recent decades, worked to revalue and popularize what he terms this "feminized" version of masculinity as a kind of "native" Jewish model that could serve as a critique and alternative to the reigning militarist, muscular model of masculinity. "In part," says Boyarin, "Jewish culture demystifies European gender ideologies by reversing their terms, which is not, I hasten to emphasize, a liberatory process in itself but can be mobilized—strategically—for liberation."[58] While valorizing what he calls "our sissy heritage," Boyarin is also appropriately attentive to the ways in which that cultural "heritage" has subordinated and marginalized women, and continues to do so:

> If the ideal Jewish male femme has some critical force vis-à-vis general European models of manliness, at the same time a critique must be mounted against "him" for his oppression of Jewish women—and indeed, frequently enough, for his class-based oppression of other Jewish men as well, namely the ignorant who were sometimes characterized as being "like women."[59]

Boyarin does not call his "reclaimed . . . Jewish male sissy" a *"yid,"* but rather promotes him explicitly as a (post?)modern *Jew*—a subject who acts as a representative and agent of difference *within* dominant cultures.

Naomi Seidman, who identifies as "a feminist and a Yiddishist both," also understands Yiddish culture as "one kind of Jewish knowledge," now largely forgotten, that could still hold critical, political potential for Ashkenazic women seeking to enact a fully realized self as *Jew*:

> But our Yiddish amnesia . . . is particularly devastating for Ashkenazic women. American Jewish feminists have struggled to make changes in the synagogue and liturgy that would seem mild by comparison with the prayers recited and composed by their grandmothers, but they have struggled with only the barest consciousness of the alternative spiritual expression of traditional Ashkenazic women or of the feminist radicality of writers like Dvora Baron. Yiddish texts can illuminate the experiences of Ashkenazic women, religious and secular, pious and revolutionary (or both).[60]

Seidman recalls that she came into her own as a "Yiddishist" at the YIVO Institute in New York City. Founded in Vilna in 1925 and relocated to New York City during the Second World War, YIVO is the largest center for Yiddish cultural studies today, providing substantial archives and public and scholarly programs to ground this field of study. Yiddish, as an academic field, is populated primarily by people who self-identify as *Jews* (or, with an acquired nostalgia, as *yidn*). Nonetheless, among the newest generation of students of Yiddish, at least two groups have caught the eye of the international press in recent years for their divergent geopolitical identifications.

Aga Ilwicka-Sheppard, a doctoral candidate in Yiddish literature at Poland's University of Wroclaw, was instrumental in procuring thousands of donated Yiddish books for several academic libraries in Poland. It seems that Poland is experiencing what some have termed a renaissance of Yiddish and Jewish studies. In an interview for the radio program *PRI's The World*, Ilwicka-Sheppard, speaking as a Pole, maintains that "Yiddish culture really belongs to Poland, it is our treasure, the biggest treasure, maybe, that we hold."[61]

Very different articulations of connection to Yiddish language and culture are cited by Palestinian Israelis studying Yiddish at Bar Ilan University's Rena Costa Centre for Yiddish Studies, where, it is reported, they accounted for about one-quarter of enrolled students in 2012 and 2013. According to Dudi Goldman in a story in *Al Monitor*, one student, Yusuf Alakili, admits being able to provide "no explanation for the fact that I have always felt a connection to this language," with "its enigmatic, refined musical tone," while another, Salam Bashara, "who hopes one day to write her master's thesis on the parallels between Arab and Yiddish literature," suggests that Yiddish stories that explore the sense of a generation's loss of its children to the surrounding secular culture "is a universal experience, something that everyone can identify with."[62] Other accounts highlight interest in Yiddish as a way to come to better understand "the other side." One of these features "Samah Jayosi, a Muslim Palestinian citizen of Israel," who "majors in Jewish literature and Arabic [and] plans to use Yiddish once she becomes a Hebrew teacher for Arab children." The story quotes Jayosi as hoping that "maybe it [Yiddish] will help them [the children] see that this language and this nation have a complicated history, and they'll understand the other side better."[63] The complex dance of self and other that *yid* has always danced continues into the twenty-first century—albeit much diminished—in both expected and unexpected places.

Jew in Jewish Studies

The study of *yidn* and of *Jew(s)* as an academic enterprise—through the study of Yiddish language and culture, Israel studies, Holocaust studies, Hebrew literature, or any of a number of other fields represented within the interdisciplinary field of Jewish studies—has, over the past several decades, become a mechanism for contributing to the meanings of Jew(s) in realms of public discourse. Jewish studies, in defining a subject of study, has also become key to a process of modern subject- or self-formation (collective and individual) by means of such scholarship.

In *Jewish Studies: A Theoretical Introduction*, the inaugural volume in the series of which the present book is a part, Andrew Bush observes: "That it is possible to be both a Jew and a self has proven to be [an] . . . enduring thesis. . . . And it is that Jew as modern self, more choosing than chosen, that provides the crucial precondition for Jewish Studies as it emerged in . . . the nineteenth century."[64] The relationship between articulations of *Jew* as self and Jewish studies remains an important and multidimensional one.

In producing knowledge about *Jew(s)*, Jewish studies provides, among other things, an ever-expanding pool of cultural resources for constructing identities. As Bush notes, "Almost any instructor in a Jewish Studies classroom will be familiar with many students who are not studying Jews as an external object, as *them*, but rather as *us*, seeking points of contact between their own lives and other Jewish experiences as the basis for grounding their sense of their own Jewish identity."[65] Similarly, for many of their teachers, studying *Jews* often informs and expresses who and what they understand themselves to be; Jewish studies frequently serves as a locus of self-exploration. For a feature in the Spring 2012 issue of *AJS Perspectives: The Magazine of the Association for Jewish Studies* (the largest professional organization of Jewish-studies scholars), the editors asked fifteen scholars to write brief, candid responses to the question "Why did you go into Jewish Studies?" Although there is some variety among responses, including "As a matter of fact, I didn't go into Jewish Studies"; "I landed there"; and "Why not?" the majority of responses resemble the following:

> Jewish Studies offers a space within which I can experiment with linking [my] family stories to collective histories.

> I began my freshman year at Columbia University with the intention of becoming a rabbi or a Jewish educator.

> One day, the rabbi at my synagogue in Madison asked me to speak to some church groups on the weekends because he had more invitations than he could handle.

> My deepest commitments were now to the Jewish people, and I wanted to find a way to insure that whatever intellectual gifts I had would leave their mark on its culture.

> Since both [Yiddish and Jews] mattered a great deal to me personally, I wondered if they might matter professionally as well. And they have.

From very early childhood, I was obsessed with the accumulation of information about a Jewish past I was convinced was utterly different from my own and my parents' American Jewish experiences.

Growing up in the years of World War II, I was haunted by what might have been in my own life, and my absorption in the topic only increased as the years went on.

I work on Jewish literature because it is what I know and where I come from. Navel-gazing, pure and simple.[66]

Notwithstanding the very real limitations of such circumscribed and anecdotal "data," these statements do gesture toward a strong connection between Jewish identification beyond the academy and creation of knowledge about *Jew(s)* within it. In some (although not all) respects, studying *Jew(s)* can be characterized as a kind of "secular" practice of Jewishness; the high percentage of college and university Jewish-studies chairs and programs endowed through private philanthropy supports this practice on a collective, institutional level.[67]

As the stories of Polish and Palestinian Yiddishists cited above remind us, however, the line between the "personal" and the "professional" is not always so (seemingly) direct, and identification with the subjects of Jewish studies and the kinds of knowledge produced in that field can take a variety of forms and inform a variety of selves and self-understandings (again, collective and individual). *Jew(s)* as the subject matter of Jewish studies not only matters differently to different subjects but also can serve as a powerful tool for theorizing subjectivity/subject formation itself.

One particular avenue on the broad map of Jewish studies in which the subject matter lends itself well to such theorizing is the flourishing subfield of examinations of *"The Jew"* in a wide range of contexts. This academic subfield emerged before the Second World War with occasional flurries of publication throughout the twentieth century. A small flood of monographs, anthologies, articles, and essays appeared toward the end of the twentieth century and continues in the twenty-first. A sampling of book titles from these more recent decades can provide a snapshot:

The Jew's Body, by Sander Gilman (New York: Routledge, 1991)
The Jew Accused: Three Anti-Semitic Affairs (Dreyfus, Beilis, Frank) 1894–1915, by Albert S. Lindemann (Cambridge: Cambridge University Press, 1991)
Constructions of "the Jew" in English Literature and Society: Racial Representations, 1875–1945, by Bryan Cheyette (Cambridge: Cambridge University Press, 1993)

The Jew in the Text: Modernity and the Construction of Identity, edited by
Linda Nochlin and Tamar Garb (New York: Thames and Hudson,
1995)

*Between "Race" and Culture: Representations of "the Jew" in English and
American Literature*, edited by Bryan Cheyette (Stanford: Stanford
University Press, 1996)

Staging the Jew: The Performance of an American Ethnicity, 1860–1920, by
Harley Erdman (New Brunswick, NJ: Rutgers University Press, 1997)

Modernity, Culture, and "the Jew," edited by Bryan Cheyette and Laura
Marcus (Stanford: Stanford University Press, 1998)

Living Letters of the Law: Ideas of the Jew in Medieval Christianity, by
Jeremy Cohen (Berkeley: University of California Press, 1999)

*A Rumor about the Jews: Antisemitism, Conspiracy, and the Protocols of
Zion*, by Stephen Eric Bronner (New York: Oxford University Press,
2000)

Chinese Perceptions of the 'Jews' and Judaism: A History of the Youtai, by
Zhou Xun (Richmond, UK: Curzon Press, 2001)

The Jew, the Arab: A History of the Enemy, by Gil Anidjar (Stanford:
Stanford University Press, 2003)

The Image of the Jew in European Liberal Culture 1789–1914, edited by
Bryan Cheyette and Nadia Valman (Elstree, UK: Valentine Mitchell,
2004)

The "Jew" in Cinema: From "The Golem" to "Don't Touch My Holocaust,"
by Omer Bartov (Bloomington: Indiana University Press, 2005)

The Jew in the Medieval Book: English Antisemitisms, 1350–1500, by Anthony
Bale (Cambridge: Cambridge University Press, 2006)

The Spectral Jew: Conversion and Embodiment in Medieval Europe, by
Steven F. Kruger (Minneapolis: University of Minnesota Press, 2006)

The Healthy Jew: The Symbiosis of Judaism and Modern Medicine, by
Mitchell B. Hart (Cambridge: Cambridge University Press, 2007)

The Jew in the Art of the Italian Renaissance, by Dana E. Katz
(Philadelphia: University of Pennsylvania Press, 2008)

*The Ridiculous Jew: The Exploitation and Transformation of a Stereotype
in Gogol, Turgenev, and Dostoevsky*, by Gary Rosenshield (Stanford:
Stanford University Press, 2008)

*Inventing the Jew: Antisemitic Stereotypes in Romanian and Other Central
European Cultures*, by Andrei Oisteanu (Lincoln: University of
Nebraska Press, 2009)

The Universal Jew: Masculinity, Modernity, and the Zionist Movement, by
Mikhal Dekel (Evanston, IL: Northwestern University Press, 2010)

The Figural Jew: Politics and Identity in Postwar French Thought, by Sarah
Hammerschlag (Chicago: University of Chicago Press, 2010)

The Other Jewish Question: Identifying the Jew and Making Sense of
Modernity, by Jay Geller (New York: Fordham University Press, 2011)
Under Postcolonial Eyes: Figuring the "Jew" in Contemporary British
Writing, by Efraim Sicher and Linda Weinhouse (Lincoln:
University of Nebraska Press, 2012)
Race, Color, Identity: Rethinking Discourses about "Jews" in the Twenty-first
Century, edited by Efraim Sicher (New York: Berghahn Books, 2013)

As is clear from these titles, subtitles, and their incorporated scare quotes, *the Jew* at the heart of these studies may name an "anti-Semitic stereotype"; an "image" or "figure"; a "construction," "representation," "performance," or an "idea." *The Jew* is a sign for "embodiment," signaled by a distinctive "Jew's Body"—although that body may be, nonetheless, "spectral." *The Jew* is a locus of "invention," "perception," "exploitation," "transformation," "conversion," "conspiracy," "accusation," and "discourse." *The Jew* may be qualified as "ridiculous," "figural," "staged," "textual," even "healthy" or "universal." And *the Jew* proves a useful lens through which to scrutinize such matters as "race," "color," "ethnicity," "masculinity," "society," "politics," "culture," "history," "literature," "postcolonialism," "enmity," and "identity" during "the medieval," "the Renaissance," "the modern," the "postwar," the "contemporary," and "the twenty-first-century" periods in France, America, Russia, Romania, Europe, Central Europe, England/Britain, Italy, the Middle East, and China. Insofar as *the Jew* is, and can accomplish, all these things (and this list is by no means exhaustive), it is indeed a powerful and illuminating artifact in the hands of Jewish-studies scholars.

Much scholarship on *the Jew* features catalogues of familiar—and less familiar—abusive and derisive caricatures. Some of these catalogues provide synchronic samplings, some diachronic, and some do both. Rosenshield's study, for example, confines itself to a single figure in the work of three nineteenth-century Russian writers. Oisteanu's, by contrast, provides "a learned inventory of the images of the Jew in the *imaginaire* of the Romanian people . . . the slow and widening accumulation of stereotypes, distortions, pictures, and slogans that nourished both the popular imagination and the approaches of many of the elite figures in Romanian culture over generations."[68]

Beyond providing catalogues of caricature, those who study *the Jew* as a cultural artifact employ a variety of analytical approaches that define and interpret their data in particular ways. Many studies explore the ways in which *the Jew* functions in the self-construction and self-representation of dominant cultures and hegemonic discourses. Those studying the medieval period, for example, inevitably attend to the ways in which *the Jew* serves the medieval Church and state. According to Steven F. Kruger,

"In recent years much work on medieval Christian engagements with Judaism has emphasized the ways in which 'the Jew' serves certain primarily ideological functions within hegemonic medieval culture. This line of inquiry has treated 'the Jew' as a fantasy construction that had as much or more to do with Christian identity as it did with actual Jews and Jewish communities."[69] Similarly, those studying the modern era have, for example, produced a rich literature exploring *the Jew*'s functions in nationalist narratives from Republican France to contemporary Israel.

Some of these studies also look to examine effects of and responses to *the Jew* on the part of those targeted as objects of caricature. Kruger's reference to "actual Jews" in the above quote finds echoes throughout scholarship on *the Jew*, as scholars attempt to understand and articulate relationships between "image" and "reality" or *the Jew(s)* as "stereotype" and "real *Jews*." Scare quotes; the use of adjectives such as *real, actual, material,* and *living*, versus *theological, hermeneutical, textual,* and *virtual*, as well as other rhetorical and orthographic strategies, are employed in attempts at distinguishing among different meanings of *Jew(s)* and differently valued subjects laying claim to the name *Jew*. Attempts to distinguish among these diverse *Jews* are complicated not only by a modern sense of the utter contingency of subjectivity, reality, and knowledge but also by the use of *Jew*, itself, to express that perplexing contingency. Brian Cheyette captures something of this Gordian knot in an essay introducing the subject matter of his monograph *Constructions of "the Jew" in English Literature and Society: Racial Representations, 1875–1945*:

> The one ironic feature of the literary representations under consideration is the protean instability of "the Jew" as a signifier. The radical emptiness and lack of a fixed meaning in the construction of "semitic" difference in this study results in "the Jew" being made to occupy an incommensurable number of subject positions which traverse a range of contradictory discourses. . . . It is precisely the slipperiness of these constructions that shall be seen to undermine fatally the supposed certainty that an author, especially of a literary realist text, might have in their ability to represent "reality." With the advent of explicitly modernist texts, the very incoherence of "the Jew" was to be a potent expression of the impossibility of fully "knowing" anything.[70]

Cheyette's important analysis, although offered specifically with regard to English literary realism and modernism, is suggestive within a much larger field of view. Given the profound significance of mediated narratives (from literature, advertising, film, popular music, social media, etc.) for modern formulations of a sense of self or subjecthood, on the one hand, and the impact of key works such as those by Freud and Marx on—and well beyond—modernist literature, on the other, Cheyette's observations capture important extraliterary dimensions of the current "state of the *Jew*[ish] question." The slipperiness, contradictions, and incoherence of *the Jew* as literary construct are every bit as characteristic of many attempts to articulate a Jewish self in a world inhabited by these preexistent constructs; a world at the same time deeply skeptical of the possibility of "fully 'knowing' anything"—not least, oneself.

Cheyette, it might be noted, has devoted much of his academic career to examining *the Jew* in European and American literature and culture—indeed, four of the volumes cited above are edited or authored by him. Cheyette's scholarly commitment to this subject, *the Jew*, is perhaps rivaled or exceeded only by that of Sander Gilman, whose work has been credited with establishing "the paradigmatic (modern) Jewish body" in work that is "extremely important and influential within Jewish studies and perhaps even more so among those working in literary studies, German studies, and the history of medicine."[71] Whereas Cheyette's focus falls largely on English-language literature, Gilman's runs the gamut from scientific through social-scientific and literary discourses in several languages in the nineteenth, twentieth, and now twenty-first centuries.[72]

Embodying the Jew

In the preface to his seminal book *The Jew's Body*, Gilman emphasizes his key concern with his subject, which persists in his more recent work:

> My concern is not only what the image of the Jew is but what the forces are which shape this image of difference and—perhaps most importantly—how those labeled as different respond to this construction of their identity. My assumption is that the Jew in the Western Diaspora does respond, must respond, to the image of the Jew in such cultures. . . . It is vital to understand that Jews (like all other groups who are labeled as different) must acknowledge the world in which they are geographically and culturally situated. This response is structured by the conception of the Jew (which may or may not be itself structured by "realities" of the self-labeling of any given Jew or Jewish community). This response may, however, take a wide range of forms. It may be internalizing and self-destructive (self-hating) or it may be projective and stereotyping; it [may] take the form of capitulation to the power of the image or the form of resistance to the very stereotype of the Jew. But there is the need to respond, either directly or subliminally.
>
> These essays are the measure of my own response.[73]

In this statement, Gilman expresses an explicit identification with the subjects of his historical studies, blurring or dismissing any meaningful line dividing him from them: "The Jew . . . does respond, must respond. . . . These essays are . . . my own response." At the same time, he enacts the conflation or imbrication of "the Jew in the Western Diaspora" with "the conception of the Jew" that he insists bears a "structured" relation to that subject. He employs the definite article and the singular for both: both are "the Jew." The agency and identity that Gilman represents as his own, as enacted in his scholarship on *the Jew*, are attributed to his subject, *the Jew*, as well. And although *the Jew* as subject may respond to *the Jew* as subject matter in any number of ways—including by internalizing self-hatred or externalizing projection—Gilman's statement presents himself, Gilman, as modeling a kind of positive, self-affirming response carried out through his scholarly mastery of his subject.

But Gilman's work has, as well, been criticized for grounding a kind of hegemonic discourse in the field of studies concerned with *the Jew*—a discourse that has the effect of occluding, if not erasing, divergent perspectives or counterdiscourses. "No single scholar has done more to disseminate 'the Jew's body' than Gilman," observes Mitchell B. Hart, "and for Gilman, the Jew's body is a diseased body. . . . Gilman's twinned phenomena of Jew hatred and Jewish self-hatred rest on the purported normative status of the abnormal. Gilman seems intent on universalizing the diseased and pathological."[74] Hart's complaint is not that Gilman's work on *the Jew* as diseased is not important, nor that Gilman ignores all evidence contrary to his theses, but rather that Gilman's work on "Jewish difference" has led to an easy equation of "difference" with "abnormality." "Different for Gilman means inferior and pathological," claims Hart, who points to the far-reaching influence of Gilman's work as rendering that generalization virtually monolithic for shaping critical analysis of *the Jew*.[75]

> But there was a counter-discourse (at least one) that constructed an image of the healthy Jew, a discourse produced by Gentiles and Jews. If we look at different texts (or even the same texts with different eyes), then we arrive at a very different image of the Jews and Judaism. . . . There did exist a significant body of literature that represented Jews and Judaism as healthy and vital, that did not feminize the male Jew, or associate him with the sorts of social and political pathologies so common in the anti-Semitic imagination.[76]

So why the emphasis on disease and abnormality? Hart avers that this persistent focus is best understood as a direct response to the Holocaust/Shoah and reflects a deeply felt need to understand the part that antisemitic images played in the success of Nazi policies. Indeed, many scholars who work on these materials address the issue explicitly, some by plotting the line that leads from point A to point B, others by explaining how and why their particular materials on *the Jew* do not belong to a continuum that leads to Auschwitz.

Not entirely convinced of the sufficiency of this explanation for what he terms the current "fascination with the abnormal," Hart proffers another, paradoxical, hypothesis that proposes a less obvious link between the distasteful subject matter that dominates studies of *the Jew* and "a continuing development within American Jewish self-consciousness." Namely, "it is precisely 'Jewish health' among American Jews today—defined, if you will, broadly enough in this case to include not merely physical health, but a general sense of well-being and security— that allows for the dissemination of images and ideas about Jewish disease in the past."[77] In other words, "American Jews today" have become the predominant creators of academic knowledge about *the Jew(s)*, and these knowledge producers feel sufficiently comfortable and secure that they can dispense with the apologetics that characterized the scholarship of earlier, more anxious, generations of Jewish-studies scholars and instead "embrace . . . 'the diseased Jew.'"[78] Hart understands "this turn to the diseased and abnormal within academic circles" well beyond Jewish studies to reflect "a broader shift in the culture, one that is now inundated and saturated with images of illness, threats from within and without one's own body to the individual and collective self."[79]

It is an odd and interesting calculus that Hart sketches here. Some might wonder how "American Jews today" could be said to feel so "healthy" and "secure" within a culture "inundated and saturated with images of illness [and] threats." Others might suggest that, far from being a thing of the past, apologetics and advocacy remain very much a part of Jewish-studies scholarship, as they do, for example, of feminist, queer, and postcolonial scholarship, and that a focus on the object of derision is in keeping with such a stance. Still others will simply question the proposed connection while suspecting that there is really no way to test such a hypothesis.

Regarding the latter, a kind of partial affirmation of *and* challenge to Hart's hypothesis comes from precisely the work—Gilman's *The Jew's Body*—that serves as the springboard to Hart's critique. At the end of the preface to his book, published as East and West Germany were commencing reunification, Gilman admits that

the further back into history my essays went, the more "real" they seemed to me. Turn-of-the-century Vienna was a more real place in my imagination than was the present-day city of Berlin. . . . Fin-de-siècle Vienna, a world and a century away, seems more real, certainly more stable in my mind's eye. Much has been written about Saul Friedländer's extraordinary work about memory, especially the memory of Jews. But historical memory *is* safer—we know how and when the story ends. It ends horribly, in the ovens of Auschwitz, but that is the past, and, as such, a safe because known past.[80]

Again, Gilman positions himself with *the Jews* of memory and history, who are more real to him, he says, than is the present-day city of Berlin. He feels, weirdly, safer and more secure in that "known past," notwithstanding the unspeakable horror toward which he knows it to be moving. Hart theorizes that "a general sense of well-being and security . . . allows for the dissemination of images and ideas about Jewish disease in the past," and Gilman's recollections corroborate a certain connection between a sense of present security and an interest in the past. But for Gilman it is *knowledge about the past*—knowledge to which he contributes through the power of his historical narrative—that provides his sense of security. That sense is not the precondition for his story of anxious Jewish bodies, he tells us; it is its result. As a historian of *the Jew(s)*, he can shape the discourse and frame the knowledge of his historical subject—and, hence, of himself as one who bears witness.

Nor does Gilman share with his imagined readers a sigh of grateful relief at their shared well-being—the rights and positions that enable them to generate and disseminate their stories in safety. Instead, he suggests, "what is more frightening" than the known past

> is the continual complexity of the present, with its last act always unseen. My own anxiety about the resurgence of right wing anti-Semitism in the wake of German reunification . . . was a response to the elimination of what I had internalized as the final act of the Shoah, the division of Germany. The fact that there are no final acts, that the anxieties of Jews present in fin-de-siècle Vienna reappear in hardly disguised form in New York and London and Bombay in the 1990s, that the fantasies about the Jews present in the sixteenth century echo in the recently liberated halls of Eastern Europe, is the lesson I continue to learn. The product of that lesson is in this volume.[81]

Gilman wants his readers to understand that it is no sense of "security," much less a real change in the condition and representation of *Jews*, that underlies his choice of subject matter. Rather, what binds him to them and leads him to tell their stories is his sense of shared and ongoing threats, present and inherited traumas.

Naomi Seidman, in reflecting on her scholarship, cited above, offers yet another perspective—perhaps closer to that articulated by Hart—on the ways in which Jewish-studies scholarship and other (American) cultural productions focused on the errant body and performance of *the Jew* (or *der yid*, or "the Yid") may be understood to be representative of—and part of what enables—the ongoing construction of *Jew* as self in the twentieth and twenty-first centuries. Citing an essay by Sidra DeKoven Ezrahi, Seidman points to Philip Roth's 1969 novel *Portnoy's Complaint* as "scandalous not merely for its sexual and excremental boldness; the scandal was that these were *Jewish* genitals and bowels being discussed on the American literary stage. These exposures were transgressive," continues Seidman,

> but they also signaled *and cleared the way for* a new openness, a genuine Jewish-Gentile rapprochement possible perhaps only in the New World. Lenny Bruce's boldest monologues and Philip Roth's raunchiest novels . . . are the hallmark of a new stage in American Jewish culture. This era eventually swept up even the cautious field of Jewish scholarship, and if I were to locate my own project within a cultural history, it would be in this one.[82]

It is neither fear nor satisfied well-being that animates projects likes Seidman's, she suggests, but it is, instead, the potential of "transgressive exposure" to enable fruitful translation across the "Jewish-Gentile" divide that for so long "separated Jewish from non-Jewish discourse."[83]

Identity and the Jew

Translation across the divide is at the heart of the modern project of formulating a sense of *Jew* as self within a history of *the Jew* as other. It is no coincidence that the vast majority of scholarship on *the Jew* is engaged with a decidedly *historical* subject, an entity of the past that has not only shaped the present but seems to function as a kind of key to unlocking and making sense of an otherwise elusive modern self. "The choice for Jews—as for non-Jews," writes Juliet Steyn in *The Jew: Assumptions of Identity*, "—is not a question of the past as given and therefore overlooked but rather what *kind* of past shall be had."[84]

Steyn, who proposes to "*banalize* the Jew," in part through a focus on "those micro-stories that constitute the lives of people and their *selves*," begins her collection of essays in nineteenth- and early twentieth-century Europe—a time and place that define the focus of much scholarship on *the Jew*.[85] Unlike the bulk of that scholarship, however, Steyn pursues her subject(s) up through early twenty-first-century America with essays on Clement Greenberg (1909–1994) and R. B. Kitaj (1932–2007). Her timeframe is not merely a function of her art-historical expertise, but is as much a strategy for achieving her end of rendering *the Jew* banal:

> My intention is neither to deny nor to elevate the history of the Jew in Modernity: rather . . . it is to banalize it, to prise it open, expose and

explore the ever-changing, yet historically grounded definitions of the Jew and identity. It is to redescribe *Jewish* identity in its "singularity" as both repetitious and subject to change and transformation. . . . My interest is also to identify and to understand the practices of institutions and discourses that both mediate and use *Jew* as a category.[86]

Steyn's immediate focus remains on *the Jew* throughout her volume; inextricable from that subject, she observes, is the category "identity"—a banal and obfuscating category that Steyn wishes not merely to explore but to explode. Jay Geller articulates a similar wariness with regard to this category that has become so central to modern culture, in general, and to Jewish studies, in particular. In *The Other Jewish Question: Identifying the Jew and Making Sense of Modernity*, Geller explains how and why he will avoid using the category altogether and will instead refer to his subjects as "Jewish-identified individuals":

> I follow Rogers Brubaker in preferring the term *identification* in order to avoid the analytical, definitional, and ontological problems associated with *identity*. The shift to *identification* "invites us to specify the agents that do the identifying. And it does not presuppose that such identifying . . . will necessarily result in the internal sameness, the distinctiveness, the bounded groupness" intrinsic to social life. Moreover, as categorizations, "'identification' calls attention to complex (and often ambivalent) *processes*, while the term 'identity' designat[es] a *condition* rather than a process." . . . I adopt such a seemingly broad analytical rubric as "Jewish-identified individuals" because no single conventional criterion is sufficient for determining an individual's Jewishness; attempts to be more selective lead either to outrageous exclusions or to troubling recollections.[87]

Both Steyn and Geller, like some of their contemporaries in this subfield, find that studying *the Jew* demands a letting-go of conventional assumptions, definitions, and categories at the same time that it invites an openness to paradox in thinking about self or subject formation. Steyn, for example, argues that "subjects are not identical with their assumed *identity*: they are not the same unto themselves." What could this possibly mean? She elaborates:

> *The Jew: Assumptions of Identity*, the title of this book acknowledges the assumptions, at the same time as dismembering the old myths of identity. It calls on us to go beyond the provocations of *identity*. It asks us to rethink identity as something made, as a process, as something that can never be complete, that is always becoming and contingent. It tells us that we should be concerned about the boundary between *Jew* as a regulating concept and real Jew and argues that the untroubled

identification of *Jew* with Jew reiterates what Theodor Adorno has characterized as "identity thinking," that is to say, an identity is presumed to be shared by subject and object. . . . Once we affirm the diverse nature of the notion of identity, then we can reappraise the ways in which we think about the self.[88]

Scholarship on *the Jew*, as a kind of "cottage industry" within Jewish studies, has served not only as a locus for exploring all of the important subjects and dynamics enumerated in the titles of the books and articles produced under this rubric, but also as a workshop for constructing, deconstructing, examining, and critiquing ideas about *Jew* as self. This workshop provides space and critical tools by which (primarily) Jewish-identified scholars come to build for themselves (and, perhaps, for others) a "native" discourse about *Jew(s)*. Undoubtedly there is a certain pleasure and satisfaction, as well as a moral and broadly therapeutic dimension, to shaping meaningful discourse around a name whose contours and content have long been set by those who have wielded the name as a weapon. The *Jew*(ish) Question that animates this subfield of Jewish studies continues to be one of how best to understand and articulate the contradictory, malleable, precarious, contingent, but nonetheless indissoluble and powerful relationship that obtains between *the Jew* and *Jew* as self.

Steyn, like so many others, cautions against an "untroubled identification" of "*Jew* as a regulating concept" with "real Jew." But the one is no more nor less "real" than the other—both have measurable impact in the world—and the rhetorical category "real Jew," as Geller's ruminations illustrate, is, itself, never "untroubled." Indeed, just as *the Jew* is "proximate other" (in the apt phrase of Jonathan Z. Smith)[89] and repressed self of Christian/Western articulations of identity, so, too, *the Jew* has become, in many respects, a kind of proximate other and repressed (or celebrated, excavated, or memorialized) self to modern articulations of Jewish identity.

Jewish studies constitutes its subjects in particular ways, employing particular tools of the Euro-American humanistic arts. The knowledge produced in studies of *the Jew* provides greater shape and dimension to *Jew* as self "within the given social reality" at the same time that it calls into question the mechanisms by which knowledge about *Jew(s)* is generated. Furthermore, any essential meaning assigned to the name (and any power to represent the object/subject claimed for that name) is undermined, in Cheyette's words, by the very "protean instability of 'the Jew' as a signifier" of anything. "Anything identified as *identity*," writes Steyn, "is already in a position of acknowledging the possibility that it is other than its representation."[90] And yet, there are *Jews*.

"Jews are a group without a single foundation, a heterogeneous link-ing of the non-identical," offers Steyn, in a formulation that is as com-monsensical as it is counterintuitive.[91] With this observation, my discussion proceeds from Jewish studies per se to political philosophy, and from historical studies to modern and postmodern theory. These catego-ries, although problematic in their own ways, signal a turn to (often more explicitly "autobiographical") materials that draw into even sharper focus the ethics and politics of thinking with, and laying claim to, *Jew* as self or subject or identity in the twentieth and twenty-first centuries.

Thinking (with) *Jew(s)*

At the midpoint of the twentieth century, a mere five years after the for-mal end of the Second World War and two years after the founding of the State of Israel, American essayist and art critic Clement Greenberg published an essay in the fledgling magazine *Commentary* entitled "Self-Hatred and Jewish Chauvinism: Some Reflections on 'Positive Jewishness.'" "Both the assimilationist and the nationalist," wrote Greenberg, "leave too little room for their native personalities. While there is no such thing as a human being in general, there is also no such thing as a complete Jew or a complete Englishman. What I want to be able to do is accept my Jewishness more implicitly, so implicitly that I can use it to realize myself as a human being in my own right *and as a Jew in my own right*."[92] These assertions and aspirations, which conclude the essay, also concisely encapsulate some of the major dynamics and chal-lenges that animate postwar reflections on *Jew*—and, indeed, on the very possibility of being or becoming a *Jew* "in one's own right."

Greenberg's juxtaposed "assimilationist and nationalist" represent two sides of the same coin. Both exemplify responses to a "self-hatred" that is the inevitable legacy of millennia of abject "othering" culminating in the "historical judgment" of the Holocaust/Shoah. For Greenberg, as for others, the hyperconformity that characterizes both nationalists and "ultra-assimilationists" is a harmfully misguided (and ultimately futile) strategy aimed at compensating for the undeniable ravages of European history. Likewise, Greenberg's juxtaposition of the myth of the "human being *in general*" with the equally mythic "*complete* Jew" or "*complete* Englishman" signals a dismissal of the false promises and dangerous exclusions that plague both sides of the timeworn universal/particular dichotomy (and, perhaps, of the homeland/diaspora dichotomy, as well). In an earnest and apparently heartfelt call for some degree of self-realiza-tion beyond these encompassing and inherited strictures, Greenberg devoutly wishes to be able to "accept [his] Jewishness . . . so implicitly" that it might become a means by which to integrate all these historical contentions and contradictions into a singular subject that can "own" itself, in its own right—as human being and *Jew*—notwithstanding the "denial of right" that has so often accompanied that latter name.[93]

To "accept my Jewishness . . . so implicitly" would mean to achieve a kind of ownership that would need not always be overtly expressed, but that might remain implicit; an ownership that would be without qualification or question: hence, absolute, a matter of implicit certainty. But such an owning of Jewishness or the name *Jew* has been anything but untrammeled and "implicit" in the postwar era. Several obvious—and some less obvious—phenomena have come to shape discourse on *Jew* in such a fashion that the word can appear far more an object of contention than the name of a self-possessed and self-realized subject. Some of these phenomena—the shadow cast by the Holocaust / Shoah, the seeming imperatives of a realized Jewish nationalism, and the persistence of age-old tropes of *the Jew* (albeit sometimes reimagined in the wake of the war)—are most significant and far-reaching. In addition, the postwar era marked a coming-into-voice of the American-born children and grand-children of the mass migrations from the *shtetlach* of Eastern Europe, as well as the rise of countercultural movements targeting racism, sexism, homophobia, and other prevailing societal dysfunctions.

"Greenberg's text," observes Steyn, "enunciated in an autobiographi-cal voice and in a confessional tone, is marked by dilemmas which reveal the paradoxes and complexities of his own position."[94] Needless to say, such dilemmas are hardly Greenberg's alone but are discernible again and again in postwar "confessional" and philosophical literature. In what fol-lows, I proffer a small but rich sampling of such works by those grappling with *Jew* as self in the present era.

Claiming Jew

In 1980, at the age of thirty, Alain Finkielkraut, French essayist and can-tankerous cultural critic, published *Le Juif imaginaire*. This book-length "autobiographical work of cultural criticism"[95] reads as a veritable orgy of recrimination and self-recrimination written by a child of Holocaust / Shoah survivors (of whom he is by turns reverential and derisive); one disillusioned with the French student activism of the 1960s and 1970s (in which he participated) and newly "converted" to a "Judaism [that is] . . . no longer a kind of identity as much as a kind of transcendence . . . a grace I cannot claim as my own."[96] In the throes of his youthful, Augustinian, confessional self-abasement, Finkielkraut nonetheless pal-pably revels in the power he unquestioningly assumes to define what *Jew* must and must not mean, as well as who does and does not merit the name. While appalled by the audacity of his own prior claim—which he also attributes to others—to be, as *Jew*, "the appointed trustee of absolute justice," Finkielkraut is more than willing to stand in absolute judgment regarding anyone else's share in or ability to define the term.⁹⁷ The force of his protestations of personal (and generational) inadequacy is matched only by the force of the prohibitions he pronounces on *Jew*: "*Jew* is a holy term: holy as in transcendent, inaccessible, in a realm beyond our grasp. This unapproachable name resists representation, remains apart from those who give it weight. The Jew may be our civilization's Other, but it is an otherness none can possess."⁹⁸

Finkielkraut delivers this "Who is like unto Thee?" in such prophetically resonant and patently devotional tones that one half expects to see the name in question spelled "*J-w*" (at least, in the English translation), as in the pious fetishization that gives rise to the spelling "G-d." *Jew*, for Finkielkraut, has come, in fact, to name a godlike "appointed trustee of absolute justice"—and, for that reason, any taking of this name cannot be other than a taking of it in vain. Taking the name *Jew* in vain is precisely the accusation that Finkielkraut aims, briefly, at his comrades of 1968 with whom he chanted, "Nous sommes tous des juifs allemands!" ("We are all German Jews!"—a student rallying cry that expressed solidarity with the banned student-movement leader Daniel Cohn-Bendit [a German *Jew*] and, at the same time, defied French self-conceptions and social conventions by asserting alignment with the figure of the alien *Jew* that haunts postwar Europe). Finkielkraut dismisses this gesture and his erstwhile comrades for a "generosity far too facile and flashy" and for striking a momentary and strategic "pose." Self-disgust ultimately overtakes that felt toward the others, however, as Finkielkraut confesses, "In judging others to be usurpers of the Jewish condition, it was impossible not to condemn myself, and belonging to the people of Israel only made things worse. Their disguise was temporary, donned for the length of a demonstration; for me every day was a costume party. I was a Jew, and frankly, I never had to take off my disguise."⁹⁹ One hears in this speech an experiential echo of Steyn's observation that "subjects are not identical with their assumed *identity*: they are not the same unto themselves."¹⁰⁰

Is Finkielkraut's transcendent, godlike *Jew* a play on, or an intentional parody of, the trope of Jewish "chosenness"? It is hard to say. Finkielkraut's essays come across as humorless and as betraying only the flattest, unidimensional sense of irony in the form of an acerbic sarcasm. What is clear is that, for Finkielkraut, the name *Jew* must be *kaddosh*—set apart—because of the singularity and untransmissibility of the event at whose center it stands. Finkielkraut concludes his benediction with a clarifying explanation: "To put it more bluntly: the Holocaust has no heirs. . . .

Among the peoples that constitute our generation, it is given to no one to say: I am the child of Auschwitz."[101] *Jew*, then, is an identity so fully identified and suffused with "Auschwitz" that it should no longer be available outside that event, not even to those whose psyches are so intimately shaped by its aftermath. "In the noun that nonetheless designates my identity," writes Finkielkraut, "nothing defines or belongs to me. To the question 'Who am I?' the answer 'Jew' is never a pertinent response."[102]

None beyond the murdered and survivors are entitled to the name *Jew*. All subsequent *Jews* are, at best, posers or trespassers. Living *Jews*, it seems, by the very fact of living, cannot inhabit the name *Jew*, much as, for Jean-Luc Nancy, "any already existing 'community' is out of consideration [as worthy of the name 'community'] by its very existence, relegated through philosophical necessity to a world we have lost or that never existed."[103] None are entitled, and yet some, like Finkielkraut, for whom the name *Jew* "nonetheless designates my identity," are entitled to feel bereft of its ownership; cannot help but feel cheated of it, "despoiled" and "sullied" when the name is taken up by others or defined otherwise.[104]

Jew, for Finkielkraut, names the Deified Victim, a "treasure," a "status too rare and distinctive" to be grasped at by unholy hands—including his own.[105] In this respect, it might be observed, *Jew* comes to resemble the figure of the crucified Christ in Christian history. Yet it is precisely the kinds of imperialist abuses that Christianity has committed in the name of its Deified Victim that writers like Alain Badiou charge the Jewish state and its supporters with committing in the name of *Jew(s)*. Badiou rails against the sacralization of *Jew* for many of the same reasons that Finkielkraut sacralizes it: both wish to set *Jew* as Sanctified Victim beyond the easy utility of "contemporary moralism"[106] or of those who would act as living "trustee(s) of absolute justice." Badiou writes:

> Indeed, what is at issue is to know whether or not, in the general field of public intellectual discussion, the word "Jew" constitutes an exceptional signifier, such that it would be legitimate to make it play the role of a final, or even sacred, signifier. . . . Today, it is not uncommon to read that "Jew" is indeed a name beyond ordinary names. And it seems to be presumed that, like an inverted original sin, the grace of having been an incomparable victim can be passed down not only to descendants and to the descendants of descendants but to all who come under the predicate in question, be they heads of state or armies engaged in the severe oppression of those whose lands they have confiscated.[107]

In his language of "original sin" and "grace," Badiou accuses his unnamed *Jew*-sacralizers of mimicking all too well the theological paradigms taught them in the pages of Christian salvation history. But where

Finkielkraut's precarious egoism leads him to include and implicate himself in his critiques and admonitions, no such self-reflection or contrition appears to trouble this other righteous accuser. Where Finkielkraut would dispossess himself and others of *Jew* as identity, Badiou, the self-professed "goy" who also proclaims, *"le juif, c'est moi,"* would possess the term as "a universalist and egalitarian" signifier *over against* "the Shoah, the State of Israel and the Talmudic Tradition," the "triplet SIT" from which he valiantly works to "liberate" *Jew*, as many have sought to liberate *Jews*—to *mach Juden frei*—before.[108] Whereas Finkielkraut holds memory of the Holocaust to be "a central injunction" associated with the term *Jew*, Badiou insists that "we must manage—and I know it's a difficult thing—to forget the Holocaust."[109] What the two men share, however, is an unselfconscious assumption of the power to bound and bind the word *Jew*, and to define, distinguish, and name "true" or "real" *Jews* over against a legion of poseurs.[110]

Admittedly, such distinguishing among *Jews* goes back at least as far as Paul, with his *Jew* "inwardly" versus "outwardly," but the modern proliferation of such arbiters and accusers remains noteworthy. Finkielkraut names himself an "imaginary *Jew*," one of the "cherubic, overnourished, pot-bellied men . . . habitués of unreality" who "live in borrowed identities." These identities are on loan from the "non-adjectived," uninflected *Jews* destroyed and sanctified by the event whose familiar moniker "Holocaust" marks both that destruction and that sanctification (unlike the Hebrew moniker *"Shoah,"* which links back through time to medieval and biblical devastations).[111] Similarly, for Badiou, "vast numbers of Jews only assert their identity, like you and me. I call them virtual Jews. They pass on virtuality." Yet occasionally, rarely, there appears "a Jew who is more than the Jews to come, such as Saint Paul for example. This Jew is the one that I call an actual Jew."[112] Badiou's citation of Paul as "actual Jew" resurrects, so to speak, the standard dualisms of universal/particular and spirit/flesh that have long characterized Christian missionary ventures—Badiou's mission included. For both Finkielkraut and Badiou, those who self-identify as *Jew(s)* are mere instances of the "imaginary" or "virtual" *Jew* that must always fall inestimably short of instantiating *Jew*, or an "actual *Jew*" whose "actuality"—or "authenticity," to use Jean-Paul Sartre's preferred term[113]—carries radically divergent meaning and content for each respective arbiter.

The Grammar of Jew

"The word *Jew*" has never been able "to take its place in ordinary language, whether neutral or profane."[114] Ordinary language has always ruled *Jew* out of order, at least—if not always, as Zygmunt

Bauman suggests, as in and of itself "the uncanny, mind-boggling and spine-chilling incongruity that rebelled against the divine order of the universe."[115] This enigmatic quality of *Jew* no doubt helps account for the felt need of those who reflect critically upon the word (myself included) to wrestle so with its orthography and grammar, while tricking it out in all manner of modifiers. What appears, at first glance, to be a proper noun—object and/or subject, individual and/or collective—(and which, following Woody Allen, I have characterized also as an interrogative) is to Badiou a "predicate" and to Jean-François Lyotard, it seems, both a collective proper noun ("real Jews") and a "common" one. In his book *Heidegger and "the jews,"* he famously begins:

> I write "the jews" this way neither out of prudence nor lack of something better. I use lower case to indicate that I am not thinking of a nation. I make it plural to signify that it is neither a figure nor a political ([z]ionism), religious ([j]udaism), or philosophical ([j]ewish philosophy) [*pénsee hébraïque*] subject that I put forward under this name. I use quotation marks to avoid confusing these "jews" with real [j]ews. What is most real about real [j]ews is that Europe, in any case, does not know what to do with them: [c]hristians demand their conversion; monarchs expel them; republics assimilate them; [n]azis exterminate them. "The jews" are the object of a dismissal with which [j]ews, in particular, are afflicted in reality.[116]

Lyotard's constructions serve to demonstrate an irresolvable ambiguity attached to the term(s) he invokes. The use of a lowercase *j* and the plural, he insists, signifies that it is neither a "nation," nor a "figure," nor any particular imagined "subject" of any particular imagined community that he has in mind, but neither is it "real Jews." He wishes, he says, to "avoid confusing" the two. But it has seemed to many that the philosopher doth protest too much. Like Finkielkraut and Badiou, Lyotard stands among a small army of (largely European, largely French, largely male) intellectuals (and their interlocutors) for whom the word *Jew* serves as a fulcrum for theorizing memory, collective identity, and a way forward from the unimaginable annihilations that mark the twentieth century and its aftermath. "The only true event of the twentieth century was the return of the name Jew," according to some members of this small army.[117] In order to serve these desired functions, the term *Jew(s)* cannot but be irresolvably *con-fusing*—that is, always eluding and eliding simple explications or applications while inextricably intermingling and fusing myriad meanings.

Much has been made of (and much consternation expressed over) Lyotard's assertion that he writes *"les juifs"* to distinguish his subject from "*une nation*" and from "*les juifs réels.*" Both Lyotard's *minuscule* gesture and the troubled critique of that gesture provide a sampling of such eluding and eliding of meaning. *Jew* "should not be thought of as a matter of identity," but as an injunction to remember, muses Finkielkraut in his native *français*.[118] In that same tongue, Lyotard affirms the injunction to remember, while proffering *juifs réels* and "*les juifs*" as gestures toward acknowledging the complexity of memory, of ways of forgetting, and of the varying subject positions of those who must remember, who must be *re-membered*, and whose debt remains.

Jonathan Boyarin quips: "While Lyotard yet lived, I fantasized inviting him to a conference on 'lyotard' and THE JEWS." Boyarin insists that his fantastic capitalization (and minusculization) does not represent "a Tayloresque claim for recognition," but rather derives from "a perceived non-invitation to critical dialogue" in the face of the "rhetorical violence inherent in valorizing only the 'figural,' that is, only the allegorical 'jew.'"[119] Similarly, Geoffrey Bennington charges Lyotard with audacious misappropriation in "position[ing] himself as able to speak for jews *and* 'jews.'"[120] Yet who among us *can* speak for *Jews* and/or THE JEWS and/ or "*les juifs*"? Who, in doing so, would not be posing, interposing, impersonating, engaging in ventriloquisms, voicing a claimed collective experience or perspective that was not always already inflected by allegory (violently or otherwise)? Who, in other words, is "actually" in a position to speak for an other, or to proffer a genuine invitation to critical dialogue between (or among) *Jews/Juifs* and/or "*jews*"/"*juifs*" and *Jews'* others? And where, finally, may one stand in order to mediate between (or usefully place oneself amid) such an "inclusive brotherhood of the common noun versus exclusive heredity of the proper noun"?[121]

Max Silverman, imagining a middle ground between proprietary disputes and impropriety, calls for "conceiving of 'the Jew' neither simply as an open-ended signifier nor as an unproblematic signified but as a real hybrid between the two, a 'Jew' in inverted commas but with an upper-case 'J.'"[122] *Jew* always points beyond the signified; it is never apropos only of itself. It is, to say the least, "a discursive site whose uses are not fully constrained in advance."[123] Nor can they be. In Silverman's usage, the "upper-case 'J'" seems to be a bid for a kind of proprietary agency, notwithstanding the "hybridity" of the "problematic signified" that is unavoidably inflected by countless prior improprieties and dismissals of agency. But the uppercase *J* as a mark of a proper self with its atomized, individualized agency is, itself, also the product of a troubled conceit.

The proper "I," first-person singular, is always capitalized in English. No other pronoun is—not even the first-person plural, "we." *En français*, by contrast, the declaration of self, "*je*," like all pronouns, presents in *minuscule.* And a *juif* as self, as "I," will still commonly name that self with a lowercase *j*. Derrida asks,

> Can one *convert*, that is to say, translate, without remainder a sentence such as *je suis juif*, a proposition in which the adjective *juif* is an attribute thus *attributed* (but attributed by whom, in the first place? and who, here, says "I"?), can one innocently convert such a *je suis juif* into this wholly other sentence, "je suis un Juif," the attributed attribute becoming an assumed name, and demanding of French this time to be capitalized?[124]

In French, *juif* is adjective and noun, the nominal form further complicated by a rule of language that calls for the lowercase *juif* to signify a "religious" identity *as distinct from* the uppercase *Juif* that signifies a "national" or "ethnic" identity—whether attributed to a self or to an other. Such distinctions clearly raise more questions than they resolve. And not just for Derrida.

In the particularly Jewish languages of Hebrew and Yiddish, not only are there no capital letters, but *yid* and *yehudi* both begin with the tiniest letter of them all, the barest intake of life's breath, the *yod, dos pintele yud,* that begins the breath and creative utterance (*yehi 'or*) of the biblical God whose revealed name (*yhwh*) begins with this letter, as well.[125] *Jew* or *jew*—singular, plural, definite, indefinite; with or without capitalization, quotation marks, or modifiers; proper or improper; and in whatever language—is a word, a signifier, a gesture held always and explicitly in common among those who claim it as an intimate and proper name for self and those who know it only as a name for other.

"Now, there are two appellations about which I have never managed to know, to know anything at all, and most of all to know how they came to me or whether they constituted names/nouns, common names/nouns or proper names/nouns," muses Derrida. "These two appellations, these two words that are neither common nor proper, are not 'Daddy' and 'Mommy,' but *God*—and *Jew*."[126]

Who can "know from" *Jew*—a word that transcends knowing and cannot but trouble attempts at appropriation, especially by those who wish to claim "historically grounded identities in those material signifiers"?[127] *Jew(s)*, as a proprietary, proper noun or proper name—one inherently (and heritably) subject to claims of ownership—is, of necessity, subject to *mis-taken* attribution. Again, Finkielkraut is most provocative: "I am a Jew, its hold is inescapable: but no sooner have I written this than I sense a mistake, that an error in grammatical attribution of person must have occurred. I am a Jew, yet the figure designated by this statement can be located nowhere."[128] Finkielkraut confesses that his attempts to appropriate *Jew* as self seem to involve "an error in grammatical attribution" of a sort similar to that which troubles Derrida, as well, when the latter asks, "Can one authorize oneself to move from 'you are Jewish' [*tu es juif ou juive*] to a 'therefore I am' [*donc je le suis*]?"[129] The difficulty, if not the impossibility, of a meaningful and moral ("authentic") appropriation of *Jew* as self has served as a major touchstone in French political philosophy since Jean-Paul Sartre's *Anti-Semite and Jew* was published immediately following the Second World War, in 1946.

Troping Jew

In her book *The Figural Jew: Politics and Identity in Postwar French Thought*, Sarah Hammerschlag positions Derrida and his ruminations on *Jew* at the near end of a line of postwar thinkers in France, beginning with Sartre and running through Emmanuel Levinas, Maurice Blanchot, Jacques Rancière, and Lyotard, who, she argues, are largely responsible for articulating a political philosophy of deracination, dissociation, and disappropriation as moral critique and counterweight to ethnic nationalisms and other problematic narratives of belonging. The "unstable figure," "wandering nomad, the foreigner," and "symbol of the improper" that animates this critical French political philosophy is *the Jew*, a revalorized literary/political "trope" that serves, according to Hammerschlag, as a potent and constant "reminder of its own deception" and therefore of the instability of all claims to collective identity.[130] *Jew*, she claims, becomes a means by which to revel in aporia, to declare "other" as a name for "self"—a declaration that can have "ethical content," but only if it is *not* "deployed as a means to characterize the Jewish community."[131] That is to say, for Hammerschlag, *Jew* can serve as an instrument of positive, ethically powerful political action, but *only* if deployed as a trope by members of (European) hegemonic majorities wishing to disidentify from their privileged positions (*Nous sommes tous des juifs allemands!*), and *only* insofar as *Jew* explicitly performs a *failure* of identity and belonging.[132]

There is much of value in Hammerschlag's discussion, and much that invites further consideration. In the present context, three points must suffice. First, the question remains open, and not well answered, to what extent the "figural Jew" of postwar French philosophy does rhetorical violence as caricature—no matter how valorized or valuable, casual or convincing any given performance of it might be. At the same time, the near "uninhabitability" of *Jew* as identity is, indeed, a theme that resonates through not a few first-person accounts—Greenberg's, Finkielkraut's, Derrida's, and Améry's among them. And Hammerschlag's provision of a "mixed" genealogy for this philosophical avatar—a lineage including, in

Jonathan Boyarin's terms, both "those who self-identify or are identified by others as Jews, and those who don't and/or aren't ('jews' or not)," fore-stalls a too-easy charge that the figure in question is a product and per-petuator of an absence of critical dialogue.[133] Second, and closely related, is the question of the obvious but largely unarticulated significance of this "ethical" trope of *Jew* with regard to postwar Jewish communitarianism—including that manifested in Zionism. Some voices addressing this ques-tion are included below. But the insistence that claims to "be" *Jew* are "ethical" *only* when such claims *exclude* identification with living Jewish communities is, to say the least, disconcerting. Finally, the emphasis on *Jew* as a tropological performance invites deeper consideration, as it finds repeated echoes in the narratives under consideration here.

Performing Jew

"Performance," as an analytical category in cultural studies, considers the ways in which identities are "performed"; are, even more, themselves products of performance. Some of the most obvious and intriguing popular notions of identity performance include "passing," mimicry, drag, and masquerade—notions found again and again in recent didactic, historiographic, and first-person writings on *Jew*. In her advocacy of *Jew* as an identity position "with which anyone, even a non-Jew might come to identify"[134] and as a tropological performance that "unravels under the paradoxical conditions of its deployment . . . exposing the ambivalences and ambiguities that are expressed when *anyone* asserts his or her Jewishness,"[135] Hammerschlag emphasizes the critical force and political potential of performing (and inevitably *failing* to perform) *Jew*.

Many first-person writers invoke the language and images of perfor-mance in exploring their own experiences of *Jew*—not only the failures and follies, but also the tolls these take and the insights they enable. Finkielkraut, for example, reflects:

> I thought I was living up to Israel's calling, and played the role of the Jew. . . . It doesn't work anymore; the drama's mainspring has unsprung. I'm an actor without parts, a laid-off tragedian. . . . Jew, to be sure, but an *indebted* Jew (because individually, I am less, always less than what the term evokes), a Jew wishing to shed the theatrical patrimony where my roots had been struck.[136]

Finkielkraut's dramatic angst here is as unmistakable as the genuine para-dox he describes. *Jew*, he insists, had once been, for him, a "pathetic and marvelous . . . self that I adored as if it were an idol,"[137] but he now sees it as a disquieting and dissembling role played on behalf of a collective—"Israel," here referring to a people, not the state—a performance in which the actor can neither "be" *Jew* nor "shed the theatrical patrimony" that calls forth the attempt to do so. Elsewhere, as we have seen, he confesses that "every day was a costume party. I was a Jew, and frankly, I never had to take off my disguise."[138]

Finkielkraut's judgment echoes but inverts the familiar antisemitic charge that *Jews* are, inherently, deceptive poseurs easily able to infiltrate social milieus by masking their true selves. In the words of Rabbi Adin Steinsaltz, to be a *Jew* is to have an "innate capacity to imitate, to become a copy . . . instinctively [to] aspire to the quintessence, the common denominator, and the very root of the national essence with which he is identifying himself."[139] In his book *We Jews: Who Are We? And What Should We Do?* Steinsaltz affirms this trope of subterfuge—so effectively exploited by the Nazis—in an attempt to warn *Jews* against the shamefulness, danger, and "spiritual consequences" of trying to "pass" or, worse yet, to "assimilate." The "quintessence" and "national essence" he invokes in his warning are those of "host cultures" and "host people" (the odd and antique phrases evoking parasitology as much as hospitality), to whom, he insists, *Jew* represents a fundamentally different, incompatible, and nonassimilable "nature" and "essence."

For many of those who, like Finkielkraut, consider *Jew* a name for self, however, it is *Jew*—a character whose story both is and is not at all one's own—that is experienced as mask, performance, artifice. And this is so regardless of whether the performance is conceived of as involuntary or voluntary, as determined legacy or worthy aspiration.

Art Spiegelman, creator of the Holocaust comic memoir *Maus* (the German, monosyllabic, four-letter title itself an effective "translation" of the Nazi *Jude*, as well as a resonant element of the wordplay "Mauschwitz" and, as it happens, an abbreviated echo of *Mauschel*), has grappled with this dynamic more publicly than most, and by means of a richly graphic self-representation and self-fashioning. Many will be familiar with Spiegelman's "author photo" of a human-like figure wearing a mouse mask, which appears on the back cover of most editions of *Maus*; the same figure also appears briefly at the start of the second volume of *Maus*. In response to a query about this particular set of images in relation to his larger project of relaying the story of his father, Vladek, a survivor of the Nazi genocide, Spiegelman writes:

> It's really implied in the first panel of the first chapter of the first volume. I had to put on a mouse head to enter into my father's story. It was only over time that I discovered the implications of that. And I elaborated the image further as the author's "photo" at the back of many editions of the book. It was my intensive rethinking of how to

get back into volume two, a story that I was trying to evade—that is, how to inhabit the oxymoron of presenting life in a death camp—that made me understand I had to fully acknowledge myself as the author wrestling with making a book. It became useful to indicate that, hey, you know what, there are human faces under these mouse heads, on the analyst's couch, grappling with my father's legacy.[140]

"Masking," says Spiegelman, enables the telling of a story "too profane to show directly."[141] Masking provides "a way into," as well as a way to "inhabit the oxymoron" at the heart of, his/his father's tale. Yet Spiegelman also speaks of his need to find the "human faces" beneath the masks as he grapples with his "father's legacy." Still, it seems that legacy— the survivor's life, and life lived in the shadow of survivors; the perplexing and often stifling notoriety that results from creatively and effectively recounting those lives—leaves Vladek's son able only to *imply* that a recognizably human face, an ordinary human self, lies beneath his mask. The mask, despite its reemphasized artifice, never does come off, so long as the story continues to be told.

As more "time flies"[142] and Spiegelman reflects further on the implications of his legacy, the question of what lies beneath the mask becomes only more haunted. In a comic sequence that serves as the introduction to *MetaMaus*, we find Spiegelman's mouse-headed avatar reflecting that "it's swell to get recognition . . . but it's kinda hard to be seen behind a mouse mask!" Hoping finally to lay to rest this chapter of his life by offering to answer, once and for all, the persistent questions raised by *Maus*, he then suggests, "And maybe I could even get my damned mask off! I can't breathe in this thing . . . unff! Urk! Oof! Grunt! [as he wrestles with it] . . . Rripp! [as it finally lets go] . . . Aah! [a sigh of relief]." The final panel reveals the author figure holding the now limp and vacant mask, while in its place we see a smiling, skeletal death's head.[143] This image brilliantly evokes multiple implications and resonances, all of them deeply disconcerting. These are rendered still more poignant by Spiegelman's choice to place a small photograph of himself as a very young child, alone, on the final page of this final *Maus* volume—a kind of "bookend" to the similar photo of his murdered brother, Richieu, on the dedication page of volume II.[144]

In 2013, a retrospective of Spiegelman's work was mounted at the Jewish Museum in New York City. Concluding his review of the exhibit, *Jewish Daily Forward* contributor Joshua Furst writes the following: "Look at Art Spiegelman, wearing his *maus* mask, slumped mournfully in front of his easel. He mined his own trauma; he mastered the metaphors of his life and became the most influential cartoonist of his era, only to discover that he'd turned into a metaphor for himself. That, as the devil could have told him way back when, is the price of success."[145] A clever assessment, to be sure. But one might wonder: is not becoming "a metaphor for oneself," rather, the price of publicly performing *Jew* at all—success or failure aside?

Finkielkraut's confessions, Derrida's unknowings, and Spiegelman's graphic musings provoke questions raised by Judith Butler about all subject formation: "Does this mean that one puts on a mask or persona, that there is a 'one' who precedes that 'putting on,' who is something other than [that 'impersonation'] . . . from the start? Or does this miming, this impersonating precede and form the 'one,' operating as its formative precondition rather than its dispensable artifice?"[146]

In his essay "On the Necessity and Impossibility of Being a Jew," Jean Améry relates that, even in his childhood, he sensed the "foolishness" of "masquerading in Austrian dress [when he wore "white half socks and leather breeches"]—although it was, after all, part of my heritage." That particular "disguise," he notes, "now lies in the attic."[147] Yet an equally unsettling sense of masquerade overcomes him as he considers how he might go about securing a "self-acquired identity" as *Jew*—another part of his "heritage":[148]

> Who would possibly prevent me from learning the Hebrew language, from reading Jewish history and tales, and from participating—even without belief—in Jewish ritual, which is both religious and national? Well supplied with all the requisite knowledge of Jewish culture from the prophets to Martin Buber, I could emigrate to Israel [under the Law of Return] and call myself Yochanan. . . . [But] a Yochanan on Mt. Carmel, haunted and spirited home by memories of Alpine valleys and folk rituals, would be even more inauthentic than was once the youth with his knee socks.[149]

Améry concludes, "To be who one is by becoming the person one should be and wants to be: for me this dialectical process of self-realization is obstructed. . . . Thus, I am not permitted to be a Jew. But since all the same I must be one and since this compulsion excludes the possibilities that might allow me to be something other than a Jew, can I not find myself at all?"[150] Améry's reflections give voice to a common tension between "compulsion" and deep identification, on the one hand, and, on the other, the competing demands of "self-realization" through performance of a nationalized identity that is too exclusive of multiple belongings and divergent memories to ever seem (for many like Améry) other than "inauthentic."

For his part, Steinsaltz would likely consider those like Améry to be the product of the inevitably failed performance of their "assimilated" parents, whose very "nature" should lead them to recognize the foolishness of masquerading as Austrian, American, French, and the like.[151] But Améry's own account highlights the even greater discomfort with which he might perform *Jew*—in particular, *Israeli Jew*—as scripted in the prescriptions and proscriptions that he attributes to that identity. A similar bemusement is expressed by the character Jascha in Rebecca Goldstein's novel *Mazel*: "If I am to believe the arguments of people like you," fumes Jascha at his interlocutor, "it is that place, and not here in the Europe of my birth, and of my father's birth, and of my father's father's birth, that I am to think of as my authentic homeland? . . . I would ask you please not to impose upon me a destiny that I could never experience, but as entirely forced and artificial and external—I would even say inimical—to my own given nature."[152]

Zionism's Conflicted Claims on Jew

Jew names a stress point between competing claims regarding nationalisms, in general, and *Jewish* nationalism or Zionism, in particular. The anti-communitarian manner in which the postwar philosophical/ethical discourse described by Hammerschlag defines and deploys *Jew* is obviously at odds with Zionism's explicitly communitarian claims on *Jew*. As noted in the discussion of *yidn*, above, Zionist narratives of ethnic identity and homeland appropriate and derogate *Jew* by turns, but all in service to building and sustaining a "Jewish nation-state" grounded, geographically and demographically, on claims of ancestral belonging.

In her book *Parting Ways: Jewishness and the Critique of Zionism*, Butler, taking what she terms her "Jewish formation" as a point of departure, explores some of the ways in which such contending claims on *Jew* are experienced as both demanding and silencing ethical relationships and dialogue. "I am trying to understand," she writes, "how the exilic—or more emphatically, *the diasporic*—is built into the idea of the Jewish (not analytically, but historically, that is, over time); in this sense, to 'be' Jew is to be departing from oneself, cast out into a world of the non-Jew, bound to make one's way ethically and politically precisely there within a world of irreversible heterogeneity."[153] But to "be"—or, more precisely, to *perform*—such a *Jew*, she suggests, is to run headlong into a prevailing nationalist discourse that subjugates both this *Jew* and its others:

> Of course, many individuals with Jewish formations and affiliations have arrived at anti-Zionist positions and concluded that they therefore can no longer be Jews. My sense is that the State of Israel would congratulate them on coming to this conclusion. Indeed, if one's opposition to the current policies of the State of Israel, or to Zionism more

generally, leads to the conclusion that one can no longer affiliate as a Jew, such a decision effectively ratifies the notion that to be a Jew is to be a Zionist. . . . There are still others with Jewish formations and affiliations who find themselves muted by the present state of Israeli politics. They very often abhor the occupation, feel appalled by Israeli military strikes against civilians in Gaza, and even sometimes wish for forms of binationalism that might provide more just and viable, and less violent, political structures for the region. But they fear that to espouse such criticism will stoke anti-Semitism, and hold that it is unacceptable to offer public criticism that might be instrumentalized to increase anti-Semitism and violent crimes against Jewish people. Indeed, this double bind has become nearly constitutive for many Jews in the diaspora.[154]

Finkielkraut describes a similar policing of *Jew* in 1970s France, but frames his description as a critique of a persistent hypocrisy of the French Left. From this leftist perspective, he reports, a neutral or pro-Zionist stance— or even the refusal to articulate an anti-Zionist stance—determines that one is not a ("real") *Jew* insofar as one is not performing rootlessness, disidentification, and a failure of belonging that are the quintessence of the French, postwar, political-philosophical embrace of *Jew*. As Finkielkraut recalls:

> They held our racism but not our race against us, saw us as the tools of a theocratic, imperialist, and militaristic state, and hated us for being colonizers and paras, not exiles or nomads. Having ceased to be a persecuted minority and become the arrogant oppressors, we were given but a single chance of reclaiming our previous image: produce our certificate of divorce from Israel. . . . To be accepted as a Jew, all ties with Zionism had to be cut, just as in the past, liberal France conferred the status of Israelite on those of the Prophet's descendants who no longer retained the slightest trace of Jewishness.[155]

By this account, the only *Jew* acceptable *as Jew* among the vocal representatives of an enlightened Left is one who actively performs a ritualized "divorce" from the Jewish state and stands in opposition to it.

The Jewish state is, itself, frequently figured—by both Zionists and anti-Zionists—as the political other, the "pariah state" in an imagined community of modern nations, just as *Jew* has long been considered other to all manner of constructions of collective self (including that of the community of anti-communitarians discussed by Hammerschlag). This representation invites the critical hypothesis that, just as the diasporic *Jew*/Jewish diaspora, in the words of the brothers Boyarin, "threatened . . . [and] constantly questioned the very attempt to organize the world polity as a neatly bounded set of so many defined, autonomous centers—[that is,] the attempt to realize what was called the nation-state system," so, too, the overt nationalism and "tortured contradictions of the 'Jewish state'" only serve to highlight what is most problematic about *all* nationalist projects and their inevitably deforming effects.[156] Outrage expressed against Israel might, then, at times, mask, sublimate, or over-compensate for discomfort with other national or homeland mythologies to which so many of us still wish to cling.

A Plural Self

Bids for and claims of ownership; the exercise of naming, defining, and delimiting; assertions, attributions, or disavowals of belonging; and explorations or accusations (including self-accusations) of usurpation, misappropriation, and masquerade—all of these represent the current state of the question of *Jew(s)* (if not also of the "Jewish Question") in the late twentieth and early twenty-first centuries. Confronted by this often fractious and disorienting dynamic, and in response to it, some have attempted expressly to craft a performance of *Jew* that not only is a ver-sion of a postmodern "fractured" self or self-divided subject, but also instantiates a multiple or plural sense of self: one that is, perhaps para-doxically, both unsituated and multiply positioned.[157]

In *First Person Jewish*, Alisa S. Lebow offers nuanced readings of a number of what she terms "Jewish autobiographical documentary films" that feature such deconstructed, plural performances of *Jew*. She identi-fies, running throughout these films, "a distinct tendency" on the part of the filmmakers to employ "self-fictionalization strategies to define a mul-tifaceted, nonessentialist, contemporary 'Jewishness' while dialogically engaging tropes of Jewish cultural identity originating in the pre- and post-Enlightenment eras."[158] These scripted, posed, framed, and edited "autobiographical" performances self-consciously draw on and seek to contribute to a wide range of critical discourses for which *Jew* may be understood to serve as a particularly productive nexus or lens:

> Questions of Jewish identity and cultural production . . . fit quite strik-ingly with larger multicultural concerns, serving as a theoretical mag-net where the politics of race, sexuality, gender, cultural and ethnic difference, political polarization, assimilation, tradition, and a host of other cultural determinants are all drawn together in one very dense, historically loaded, cultural location: *Jewishness*. Jewishness is, of course, itself a manifold and polysemous cultural site. Better known for its unsituatedness or disaggregatedness (otherwise known as Diaspora), Jewishness provides dynamic and variegated vantage points from which to explore [a] range of concerns.[159]

Not only do these performances, in Lebow's reading of them, participate in broader, multidimensional cultural conversations about the politics of difference and relation, but they often incorporate old tropes of the Jew in a manner that signals a kind of subverted revaluation of these tropes. In this way, the films' characters might be understood to be engaging in the "tropological performance" of Jew celebrated by Hammerschlag as a product of postwar political philosophy:

> The slippery, contradictory image of the Jew formerly found in the lexi-
> con of the anti-Semite has come to yield a new meaning in the context
> of postmodern identity, basking in the cultural approbation of a cur-
> rently sanctioned discourse. In this redemptive, culturally affirming
> shift, traditional Jewish stereotypes drawn from a vast antipathetic cul-
> tural cache have been transformed into a positive conception: the self
> as open-ended figure.[160]

The resemblance between this Jew and that described by Hammerschlag is immediately evident. Moreover, the ethical/political potential of this filmic Jew is every bit as viable as that of the figural one articulated by the philosophers. Lebow echoes Faye Ginsburg's assessment that Jewish ethnographic films like these "are not simply filmic texts, but are *mediating* documents, part of the process of the re-invention(s) of contemporary Jewish identity."[161] Yet, as this formulation illustrates, there are some crucial differences between the one Jew and the other. Whereas the figural Jew of postwar political philosophy emblematizes disaffiliation and disidentification with all communitarianisms, many of these filmic performances of Jew are deeply involved in negotiating identification with—as well as disidentification from—an imagined Jewish community toward which the performances might be oriented (and to which they might even be addressed).[162]

Lebow's own autobiographical film *Treyf* represents one such set of performances. In an "autocritique" of her film, Lebow describes the variety of strategies she and her co-filmmaker Cynthia Madansky employed to portray the unsituated, yet multiply positioned, plural self and subjectivity that float—embodied and disembodied—through their narrative. The film's title, itself, encodes the sense of uneasy negotiation, of identifications and disidentifications in which this subjectivity is enmeshed:

> *Treyf* is predicated on a formulation of queer, secular, politically pro
> gressive Jews as being outsiders in the Jewish world yet still having
> antecedents in modern Jewish history. . . . To be treyf in the context of
> this film is to maintain a delicate balance between being integrated into
> one's identities and being radically alienated from them. As my charac
> ter says, in direct address, early in the film, "'Treyf' is an insider/

outsider term: you have to be insider enough to know what it means, yet to be treyf is to be an outsider."[163]

In addition to explaining the metavalue encoded in the word *treyf* (recall Seidman's parsing of her father's *"Yidn!"*), Lebow here characterizes her performance of *Jew* as "treyf" (unkosher) because it holds in "delicate balance" queer *and* normative, past *and* present, integration *and* alienation, self *as* other. She even admits, wryly, "We insist, in contrarian fashion, on being treyf, and then proclaim treyf to be a quintessentially Jewish value."[164]

In performing *Jew* as a balancing act of insider/outsider, as a constantly evanescing "plural self" constituted (and contested) in relation, Lebow invites her viewers to perceive *Jew* as a self that is never so "in its own right." Greenberg's mid-twentieth-century longing to be a *Jew* in his own right is met, in this twenty-first-century response, with a powerful performance of agency and ownership that is nonetheless always plural, always contingent, always mediated and mediating, never "proper" or "authentic" but, instead, "treyf."[165] Even Finkielkraut, writing at a temporal midpoint between Greenberg and Lebow, seems ultimately to glimpse something of this *Jew*: "The word *Jew* is no longer a mirror in which I seek my self-portrait," he writes in the final pages of *Le juif imaginaire*, "but where I look for everything . . . I'll never be able to glimpse by taking myself as the point of reference."[166] In the end, however, it is Butler who, engaging Levinas, perhaps best summarizes the ethical implications of this complex, necessarily plural identification of self as *Jew*:

> The relation to alterity becomes one predicate of "being Jewish." . . .
> That very relationship . . . challeng[es] the idea of "Jewish" as a static
> sort of being, one that is adequately described as a subject. . . .
> Moreover, the kind of relationality at stake is one that 'interrupts' or
> challenges the unitary character of the subject, its self-sameness and its
> univocity. In other words, something happens to the "subject" that dis-
> locates it from the center of the world; some demand from elsewhere
> lays claim to me, presses itself upon me, or even divides me from
> within, and only through this fissuring of who I am do I stand a chance
> of relating to another. If one tries to say that this is [a] formulation of
> "Jewish ethics" . . . one would only be partly right. It is Jewish/not
> Jewish, and its meaning lies precisely in that conjunctive disjunction.[167]

Jew as self inhabits precisely this space of "conjunctive disjunction," a space where unity and difference, belonging and alienation, longing and being hover in a delicate—and sometimes indelicate—balance.

The appropriation of *Jew* as a name for self in the dominant languages and discourses of the West has been a multifaceted and centuries-long process—one that is still unfolding, not always successfully. From the doubled internal and external bilingualisms of *der yid*, through the "incommensurate number of subject positions" and "contrary discourses" contrived for *the Jew* and identified by Jewish-studies scholars, to the self-consciously tropological and *treyf* performances of a postmodern proliferation of selves, *Jew* has come to name a multiply positioned and inflected subject/object. *Jew* remains an open and irresolvable question. But it is a question that, as I hope to have intimated here, rewards the asking with an endless array of fascinating, provocative, and ethically meaningful responses.

3 In a New Key

> A current generation of Jewish activists, whom
> some call "the New Jews," are providing a new
> Jewish imaginary that is far more flexible and
> inclusive than that of prior generations.
>> Faye Ginsburg, "The Canary in the
>> Gemeinschaft?"

> I may not have known I was Jewish, but I carried
> the gene.
>> Stephen Frears, quoted in "Hidden Heritage
>> Inspires Director"

> Are Muslims Europe's new Jews?
>> Shireen M. Mazari, *Pakistanpal's Blog*

This final chapter takes as its starting point the word *new* as a key word modifying *Jew(s)*. At the turn of the twentieth century, the phrase "new *Jew*" most forcefully served "to denote the growing distinction that Zionists made between the Jew of the Diaspora and the 'new Jew'—the native Jew of Palestine," popularly termed "Sabra."[1] In his book *The Sabra: The Creation of the New Jew*, Oz Almog cites among prominent "Sabra characteristics" at that time: "a hatred of the Diaspora [and] a native sense of supremacy" over the land, over other peoples of the land, and especially over "Diaspora *Jews*." Almog's translator, Haim Watzman, adds that "Sabra society was very much based on masculine ideals. . . . The classic, influential, and familiar Sabras were men, and the mythic Sabra ideal . . . was explicitly a male one."[2]

At the turn of the twenty-first century, the phrase "new *Jews*" has gained currency in formulations quite different from this earlier, Zionist usage. In the "New Europe," for example, "new *Jews*" now often describes a growing "Muslim diaspora" that poses fundamental challenges to experiments in collective identity and democracy in the emergent postcolonial, post-Holocaust, supranational society of the European Union. On the other side of the North Atlantic, in the United States, notions of "new *Jews*" are intertwined with what some have called "postethnic" affiliations and identifications that signal a critique, rejection, and dissolution of standard dichotomies—including us/them, homeland/diaspora, religious/secular, masculine/feminine, even *Jew*/Gentile—that have heretofore seemed to delimit the contours of *Jew*.

Generally speaking, the adjective *new* connotes a specifically temporal attribute. Yet, as the preceding examples indicate (and as monikers like "New Europe," "New World," and "New York" ought to remind us), *new* is always geopolitically contingent and conditioned, as well. The new *Jews* explored in this chapter, then, constellate within and between distinct—albeit deeply interconnected—geopolitical spaces: Israel, Europe, and the United States. And the newness of which they partake represents, in the words of Homi K. Bhabha, "not a smooth passage of transition and transcendence," but rather "a sense of the new as an insurgent act of cultural translation" realized through "spaces [that] provide the terrain for elaborating strategies of selfhood—singular or communal . . . in the act of defining the idea of society itself."[3] The United States, Europe, and Israel provide radically different terrains, spaces, and ideas of society within which new *Jews* come to represent a variety of strategies for negotiating selfhood and otherness.

Accounts of new *Jews* are bound up with diverse and multifaceted narratives of history and affinity that, at times, combine into new "genealogics" of *Jew*. By "genealogics" I mean to signify interconnected ways of formulating, thinking about, and articulating collective identifications and relationships among people(s) using conceptual categories such as "kinship," "legacy," "influence," "blood," and the like. Just as "new *Jews*" is of a piece with *and* in tension with received understandings of *Jew*, so, too, are these "new genealogics" of a piece with and in tension with earlier, more familiar genealogics of *Jew*.

Key factors contributing to new genealogics of *Jew* include legacies of the Nuremberg Laws and related policies that have expanded, fractionalized, and racialized definitions of *Jew*; developments in Halacha (for example, the restoration of patrilineal—alongside matrilineal—definitions of birthright in many contexts and communities); high and growing numbers of so-called intermarried families in the United States and elsewhere; popularization of digital media; feminist and LGBTIQ activism; transnational movements and migrations; postwar European political projects; and Israeli demographic, religious, and military policies, along with collective responses to these.

Another contributing factor is the burgeoning of programs of genetic research, with their associated discourses and other practices in which *Jew(s)* is treated as a biological, scientifically legible category. This is the case, for example, in "genetic ancestry" studies that led to isolating, naming, and capitalizing on the much-hailed and much-contested "Cohen Modal Haplotype."[4] It is likewise expressed in genetic medical projects like those focused on managing Tay-Sachs and other so-called Jewish genetic diseases, including the gene mutations in BRCA1 and BRCA2 associated with breast and ovarian cancer.[5] "Genomic *Jews*" are among the newest of the new *Jews* examined here.

As with the subjects introduced in the previous parts of this book, this chapter makes no pretense of addressing the entire range of new *Jews* and all of the new genealogics by which they are constituted. Still, the "insurgent act," or disruption, that the attribution of "newness" implies serves here not only to highlight the continued currency and malleability of *Jew(s)*, but also makes of new *Jews* a powerful lens through which to perceive ongoing and emerging patterns of self-understanding and attributions of otherness.

Zionism's New *Jew* and the Birth of the Genomic *Jew*

Zionism's new *Jew* was formed at the intersection of nineteenth- and early twentieth-century race science/eugenics with romanticized, racialized, ethnic nationalisms. He—a paragon of dominant Western masculinism—was a rejoinder to the neurotic, degenerate, effeminate, rootless, and money-grubbing "old" *Jew—Yid, Jude, Mauschel*—whose odious condition was the result, according to some "scientific" theories of the day, of a distinct, substandard evolutionary lineage sustained and degraded by inbreeding. According to other theories, this old "Diaspora *Jew*" was the result of millennia-long population concentration (involuntary or voluntary) in urban centers or in trades and lifestyles divorced from contact with the salubrious effects of landedness and agrarian labor.

For those who generated and subscribed to the first variety of these theories, there seemed two viable options for responding to the diagnosis. One would be to disrupt the custom of endogamous marriage among *Jews* and thereby cease the destructive pattern of inbreeding, diversify the gene pool, assimilate the population, and hence dissipate the perceived genetically transmitted defects. The other option would be to isolate the "pathogenic race" through campaigns of public education (a kind of inoculation) and laws against intermarriage and intermixing designed to stop its spread and its contamination of other, healthier, gene pools.

Once isolated, the danger could be excised, amputated, and ultimately destroyed. The results of this latter analysis, with its implemented "final solution," are widely known: unspeakable atrocity whose devastating effects are enduring and irremediable.

For those who subscribed to the second variety of explanation, by contrast, amelioration of the environmental harms accumulated by diaspora Jews required a collective change in lifestyles and livelihoods. Such a change might take the form of full integration into the worldwide proletarian class (a communist solution)[6] or, conversely, relocation to a place where Jews could practice ethnic political sovereignty, as well as landed labor. Statist Zionism promoted the second of these models, as exemplified by the Zionist Organization Statement on Palestine at the Paris Peace Conference in February 1919:

> The conditions of life of millions of Jews are deplorable. Forming often a congested population, denied the opportunities which would make a healthy development possible, the need of fresh outlets is urgent, both for their own sake and the interests of the population of other races, among whom they dwell. Palestine would offer one such outlet.[7]

Fin-de-siècle Zionism's new Jew, then, although set forth as a proud countermodel and bold response to the unhealthy, degenerate Jew of early race science and European romantic nationalism, is, itself, clearly a product of those same discourses. The following analysis, penned in 1904, is another unmistakable artifact of such discourse:

> A Jew brought up among Germans may assume German custom, German words. He may be wholly imbued with that German fluid but the nucleus of his spiritual structure will always remain Jewish, because his blood, his body, his physical-racial type are Jewish. . . . It is impossible for a man to become assimilated with people whose blood is different from his own. In order to become assimilated, he must change his body, he must become one of them, in blood. . . . There can be no assimilation as long as there is no mixed marriage. . . . An increase in the number of mixed marriages is the only sure and infallible means for the destruction of nationality as such. . . . A preservation of national integrity is impossible except by a preservation of racial purity.[8]

The author's argument, to this point, is indistinguishable from so many others that became tragically familiar in the wake of the paroxysms of the first half of the twentieth century. Romantic/mythic and scientific notions are indistinguishable here among talk of "fluid" and "nucleus," "blood" and "body," "physical-racial type" and "preservation of racial purity." A Jew may be "wholly imbued with that German fluid," and yet "the nucleus of his spiritual structure will always remain Jewish" and, thus, unassimilable into a European nation-state, because "his blood, his body, his physical-racial type are Jewish." There is, in this conception, no German *Jew*, no French *Jew*, no Polish *Jew*. A *Jew* born in Europe to a long line of progenitors born and raised in Europe remains, nonetheless, not of "European blood." A *Jew* is, in essence, sui generis.

Even so, "mixed marriage" might serve the aim of assimilating the *Jew* into a European nation-state; in fact, it is the only "sure and infallible means" to that end. But it would also destroy the "nationality" and "national integrity" of the racially pure peoples at the heart of nation-states, thus conceived. National (or "ethnic") integrity, in this understanding, relies on "racial purity," "and for that purpose we are in need of a territory of our own where our people will constitute the overwhelming majority."⁹

So wrote Vladimir (Ze'ev) Jabotinsky, prominent architect and theorist of early statist Zionism. That movement's new *Jew*, then, represented not a rejection of, but rather an embrace of, racialist ethnic nationalism. Jabotinsky's is hardly the first or only rationale for Zionism, which became a multipronged movement with some degree of ideological diversity and disagreement among its base. Even so, Jabotinsky remains one of the most highly honored founders of early Zionism and of what became Israel's Likud Party.¹⁰ His were not marginal perspectives.¹¹

Jabotinsky was a great admirer of the work of Max Nordau—scientist, physician, and cofounder with Theodore Herzl of the World Zionist Organization. Perhaps best known for his book *Degeneration* and for his conception of a new, "muscular" *Jew*, Nordau called for the biological and anthropological study of *Jew(s)* as the raw material (*das Volksmaterial*) for Zionism's nation-building project. In his address to the Fifth Zionist Congress in Basel in 1901, Nordau asserts the need for scientific precision in measuring the "exact anthropological, biological, economic, and intellectual statistic of the Jewish people."¹² He continues:

> We [Zionists] must have quantitative answers to the following questions: How is the Jewish people physiologically constituted? What is the average size (of the Jew)? What are his anatomical characteristics? What are the numbers of diseased within it? What are the death rates? How many days, on the average, is the Jew ill during a year? What is the average life span? From which diseases do Jews die? . . . How many criminals, insane, deaf and dumb, cripples, blind, epileptics are there among the Jewish nation? Do the Jews have their own particular characteristic criminality, and if so, what is it?¹³

Nordau's program—sketched here and subsequently put into practice—is notable both for its Zionist impetus and for its preoccupation with disease, disability, and criminality. His pleas, as Mitchell B. Hart observes in *Social Science and the Politics of Modern Jewish Identity*, "spoke to a more general belief or conviction that Jewish nationalism must become 'scientific' in order to achieve its goals. A mass movement, if it was systematically to reconstitute a *Volk*, required the tools by which mass phenomena could be known and understood."[14] In a very real sense, then, *the Jew(s)* is here constituted by the Zionist project as, at one and the same time, a modern scientific subject *and* object, a modern ethno-national self *and* other, and an encompassing collective modern subject *tout court*. These are, each and all, new *Jews* whose emergence within Zionism is quite explicitly "an insurgent act of cultural translation." The generation and amalgamation of scientific data about disparate individuals and collectives here becomes the means for "elaborating strategies of selfhood—singular [and] communal" toward the end of realizing a Zionist "idea of society itself."[15]

Reconceiving the Land and Its Jews

Zionism's new *Jew* is an insurgent, "regenerate" species that would be developed to supersede the "degeneration" caused by millennia of "exile" from a homeland that, as well, needed to be newly reconstituted and regenerated to the standard of its ancient biblical kingdoms. In fact, just as centuries of midrash retrojected sagacious rabbinic ideals back into the biblical stories and reconceived biblical heroes in the "image and likeness" of the rabbis, so now, too, did the architects of Zionism translate their militant and muscular new *Jews* back into biblical tales and times.[16] As a result, biblical and other ancient heroes came to bear a striking resemblance to the Zionist ideal. Herzl's fictional David and Jabotinsky's Samson are but two of Zionism's biblically inspired new *Jews*, while Nordau's Zionist gymnastic club in Berlin was named "Bar Kochba" in a similar vein.[17] "The new Jew was to be symbolic of the Jewish national character as it had existed in ancient times and must exist again in the future," observes George L. Mosse.[18] In these Zionist visions, the ancient *Jew* of a reconceived biblical and postbiblical past becomes one with his (masculine, militant) new-*Jew* descendant in a telescoping of time and space that renders a score of intervening centuries and worldwide habitation, at best, irrelevant.

To create the new *Jew* as a "native" *Jew* in Palestine, Zionism needed first to create the conditions for this *Jew*'s birth. This, of course, required establishing settlements of *Jews* in, first, Ottoman and, later, British Mandate Palestine alongside and despite its existing inhabitants. Among documents from the early years of cohabitation and conflict, Jabotinsky's are, once again, most impressive for their candor—in this case, about the armed force required to colonize and hold a land against the wishes of its

"natives." In his famous "Iron Wall" essay, Jabotinsky challenges his readers to "see whether there is one solitary instance of any colonization
being carried on with the consent of the native population." He concludes, "There is no such precedent."

> The native populations, civilized or uncivilized, have always stubbornly
> resisted the colonists, irrespective of whether they were civilized or
> savage. . . . The Palestinian Arabs . . . feel at least the same instinctive
> jealous love of Palestine, as the old Aztecs felt for ancient Mexico, and
> the Sioux for their rolling prairies. . . . Every native population in the
> world resists colonists as long as it has the slightest hope of being able
> to rid itself of the danger of being colonized.[19]

The bluntness of Jabotinsky's prose is startling as he identifies the settlers
as dangerous "colonists" on the order of "Cortez and Pizarro . . . Joshua
ben Nun [and] the Pilgrim Fathers . . . of North America," notwithstanding the reigning messianic and Zionist rhetoric of simple "return from
exile." Jabotinsky insists that the new *Jew* be recognized as a militant settler and the Zionist project as a conquest—one he insists is "moral and
just"—over the "native-born population" of the land.[20]

Other Zionists, perhaps by way of tempering the colonialist nature of
the enterprise described by Jabotinsky, sought to discover a surviving lineage of "native" *Jews* in the land who might more securely anchor a nativ-
ist claim to shared belonging there. Yitzhak Ben-Zvi, historian and second
president of Israel, for example, made a four-decade career out of "prov-
ing the continuity of Jewish settlement in Eretz Israel."[21] Ben-Zvi believed
he had located just such a line; one that, although quite tiny, could serve
as a kind of flesh-and-blood, ancestral umbilical cord for the new "natives":

> The thread connecting the entire nation, wherever it was, to its home-
> land was never broken, not for one moment in the history of our peo-
> ple, and the thin strands of the remnant Yishuv [Jewish settlement]
> served as *a living, palpable channel for this eternal connection.* . . . Indeed,
> the small Jewish settlement [of Peki'in] . . . fulfilled a momentous role
> as *the* link connecting the illustrious historical past of the nation with
> its grey present and with the longed-for future.[22]

Ben-Zvi and his close collaborator David Ben-Gurion also pursued a
theory of "Jewish roots among the Arab *fellahin* [peasant farmers] who
lived in Eretz Israel," and both claimed that their research pointed to
these peasants' Jewish ancestry. "According to Ben-Gurion and Ben-Zvi,
the new Jew was thus a man whose identity was formed by the Land of
Israel" in a variety of ways.[23] Zionism's new *Jew* became "native" by a
kind of "chemistry" between his very body and the land he came to

occupy; by the recovery and regeneration of a glorious ancient past of Jewish political sovereignty in the land (bolstered by the scientific documenting of that past through archaeology); and by a biologically traceable thread of blood running in the veins of past, current, and future *Jews* "native" to the land. Not coincidentally, images of Ben-Zvi and of Peki'in adorn Israel's current hundred-NIS (new Israeli shekel) bill, replacing the old hundred-shekel bill that, before revaluation, bore Jabotinsky's image.

Scholarship on Zionism might differentiate among diverse visions of the new *Jew* articulated by various activist-thinkers of different eras and dispositions: for example, by romantics versus rationalists; by mystical messianists seeking rebirth and redemption in the Holy Land versus Darwinian survivalists championing regeneration through physical and moral fitness; by those who called for a complete break with the diasporic past versus those who imagined the new age and its new *Jew* as the latest flowering in a long history of creative Jewish adaptation. But the overlap and synergies among all these are measurable in the people, institutions, and popular ideologies through which the new *Jew* as Zionist ideal was pursued in the *Altneuland* of Palestine and then Israel.[24]

Since the founding of Israel, the nation-state has been concerned with, among other things, absorbing and assimilating large numbers of immigrants, and with developing and refining the institutions, laws, and bureaucracies needed to make this possible. In the process, Israel has produced a dizzying array of divergent and contending new legal, bureaucratic, and de facto permutations of *Jew.* An entire volume might easily be devoted to *these* new *Jews* alone—one that would need to be updated frequently, given the modifications and contestations that constantly arise over the now perennial questions "Who is a *Jew*?" and "Who decides who is a *Jew*?" I have provided a very partial catalogue of these new (Israeli) *Jews* in chapter 1; others have provided more extensive analyses.[25] Rather than elaborate upon these here, I wish to focus instead on the ongoing story of just one new *Jew*: the modern, scientifically constituted and measured *Jew* that emerged at the turn of the twentieth century and has become, by the turn of the twenty-first, among the newest of the new *Jews*—the "genomic *Jew*."

Genomic Jews

Like Zionism's new *Jew* that emerged from nineteenth-century European race science, the genomic *Jew*, a product of "population genetics," springs from the same milieu. According to Israeli geneticist Raphael Falk, although the prewar categories "race," "racial purity," and "eugenics" became taboo following the Nazi genocide, "scientific discussions about race" did not disappear but were merely "transformed. Population genetics now largely replaced anthropological types in tackling issues of race."[26]

Human population genetics is a discipline devoted to exploring persistent and changing polymorphisms in genes and genotype frequencies within and between human "populations" over multiple generations. It has been called "the most widely misused area of human genetics"[27] largely because findings are readily appropriated into preexisting cultural narratives (like those about "racial characteristics" such as intellectual or athletic aptitude), where they may be presented as "proof" in support of a variety of sociopolitical agendas. In addition, determination of what constitutes a "population" and what constitute "discrete and comparable populations," critical decisions for the purposes of designing or interpreting genetic studies, can also be deeply entwined with popular concepts of race and other essentialist notions of identity. Given these issues and the veritable explosion in genomic research and its applications in recent decades, some scholars have expressed concerns that we have entered an era of the "molecularization of race."[28]

Population genetics or genomics is not, itself, race science, although current genetic research does, in fact, contribute to the production and marketing of racialized biotechnologies, such as "targeted" pharmaceuticals.[29] Just as *Jew* first became a biological classification in the "discipline" of race science, in more recent population-genetics and genetic-disease studies, *Jew*, likewise, has often been treated as a biological classification. Whereas race science undergirded narratives of biological determinism and fitness for survival, population-genetics and genetic-disease studies have come to undergird narratives of "Jewish genetic identity"[30] and marketing campaigns that nationalize, medicalize, and monetize, for example, "genetic markers" of "Jewishness."[31]

Genome biology has been harnessed to creating and sustaining a Jewish genetic-identity discourse through popular dissemination of claims for a "biological basis for Jewishness,"[32] a "genome-wide structure of the Jewish people,"[33] and a "genome-wide genetic signature of Jewish ancestry [that] *perfectly separates individuals with and without full Jewish ancestry*."[34] Such formulations as "genetic identity" and "with and without full . . . ancestry" can read eerily as the latest iterations of racialist and racial-purity discourses. How population-genetics studies are designed, how their findings are narrated and meanings assigned to them, and how these latter are translated into popular discourse and broadly disseminated—all of these elements serve to constitute the new genomic *Jew* as representative of a range of cultural concerns and aspirations, and as an instrument able to serve multiple ends.

That *Jew* has become, once again (or still), a biological classification is, to some, a deeply perplexing development. Shortly after the turn of the twenty-first century, for example, Sander Gilman wondered about "The New Genetics and the Old Eugenics."[35] More recently, he warned that, while "all science is ideological . . . some science is less tendentious than others," and that, "sadly, some of the models [of genetic analysis focused on new data about *Jews*] revert to older patterns or to older belief systems."[36] Petter Hellström has put the matter more bluntly:

> Scientific investment in a "Jewish" biology—essentially to define Jewishness as racial—should, I think, be described in terms of an obsession. Employing sacred texts, philological analysis, nose and cranium measurements, fingerprints, facial expressions, antigen, enzyme and blood-group analysis, and what not, the "Jewish" body has remained under scrutiny at least since the nineteenth century. DNA [mapping] is not likely to be the last technology bent for the purpose.[37]

Recent popularizing publications associated with the "Jewish Hapmap Project" (an international consortium devoted to "Jewish genetic research") do, indeed, explicitly trace their scientific genealogy to turn-of-the-twentieth-century research "about whether the Jews constitute a race," as well as to early Zionist aims of creating the new *Jew* as a "native" of Eretz Israel.[38] According to Harry Ostrer, director of the Human Genetics Program at New York University and one of the lead geneticists of the Jewish Hapmap Project,

> In 1911, the forces of social cohesion were religion, race science, and Zionism. Often, race science and Zionism went hand-in-hand, and the identification of a Jewish race provided justification for an ancestral homeland. The issue was addressed head-on in the Paris Peace Conference of 1919, and the consensus on a Jewish race led to the mandate for the creation of a Jewish state in Palestine. . . . The issues that preoccupied the Jewish intellectual leaders of 1911 are the same ones that preoccupy the leaders of today.[39]

Ostrer concludes his book *Legacy: A Genetic History of the Jewish People* with an even stronger claim: "The stakes in genetic analysis are high. It is more than an issue of who belongs in the family. . . . It touches on the heart of Zionist claims for a Jewish homeland in Israel. One can imagine future disputes about exactly how large the shared Middle Eastern ancestry of Jewish groups has to be to justify Zionist claims."[40]

In Ostrer's linking of genetics to "Zionist claims" and his anticipating debate over "how large the shared Middle Eastern ancestry of Jewish groups has to be to justify" them, one hears a distinct echo of Ben-Zvi's earlier assertion of "Jewish roots among the Arab *fellahin* who lived in Eretz Israel" and of the existence of a "living, palpable channel for this eternal connection" between *Jews* and the land. Yet, in Ostrer's case, the peculiar formulation "exactly how large the . . . ancestry" does not merely reflect a scientist's preoccupation with quantitative biometric data on *Jew(s)* as research subject (à la Nordau). Rather, it points to his and others' inclination to privilege genetic/genomic evidence of just such "shared Middle Eastern ancestry" among modern *Jews* over all other geo-politically defined lines of "Jewish genetic ancestry."[41]

"Abraham's Children in the Genome Era: Major Jewish Diaspora Populations Comprise Distinct Genetic Clusters with Shared Middle Eastern Ancestry" is the title of one widely cited article in this field, published in the *American Journal of Human Genetics* in 2010.[42] The title, itself, like the report that follows, is an amalgam of biblical, historiographic, sociological, and biological narratives, each serving as interpretive key for the others. The first sentence of the article informs the reader that "Jews originated as a national and religious group in the Middle East during the second millennium BCE and have maintained continuous genetic, cultural, and religious traditions since that time despite a series of Diasporas."[43] The report concludes with a similar assertion: "Over the past 3000 years, both the flow of genes and the flow of religious and cultural ideas have contributed to Jewishness."[44]

In defining its subjects and framing its findings in this fashion, the study establishes what Moshe Rosman calls an "*a priori* . . . metahistory"[45] within which data are generated and for which these data are then presented as scientific confirmation. Describing their materials and methods, the "Abraham's Children" authors note that research subjects "were included only if all four grandparents came from the same Jewish community" (delineated variously by country or geographic region), thereby preselecting for the "distinct Jewish population clusters" that the study reports in its findings.[46] Yet the study also discerns genetic evidence for "two major groups [that] were identifiable that could be characterized as Middle Eastern Jews and European/Syrian Jews."[47]

The former "group" exclusively comprises "Iranian and Iraqi Jews" who are later hypothesized to be descendants of "populations [that] were formed by Jews in the Babylonian and Persian empires who are thought to have remained geographically continuous in those locales."[48] This hypothesis interprets the genetic data through a creative extrapolation from positivist biblical historiography, albeit in a way that seems to disregard the geographical extent and overlap of the two successive ancient empires, mistakenly treating them as discrete "locales" and distinct from "Syria." The latter category, "European/Syrian Jews," is likely to strike the modern reader as curious, given that current geopolitical understanding locates Syria in the "Middle East." But this category, too, is provided a hypothetical origin among "Jews who migrated or were expelled from Palestine and . . . individuals who were converted to Judaism during Hellenic-Hasmonean times, when proselytism was a common Jewish practice."[49] Again, the new genetic findings become part of a familiar (albeit faulty)[50] historiographic narrative, telescoping time and geography to reveal a "living, palpable channel" connecting modern *Jews* to a biblical and national past in what is now called the "Middle East."

According to the authors of "Abraham's Children," the primary division between these two genetically distinguished "groups" of *Jews* relates to what, in this field, have come to be called "European admixtures," or "genetic contributions" from "European ['non-Jewish'] populations." This is where estimated percentages of varying "ancestry" come into play, as genetic measurements of *Jews* are compared and contrasted with genetic data about "Europeans"—that is, data derived from "individuals of *unmixed ancestry* . . . from a wide variety of European countries."[51] The juxtaposition of *Jews* with "Europeans of unmixed ancestry," needless to say, conjures up a host of racialist and other theological/political ghosts—to say nothing of the deeply problematic nature of such essentializing definitions and distinctions. Nonetheless, these are standard terms of the trade in twenty-first-century population genetics.

The authors go on to report a "high degree of European admixture (30%–60%) among the Ashkenazi, Sephardic, Italian, and Syrian Jews." These figures derive from data about "haplogroups"—that is, from Y chromosomal polymorphisms (indicating only father-to-son transmission of genetic material) or from mitochondrial DNA (indicating only mother-to-child transmission of genetic material). Referencing earlier, widely hailed studies, the authors report that "up to 50% of Ashkenazi Jewish Y chromosomal haplogroups . . . are of Middle Eastern origin, whereas the other prevalent haplogroups . . . may be representative of the early European admixture."[52] Furthermore, "four founder mitochondrial haplogroups of Middle Eastern origins comprise approximately 40% of the Ashkenazi genetic Jewish pool, whereas the remainder is comprised of other haplogroups, many of European origin and supporting the degree of admixture observed in the current study."[53]

The primacy given to haplogroups of "Middle Eastern origins" over those reflecting "European admixture" or "European origin" is notable in the reportage, notwithstanding the unspecified but apparently higher percentages of the latter. This, again, is in keeping with the dominant metahistorical framework of *Jew* as "native Middle Easterner" within which this genetic discourse operates. Yet, one begins to see, perhaps, why those who play in the field of ancestry-by-the-numbers might be anxious about "how large" a percentage each geopolitically freighted identity category gleans.

As it happens, even the 40 percent figure of "mitochondrial haplogroups of Middle Eastern origins" cited in the "Abraham's Children" report no longer holds. A 2013 study that used "a much larger database from potential source populations" determined that

> at least 80% of Ashkenazi maternal ancestry is due to the assimilation of mtDNAs [mitochondrial DNAs] indigenous to Europe, most likely through conversion. . . . The Ashkenazim therefore resemble Jewish communities in Eastern Africa and India, and possibly also others across the Near East, Caucasus and Central Asia, which also carry a substantial fraction of maternal lineages from their "host" communities. . . . Y-chromosome studies generally show the opposite trend to mtDNA (with a predominantly Near Eastern source) with the exception of the large fraction [greater than 50 percent][54] of European ancestry seen in Ashkenazi Levites.[55]

Given that "Ashkenazim" represent, by far, the majority of *Jews* as defined by genetic databases and studies, the findings reported here (if they continue to hold up) appear to indicate that the vast majority of contemporary *Jews* are descended from new *Jews*—that is, from "European women" who somehow became new *Jews* through marriage and motherhood. There is no evidence that these mothers were subjected to any process that would pass Orthodox rabbinic muster as "formal conversion" today—especially in Israel—nor could any amount of DNA testing provide evidence of such conversion. One wonders what effect, if any, this "new matrilineal principle" (if we might—with tongue in cheek—call it that), discovered among genomic *Jews*, will have on future conceptions of identity and on the narratives that undergird and sustain them.

The foregoing analysis of how genetic/genomic findings are framed and narrated in such studies as "Abraham's Children in the Genome Era" has not been aimed at assessing the genetic data—much less at assessing their putative ability to "justify Zionist claims" (or not), or to ground contemporary identities.[56] Rather, my interest has been in briefly examining some of the ways in which this new *Jew*, this genomic *Jew*, is being constituted both through the measuring, compiling, and comparing of genetic data and through the framing and narrating of the findings thus derived. I touch on other dimensions of the genomic *Jew* in the final section of this chapter.

In both the early-Zionist new *Jew* and his older/younger genomic sibling, we encounter *Jews* as a product of scientific, nationalist, and biblical discourses so tightly interwoven as often to seem to form a single strand or tell a single, if complex, story. Yet the more we scrutinize this new genomic *Jew*, the more we may be surprised at what it can signify—not only about buried histories of connection, division, and even recombination, but also about the fears and desires that animate *Jew* in the present and that frame its future. Generating and interpreting biological data about *Jews* has become new "terrain for elaborating strategies of selfhood—singular or communal" (to invoke Homi Bhabha's phrase, once again). Within this novel, scientifically constituted terrain, other, geopolitical, terrains (and terrains of otherness) like the "Middle East" and "Europe" appear to loom especially large. Exactly how large remains to be seen.

New *Jews* in a New Europe

In a 2005 blog post entitled "Europe's New Jews," Israeli writer Shmuel Ben David Vaknin offers the following eerie description of targeted minority communities in Europe:

> They inhabit self-imposed ghettoes, subject to derision and worse, the perennial targets of far-right thugs and populist politicians of all persuasions . . . accused of spreading crime, terrorism and disease, . . . of refusing to fit in. Their religion is atavistic and rigid, insists on ritual slaughter and male circumcision. They rarely mingle socially or intermarry . . . are subject to police profiling and harassment and all manner of racial discrimination. They are the new Jews of Europe—its Muslim minorities.[57]

This same trope is picked up four years later by Pakistani political scientist Shireen M. Mazari when she asks, "Are Muslims Europe's New Jews?" in a piece decrying the stabbing death, earlier that month, of Egyptian-born pharmacist Marwa al-Sherbini in a German courtroom.[58] Al-Sherbini was testifying against Alex Wein for his having verbally assaulted her at a public playground in Dresden where she, wearing hijab, had been playing with her young son. After al-Sherbini had completed her testimony and rejoined her husband and child, Wein, who had used the proceedings to rail against "Muslims" and "foreigners," lunged at her with a knife that he had smuggled into the courtroom, striking multiple deadly blows before he was subdued. In her article, Mazari chastises the West for insufficient attention to the horrifying story: "Of course had it been the murder of a Jewish lady specifically for displaying her cultural/religious Jewishness, the western media would have gone to town crying foul and the German government would have been put fairly and squarely in the dock."[59] In the next paragraph of her essay, Mazari observes that "European secular 'liberalism' is being defined increasingly in terms of non-acceptance of the new multi-religious and multi-ethnic Europeans by the old white Christian Europeans. When European leaders display this characteristic in public statements, it gives leeway to the racist bigotry that still pervades in Europe—only now the Muslims have replaced the Jews as the bête[s] noirs."[60] In yet a third invocation of *Jews* in the piece, Mazari writes:

> Ironically, apart from the Central Council of Muslims' leadership, it was the Central Council of Jews General Secretary, Stephan Kramer who decried the "inexplicably sparse" reaction of the media and German politicians [to al-Sherbini's murder]. After all, the Jews of Europe know only too well that it begins with one incidence [sic] after another and, if one remains silent, the victimization becomes collective.[61]

Mazari's final such invocation—at once more oblique and more encompassing—comes in the essay's last sentence, which conjures the specter of Muslims becoming "the next victims of European history."[62]

What does *"Jew"*—and, specifically, *"new Jews"*—signify when invoked with reference to *Muslims* in late twentieth- and early twenty-first-century Europe? And what ideas about *Europe* and *European-ness* (as well as about *Jews, Muslims*, and, perhaps, *Semites*) play a part in these significations?

The phrase "the next victims of European history" clearly invokes *Jews* as collective "victims of European history." Hence, insofar as Muslims, as an identifiable minority in Europe, fall victim collectively to widespread, systemic, and historically conditioned harms through the actions and inactions of (other) Europeans, they, too, become "victims of European history" and, therefore (so goes the analogy), the continent's next or new *Jews*. The phrase "new *Jews*," in such formulations, appears most often designed both to effect moral rebuke of an uncaring, if not hostile, European society and to raise a clarion call against a growing potential for collective disaster. "After all," to reiterate Mazari's assertion, "the Jews of Europe know only too well that *it begins* with one incidence [sic] after another and, *if one remains silent*, the victimization becomes collective."[63] "New *Jews*," as a kind of shorthand for moral reproach and recollection, has great currency in Europe—in implicit, as well as explicit, articulations. A German press account of the trial at which al-Sherbini's murder took place, for instance, reports that, in response to Wein's repeated extreme anti-Muslim statements in court, the presiding judge pointedly asked him whether he had ever visited a concentration camp.[64]

Germany is hardly alone in Europe in drawing such cautionary connections among collective victims of what it identifies as racism and xenophobia. In 2003, the European Monitoring Centre on Racism and Xenophobia (EUMC), with the support of the European Union's European Commission, sponsored a series of meetings under the rubric "The Fight against Anti-Semitism and Islamophobia: Bringing Communities Together." In her opening speech at one of these meetings, Odile Quintin, director general for Employment and Social Affairs of the European Commission, suggested that "in Europe . . . Islamophobia has a history almost as long as that of anti-Semitism."[65] In an earlier speech, she held that, even so, "the problem [of anti-Semitism] itself has a *special significance for all Europeans*. This is because anti-Semitism is *not the same thing as racism and xenophobia*. The *experience of the Shoah* has made it impossible to treat anti-Semitism as just another social problem."[66]

Quintin's insistence on the historical specificity and exceptional significance of *Jew*-hatred in Europe stands in tension with her and others' recognition of the ways in which hate speech and acts targeting *Jews* share important attributes with (other) instances of systemic racism and xenophobia, past and present, in Europe and its colonies. This tension comes to the fore, in particular, in popular-periodical essays directed at *contesting* the labeling of Muslims as Europe's new *Jews*. "Muslims are not the new Jews," asserts David Cesarani in a piece for the *Jewish Chronicle*, because "the racism they face and the current surge of prejudice against Islam have their own specific causes and contexts, and however seductive the parallels may appear they tend to be shallow and anachronistic. Britain today is not the late Victorian and Edwardian country into which Jews immigrated from Eastern Europe. Europe has not slipped back into the 1930s."[67]

"Anachronistic" seems a particularly odd charge to bring against a phrase that features the term "new." Given that the adjective *new* points precisely toward temporally *later* "causes and contexts," and that the name *Jew* remains a live signifier in the twenty-first century, an objection to the phrase "Europe's new *Jews*" on the grounds that "Europe has not slipped back" to an earlier time appears curiously misdirected.

Perhaps sensing this, Cesarani tries another tack. He insists that his assertion that "Muslims are not the new Jews" is "not in any way intended to minimize the fact that Muslims today suffer appallingly from Islamophobia and racist violence." He then continues, "But while racism has generic qualities, it has particular variants and these can only be fought by grasping what is specific about them."[68] That may be so. Yet Cesarani devotes no space in his essay to providing any specifics about the particular variants of racism from which Europe's Muslims suffer, and what makes those variants qualitatively distinct. Others who contest the phrase, however, prove more than willing to do so.

In a 2014 essay entitled "Meet the New Jews, Same as the Old Jews: Why 'Islamophobia' in Europe Cannot Be Equated with Anti-Semitism, Either in Nature or Degree," James Kirchick rejects the phrase "*new Jews*" in large part because it gives the impression—to his mind, false—that "Islam itself and the behavior of Muslims play no part in generating negative views."[69] In a move familiar from its antisemitic and other racist applications, by which the acts of some are held to reveal the character of all, Kirchick elaborates: "Jews never carried out terrorist attacks against civilians . . . or openly boasted of their goal to 'conquer' the European continent, as prominent Muslim spokesmen have repeatedly done. Jewish schools did not indoctrinate their charges with hatred of Western civilization," nor with "reactionary attitudes . . . about women."[70] For Kirchick, Muslims cannot be Europe's new *Jews*. "The 'new' Jews, it turns out, are the same as the old ones: Jews."[71] *Jew*, unlike *Muslim*, is a name "never" tarnished in Europe by violent revolutionary, reactionary, or terrorist associations.

Au contraire. Although the potential pitfalls of analogical moral reasoning are not insignificant, the pitfalls of selective historical memory may be even deeper and more dangerous. What Maleiha Malik has termed "uncanny echoes" between "today's anti-Muslim racism" and the "treatment Jews had a century ago" suggest that meaningful "parallels" are perhaps not quite so few or so shallow as Cesarani has warned, nor *Jew* quite so exceptional as Kirchick has claimed. With a particular focus on her own specific British context, Malik offers the following historical narrative:

Migrants fleeing persecution and poverty settled with their children in the East End of London. As believers in one God they were devoted to their holy book, which contained strict religious laws, harsh penalties and gender inequality. Some of them established separate religious courts. The men wore dark clothes and had long beards; some women covered their hair. A royal commission warned of the grave dangers of self-segregation. Politicians said different religious dress was a sign of separation. Some migrants were members of extremist political groups. Others actively organised to overthrow the established western political order. Campaigners against the migrants carefully framed their arguments as objections to "alien extremists" and not to a race or religion. A British cabinet minister said we were facing a clash about civilisation: this was about values; a battle between progress and "arrested development."

All this happened a hundred years ago to Jewish migrants seeking asylum in Britain. The political movements with which they were closely associated were anarchism and later Bolshevism. As in the case of contemporary political violence, or even the radical Islamism supported by a minority of British Muslims, anarchism and Bolshevism only commanded minority support among the Jewish community. But shared countries of origin and a common ethnic and religious background were enough to create a racialised discourse whenever there were anarchist outrages in London in the early 20th century.

Most anarchists were peaceful, but a few resorted to violent attacks such as the bombing of Greenwich Observatory in 1894—described at the time as an "international terrorist outrage." Anarchist violence was an international phenomenon. In Europe it claimed hundreds of lives, including those of several heads of government, and resulted in anti-terrorism laws. In the siege of Sidney Street in London in 1911, police and troops confronted east European Jewish anarchists. This violent confrontation in the heart of London created a racialised moral panic in which the whole Jewish community was stigmatised. It was claimed that London was "seething" with violent aliens, and the British establishment was said to be "in a state of denial." East End Jews were said to be "alienated," not "integrated," and a "threat to our security" a long time before anyone dreamed up the phrase "Londonistan."[72]

By pointing to specific historical events while highlighting particular recurrent typologies, tropes, and popular formulations, Malik's paralleling narrative works as a rhetorically provocative cautionary tale. Her assertion that marked signs of otherness served to "create" (or, more accurately, to mobilize a preexisting) "racialised discourse" and a "racialised moral panic" is borne out by the evidence she presents. Where Cesarani argues that racism's "particular variants . . . can only be fought by grasping what is specific about them," Malik counters that, "despite important differences, . . . there are recurring patterns . . . that racialise Jews and Muslims, which we need to understand if we are to develop an effective strategy for national security."[73]

Both authors share a recognition that *Jew* is a signifier that carries a particular kind of moral/analytical force in a specifically European geopolitical context. But that does not make it a simple or unidimensional signifier. In fact, my interest in exploring recent arguments for and against characterizing Muslims as "Europe's new *Jews*" is not to adjudicate the merits of the conceit, nor to opine on the appropriateness of its deployment in any or all instances (certainly, reasonable and compassionate people can disagree about these matters). Rather, I am interested in the complex nature of the rhetorical power vested in *Jew* in twenty-first-century Europe as exemplified by such appeals to the idea of "new *Jews*." In other words, this discussion concerns the genealogics that give birth to Europe's new *Jews*.

Europeanism's Jews

In simplest terms, we might begin by recognizing that, as noted above, the phrase "new *Jews*" functions in contemporary Europe as a kind of moral reproach, a call to mindfulness, and an urgent warning against the dangers of a scapegoating or racializing xenophobia. To my knowledge, none who have invoked the phrase there—explicitly or implicitly—have claimed that another European genocide is either likely or imminent, much less presently occurring. This point is conceded even in published objections to the labeling of Muslims as Europe's new *Jews*. Kirchick, for example, acknowledges, "To be sure, those asserting that Muslims have replaced Jews as the continental scapegoat are not claiming an exact likeness between the past experience of Jews and that of today's Muslims. Rather, their argument invokes the slippery slope" by which scapegoating can slide into genocide.[74] Tellingly, Kirchick nonetheless first decries the claim that he admits none have made: "The claim that Muslims are experiencing anything resembling the Holocaust of European Jewry is of course absurd."[75]

But the rhetorical power of the concept "new *Jews*" is only partly captured in the observation that it gestures toward such a "slippery slope" of the escalating endangerment of a significant European minority. Still more so, it is the fate of the European majority—of Europeanism itself—that is called into question by the idea of "new *Jews*." This is because *Jew(s)* plays no less significant and foundational a role in the conception of the "New Europe"—the secular, progressive European Union founded on the postwar ashes of the "Old Europe"—than it did in the conception of Christendom or in the unholy visions of the Third Reich.

Diana Pinto, one of the more incisive observers of this key role, describes it as arising out of the postwar, continent-wide *cri de coeur* of "Never again!" that came to serve as an ideological core element fueling the construction of a New Europe:

> For Europe's founding fathers, this ["never again"] meant never again to go to war, no to any Volkgesetz or legal ethnic or religious definitions of a nation state, combined with a commitment to universal values and supra-national institutions. The entire edifice was based on two key pillars: a call to historical reconciliation, and democratic citizenship as the building bloc[k] of national identity. These principles were meant to preclude the return of fascism and any racial discrimination.[76]

The significance of *Jews* for the founding, maintaining, and assessing of these pillars or principles lies, on the one hand, in the necessity of confronting and commemorating Europe's genocidal past as a means to genuine "historical reconciliation," and, on the other, in the combatting of religious and/or racialized conceptions of identity that, when mobilized in ethno-nationalist partisanship, can undermine genuine "democratic citizenship." *Jews*, then, speaks to both the commemorative and the nonexclusionary, democratic elements of the European experiment.

In an essay in which she observes that "through nearly a quarter of a century of Holocaust commemorations the Jewish story has become an integral . . . part of Europe's own self-understanding and democratic organisation," Pinto elaborates:

> Unwillingly and unwittingly, Jews have become "icons" in Europe's new commemorative pluralist democracies. They have now set the standard for national commemoration of specific historical wrongs, for victimhood, for public visibility, for community organization, for the right to multiple loyalties, and for a position that one can call selective national belonging; in brief, for real but also highly symbolic power.[77]

Many have echoed this assessment, although most would likely contest Pinto's assertion of Jewish passivity in the process of iconization. Matti Bunzl, for example, has observed that "in the supranational context of the European Union . . . Jews no longer figure as the principal Other, but as the veritable embodiment of the postnational order."[78] He cites as evidence a statement made by Romano Prodi while serving as president of the European Commission:

> I believe we can learn a lot from the history of the Jews of Europe. In many ways they are the first, the oldest Europeans. We, the new Europeans, are just starting to learn the complex art of living with multiple allegiances—allegiance to our home town, to our own region, to our home country, and now to the European Union. The Jews have been forced to master this art since antiquity. They were both Jewish *and* Italian, or Jewish *and* French, Jewish *and* Spanish, Jewish *and* Polish, Jewish *and* German. Proud of their ties with Jewish communities throughout the continent, and equally proud of their bonds with their own country.[79]

Bunzl notes that, "symbolic window dressing" or not, "statements like this . . . are legion in the new Europe."[80] Nor are they the exclusive purview of spokespeople for the supranational European Union. For some, like Spanish-born Manuel Valls, elected prime minister of France in 2014, *Jews* can now also function as specifically emblematic of French national identity, insofar as French national pride is historically bound up with the championing of enlightened "universal values." Calling France "the Jews' land of emancipation two centuries ago but also, seventy years ago, one of the lands of their agony," Valls declared in a speech to the French National Assembly on January 13, 2015: "History has shown us that a reawakening of anti-Semitism is the symptom of a crisis of democracy, a crisis of the Republic. . . . Without the Jews of France, France would no longer be France. . . . When the Jews of France are attacked, France is attacked and the universal conscience is attacked. Let us never forget that!"[81] The European "never again," French Republican honor, and the health of democracy itself, according to Valls, stand or fall with *the Jews*.[82]

In this sense, *Jew(s)* belongs to Europe as part of the European Union's very raison d'être, its narrative of origins, its recollection of conscience, its confession of sin, and its promise of redemption. In addition to all the other meanings it retains and accrues, *Jew(s)* now also invokes a peculiarly European memory and memorialization, a sacred trust and an honorable aspiration. Hence, to identify harm to Europe's *Jews*—or to Europe's new *Jews*—calls the European Union to account in a profoundly meaningful way. Insofar as there can even *be* new *Jews* in Europe, there can be no New Europe, for the newness of a New Europe is predicated on there being no new mythologized and targeted collective "victims of European history." "New *Jews*" thus stands alongside *Jews*, neither replacing nor superseding the latter—*pace* the common complaint or implication that "Muslims as the new 'Jews' . . . erases real Jews."[83] As an example of what Bhabha has called "an insurgent act of cultural translation," "new *Jews*" partakes of the very "act of defining [and defending] the idea of [a New European] society itself."[84]

A major part of what *Jew*/new *Jew* has come to represent in the New Europe of the European Union, then, is a promised dismantling of the ethnic nation-state model that institutionalizes the privileging and disprivileging of citizens and residents according to race/ethnicity/religion (the opposite of what *Jew* represents in Israel). "The main benefit of accepting Islam as an integral part of Europe and of fighting anti-Muslim discrimination," asserts ethnologist Esra Özyürek, "would be the creation of the conditions for the possibility of achieving a democratic European Union, in which Europeans of diverse backgrounds recognize everyone's right to exist as equal members."[85] The stakes that Europe's *Jews*/new *Jews* have in the European Union's promise are those shared, in theory, by all Europeans.

It is precisely the difference between the earlier ideological project of defining and perfecting discrete ethnic nation-states and the current project of creating and sustaining a democratic, supranational European Union that, according to Bunzl, represents the key qualitative difference between antisemitism and Islamophobia. The racializing exclusion of *Jews*, notes Bunzl, "was connected to the project of nationalism, with the champions of anti-Semitism seeing themselves, first and foremost, as guardians of the ethnically pure nation-state. Given their racial difference, Jews could never belong to this national community."[86] By contrast, what stands "at the heart of Islamophobic discourse is the question of civiliza-tion, the notion that Islam engenders a world view that is fundamentally incompatible with and inferior to Western culture."[87] Notwithstanding the supranational claims of (the profoundly antisemitic) Aryan ideology and its Europe-wide reach, it is this important nationalist-versus-internationalist distinction, Bunzl insists, that demands the recognition that

> Islamophobic claims are actually quite different from those of modern anti-Semitism. Whereas anti-Semites questioned Jews' fitness for inclu-sion in the national community, Islamophobes are not particularly wor-ried whether Muslims can be good Germans, Italians, or Danes. Rather, they question whether Muslims can be good Europeans. Islamophobia, in other words, functions less in the interest of national purification than as a means of fortifying Europe.[88]

In fact, Bunzl goes so far as to hail "the thorough insignificance at the current time of the modern [i.e., nationalist] variant of anti-Semitism," claiming that it has "become obsolete in the supranational context of the European Union."[89]

Others concur with this broad assessment and have recognized, in what is now widely (albeit not unproblematically)[90] termed "Islamophobia" throughout the European Union, the same dynamic of "othering" that has long characterized animus toward *Jew*, now instead strategically directed at a *new* other designed as a perfect foil for a New Europe:

> The discreditation of the nation-state is not sufficient to buoy the imagination of new Europe. The enemy within is one thing, but the big enemy outside is even more efficacious. . . . [A] new principle of alterity has already been mobilized by supranational Europe, a new medium and foil for the future of Europeanness. Welcome to the new Europe, in which the Jews are no longer persecuted but revered as cosmopolitan ancestors, but one that has reserved the right to define and exclude new supranationals for their very intolerance to the tolerance of the new Europe.[91]

Inasmuch as anti-Muslim animus represents a Europe-wide discourse of "othering" in the service of constructing and maintaining a collective identity, the label "Europe's new *Jews*" for the maligned entity seems not inapt.

Moreover, when these new *Jews* are utilized in this familiar fashion by ethno-nationalist movements—like France's National Front, headed by Marine Le Pen, or its German counterpart, represented by Thilo Sarrazin, among others[92]—that newly claim sympathy and common cause with *Jews*, a stunningly new and deeply cynical form of political supersessionism is on full display. As Yascha Mounk observes in a piece entitled "Europe's Jewish Problem," this dynamic is hardly confined to far-right groups in Europe:

> To signal how different they are from their predecessors, liberal Islamophobes also embrace Jews. There is a clear logic to this strategy. Because of their past persecution, Europe's Jews have become . . . mainstream society's litmus test for tolerance. To ward off accusations of racism, populists across the continent . . . have thus learned to preface their incendiary remarks about Muslims with a marker of tolerance and enlightenment: lavish praise of Jews and Judeo-Christian civilization. . . . Doing so allows them to claim the mantle of tolerance even as they sow hatred.[93]

If we recall Mazari's comments above, some of the emotional reasoning behind her labeling as "ironic" the public chastisement offered by Stephan J. Kramer, then general secretary of Germany's Central Council of Jews, regarding the scant media coverage of al-Sherbini's murder comes into clearer focus. One might otherwise wonder whence the sense of irony, given the obvious moral calculation by which Mazari herself articulates Jewish stakes in naming and countering instances of violence against an increasingly targeted minority. Mazari's palpable bitterness becomes more understandable "in a European context of apparent double-standards—where oblique anti-Semitic remarks are criminalized while blatantly Islamophobic cartoons are protected under freedom of speech laws, and where toleration of Jewish (but not Muslim) difference becomes the *sine qua non* of Europeanness."[94] The fact that such "toleration" can be, and is, so readily instrumentalized by those who use it to sow hatred and fear of all Muslims is more than ironic. The same sense of a double standard is evident in Mazari's claim that "of course had it been the murder of a Jewish lady specifically for displaying her cultural/religious Jewishness," the story would have received more press coverage in the West and in Germany greater censure.[95]

For his part, General Secretary Kramer reserves his "annoyance" and even disgust for the "almost smug, patronizing satisfaction" of "some editors [who] found the murder of a Muslim woman much less notable than the joint appearance of two general secretaries, one Muslim the other Jewish," at the bedside of al-Sherbini's husband, who was also critically injured—in his case, by a responding police officer who took him to be the assailant.[96] In a statement titled "In Solidarity with All Muslims," Kramer follows up his criticism of the press with "a few words of clarification" about his action:

> I did not travel to Dresden because as a Jew I belong to a minority. I made the journey because as a Jew I know that anyone who attacks a person because of their race, nationality, or religion is not only attacking the minority, they are attacking democratic society as a whole. The relevant question is therefore not why a representative of the Jewish community paid his condolences and showed solidarity with Elwi Ali Okaz [al-Sherbini's husband], but why there was not a steady stream of visitors or statements of solidarity from representatives of the social majority in Germany. . . . Society's inadequate resistance to racism threatens to encourage further acts of terrorism—the word is wholly appropriate—such as this cowardly murder in Dresden.[97]

The resonance between Kramer's first-person speech "as a *Jew*" in the name of "democratic society as a whole" and Prime Minister Valls's speech in defense of France's "universal conscience," excerpted above, is obvious. Yet the former differs, importantly, in the way that Kramer redirects the moral force of his appeal "as a *Jew*" to speak specifically on behalf of *Muslim* targets of white, Christian, European terrorism. Kramer's gesture of solidarity with Europe's new Muslims encapsulates precisely some of the rhetorical force carried by the phrase "Europe's new *Jews*" while also demonstrating the enduring, singular nature of *Jew(s)* as a privileged European icon.

Icons and Identities

The fact that *Jew(s)* has become so iconic in discourse about the postwar European experiment, in so many ways—with regard to the victimization of vulnerable minorities, the development of models of community organization and integration, and the acceptance of multiple loyalties and diverse senses of belonging—is not surprising nor, in itself, troubling. Quite the contrary.

Nonetheless, such iconism—not to say idolatry—can easily beget the kind of bitter irony expressed by Mazari, as well as the cynical philosemitism affected by ethno-nationalists like Le Pen, Sarrazin, Nigel Farage, and others. Additionally, many have observed that it can lead, among younger generations of Germans, to an "impatien[ce] with the ubiquitous memorials attesting to their nation's past crimes" that are such a "prominent part of public life" and, more broadly, to a kind of reflexive iconoclasm that fixates on violence committed by *Jews* elsewhere:

> Given the strange role Jews have been assigned in Europe's societal morality play, it gives nationalists special comfort to claim that Jews are ultimately no better than the fascists and collaborationists of the continent's past. By showing that Jews are themselves capable of perpetrating violence, they hope to lighten their nations' heavy historical burdens. When Israel began bombing Gaza this summer [2014], European nationalists seized the opportunity to do just that.[98]

The iconic quality of Europe's *Jews* may also, according to Bunzl and Paul A. Silverstein, account, in part, for the targeting of *Jews* by disaffected, militant Muslim youth who come to "regard Jews as fully integrated European insiders and indeed as iconic of all which is intolerable in their own lives."[99] (Other significant factors include anger over belligerent actions by an Israel that claims to represent all *Jews*, as well as hatemongering by clerical extremists.) This "new anti-Semitism," as some have dubbed it, is a limited but growing phenomenon in contemporary Europe, and one that is intimately interwoven with Islamophobia in ways that include but go beyond what can be touched on here.[100]

Jew as European icon not only elicits the expressions of irony, impatience, iconoclasm, and intolerable marginalization highlighted by Mounk, Silverstein, Bunzl, and others, but also calls forth, among some, a kind of doctrine of "exceptionalism" that can be even more discomfiting. There are any number of commentators on Europe and its future, says Silverstein, who "effectively reject the possibility that Muslims, like Jews, can become insiders to France or Europe more broadly. More precisely, such a defense of Jews' exceptional incorporation in Europe is a claim to an ownership of victimhood. . . . Alarmists tend to write as if there is a zero-sum game of suffering, as if the recognition of Islamophobia will somehow dilute a narrative of Jewish persecution."[101]

Cesarani, whose rejection of the phrase "new *Jews*" frames an essay marking Britain's Holocaust Memorial Day, is clearly aware of this odd arithmetic by which "exceptional incorporation" is linked to "ownership" of exceptional victimhood, and he works to distance himself from it. "I have not argued that the Holocaust is unique (as distinct from being specific), nor that other folks should leave our genocide alone," Cesarani insists. And he goes on to excoriate those who, by virtue of identifying as *Jew*, "think they know what's going on [with regard to anti-Muslim animus in Europe] (they don't), or they aren't bothered because, well, we Jews had it worse."[102] One hears in Cesarani's statements the critique of affected, inherited victimology similarly proffered by Finkielkraut and

Badiou. Yet, hand in hand with that critique, one finds, nonetheless, the uncritical assumption of an *ownership* of victim narratives that can be bartered among minorities in a kind of marketplace of reciprocal empathies. As Cesarani urges,

> If we [Jews] expect others to empathise with the extraordinary nexus of social tension, supersessionist Christianity, "scientific" racism, and political messianism that eventuated in genocide, then we have to reciprocate. We may know about the Holocaust, but that does not mean we know about the horrors of the transatlantic slave trade or the ravages of colonialism. Once it is established that Muslims are not the new Jews, there is no excuse for failing to get to grips with Islamophobia and the daily racism Muslims suffer, which Jews thankfully do not.[103]

Cesarani appears to embrace victim narratives as a kind of proprietary cultural currency usable for bartering among discrete minorities. Silverstein similarly characterizes these narratives as tokens—albeit of a sort deployed in a "proxy" field of bad-faith political gamesmanship whereby "increased attention to European Muslim (or Palestinian) discrimination . . . [threatens to] break the Jewish monopoly on victimization, and hence threaten the recognized need for a Jewish state."[104] Pinto, dismayed by both forms of appropriation, would have all parties cease and desist from all such trade in "exacerbated" identities:

> The pendulum has swung too far in the direction of sanctified specific identities. . . . Commemoration should lead to reconciliation, overcoming of the past, and healing, not to exacerbated identities. And Jews, precisely because of their iconic quality, now hold the keys to such a swing back. Otherwise we should not be surprised if *Europe's Muslims follow the Jews* in the path of declared victimhood, selective belonging, even dis-integration through an implicitly hostile reading of the larger society outside.[105]

While reiterating the "iconic quality" of Europe's *Jews*, Pinto warns that misappropriating that status in service to a politics of exceptionalism and exclusivism poses risks to the European Union far beyond what simple demographic trends might portend. Her forecasting of a dynamic by which "Europe's Muslims follow the Jews" in dis-identifying from a European common cause highlights yet another dimension of the provocative label "Europe's new *Jews*."

For Pinto, the Shoah, or Holocaust, must remain a collective European memory, a story that, tragically, belongs to Europe, to European-ness in *all* its constituencies—as do accounts of the transatlantic slave trade and of European colonialism (although these latter have yet to be integrated into the collective self-consciousness of the postwar "pluralist commemorative democracies").[106] If these stories become merely atomized emblems of essentialized, reified, subcultural identities rather than spurs to broader, collective change, then the zero-sum game that Silverstein invokes and the "power brokerage with other minorities" that Pinto deplores play out as a high-stakes contest that all parties stand to lose.[107]

In fact, these two alternative responses to Europe's troubled history—identitarian withdrawal and commitment to collective change—are presaged in what she refers to as "a parting of the two 'never agains'":

> The European understanding of the post-war 'never again' became a 'never again' to war, xenophobia, to racial discrimination and to colonialism with a positive commitment to human rights. The Israelis' . . . understanding of the 'never again' became instead one based on the credo that 'never again' would the fate of the Jews depend on anyone but themselves, be it another country or international body, in the daily equivalent of an all out existential war.[108]

The Israeli "never again," Pinto observes, was "based on the absolute need to have a state created by the Jews for the Jews. Such a state had as primordial responsibility to ensure that its Jewish citizens and Jews around the world would never find themselves again in a situation of total powerlessness over their own collective fate."[109] In the wake of the European genocide, the logic of this "absolute need" seemed unimpeachable. Nonetheless, the creation of a new ethnic nation-state, Israel, in response to the catastrophic abuses of uncontrolled ethno-nationalism on the European continent, stands fundamentally at odds with the postwar European "never again," which Pinto describes as a "no" to any "legal ethnic or religious definitions of a nation state."[110]

This basic ideological divide between the two postwar visions continues to widen, observes Pinto, as Europe further institutionalizes its secular, supranational Union and Israel continues to harden "its ever more Orthodox religious identity and its ever more ethnic nationalist outlook."[111] The divide is further exacerbated by Israel's frequent insistence that it is the political representative of the interests of all *Jews* worldwide, and that it is the national homeland of all *Jews*. Since its founding, Israel has directed recruiting efforts to Europe that, to this day, characterize the continent as a place that can only ever be a graveyard of *Jews* and a locus of ongoing danger to "its few remaining *Jews*." Over the past quarter-century, Israeli heads of state have repeatedly issued public appeals to Europe's *Jews* to "return home" to Israel, to "move out immediately," and to "get out [of Europe] before it's too late."[112] Significantly, such overtures are unfailingly criticized by those at whom they are directed.[113]

This Israeli campaign, a curious version of Jewish supersessionism, presents Israel's militant new *Jew*—one who is native to, and only at home in, Israel—as utterly and necessarily superseding the perpetually victimized "old *Jew*" of an unchanging Europe. Israel's "March of the Living" identity-travel program brings thousands of young people each year to Poland's Nazi-era death camps and then on to Israel, in order to reinforce this "Zionist narrative of history that moves from European death in the past to Israeli life in the future."[114] From this fiercely Zionist perspective, there can be no such thing as a New Europe and no real future for European *Jews*, who, after all, are nothing but "mere remnants of the murdered European Jews of yore,"[115] survivors of an unbroken history of diasporic suffering in the "all-out existential war" of a hostile world pitted against *the Jews*. "This split" between Israel's vision and Europe's vision, notes Pinto, "has become ever more visible with respect to Israel's situation, but also, through Israel, with respect to Jewish interactions with Europe's 'others.'"[116] She describes, with a sense of dismay, the collateral supersession that the Israeli vision threatens to effect in Europe itself:

> The old humanist, intellectual Jews interested in universal values and human rights, and seeking reintegration in their respective countries have given way [in Europe] to another type of Jew with visible community power who feels far more ethnically Jewish, whose motto is toughness against dangerous "others," and who is slowly becoming the equivalent of an Israeli patriot abroad. In what can be perceived as the belated poisoned fruits of the Holocaust, it is those who did not experience it, rather than its survivors, who are turning their backs to the European world. The survivors did not think of themselves as sanctified victims, but their successors (whether direct or not), increasingly think of themselves in these terms, with respect to a hostile outside world.[117]

Israel's new *Jew*, it seems, has spawned "another type of [European] Jew" whose self-conception bodes ill, in Pinto's analysis, for the promise of a New Europe. If Europe's iconic *Jews* and its vulnerable new *Jews* choose a common path of disconnection and disintegration over one of multiple belonging, deep engagement, and shared struggle, then the European experiment fails. In an opinion piece in *Haaretz*, Pinto questions whether "Israel, by its actions, is truly protecting the Jewish people," as it perennially claims.[118] "Or is it," she asks, "the Jews outside Israel who . . . feel the need to protect *it*, often at the cost of a European and international 'never again' that lies at the heart of their own legitimacy as Jews in democratic countries?"[119]

Ultimately, the contested idea of "Europe's new *Jews*" provides a fruitful lens into the many dimensions and meanings of *Jew* in contemporary Europe—a New Europe still finding and building its way out of a rich but troubled history. *Jew / new Jew* names a key nexus at which Europe's past, present, and potential futures intersect, and I close this discussion with two snapshots that provide a sort of condensed cross-section of this distinctively European nexus.

In January 2015, four *Jews* were gunned down at a kosher market in Paris by a young, French-born Muslim man of West African descent, Amedy Coulibaly, while another young Muslim man, Lassana Bathily, an immigrant from Mali who worked at the kosher market, sheltered several other *Jews* by hiding them away from the gunfire in a basement cold-storage locker. In the wake of the assault, France awarded Bathily immediate citizenship, and Muslim leaders and a local rabbi appeared together to lay flowers at the site of the murders in a gesture of solidarity and rejection of divisive violence, while bystanders chanted, *"Tous ensemble"* ("We're all in this together"); Israeli prime minister Benjamin Netanyahu responded by calling on French *Jews* to give up on Europe and "come home to Israel."[120]

Elsewhere on the continent, that same month, Portugal announced that its "law of return"—similar to one previously passed in Spain—would soon take effect, offering immediate citizenship and nationality to descendants of Sephardic *Jews* who had been expelled half a millennium ago. These laws serve, as it were, as an act of memorialization and reparation, as well as a belated invitation to *Jews* to "come back home" to Portugal and Spain. Both members of the European Union, Portugal and Spain disallow preferential treatment on the basis of religion, but the laws pose no problem in this regard, according to the secretary-general of the Federation of Jewish Communities in Spain, Mauricio Toledano: "'The question is, were your ancestors Spanish Jews in 1492?' he says. 'If the answer is "yes," whether you're Jewish, Christian, Muslim or whatever today, that has nothing to do with it.'"[121]

As of this writing, Porto and Lisbon have certified the Sephardic ancestry of hundreds, perhaps thousands, of applicants under Portugal's law of return. Spain's application process opened in October 2015. The president of Lisbon's Jewish community, Jose Oulman Carp, reports that, in Lisbon, the majority of applications for citizenship come from Israelis. The obvious, if ironic, question then arises: Will Israelis responding to Spain's and Portugal's new laws of return become the newest of Europe's new *Jews*?[122]

New *Jews*: A View from the New World

> Irving Howe described America as a place where "the new" was more
> than an American value; it was an ethos. In such a society, even as tradi-
> tion has a place, its place will always be refracted through the lens of
> the new.[123]

In the preface to *New Jews: The End of the Jewish Diaspora*, American scholars Caryn Aviv and David Shneer insist that, "rather than write about
fears of displacement and violence . . . we have written about Jews' *rootedness* in the places they live and about their ability to move around the
world because they *choose* to. . . . We have written about a new Jewish
map populated by New Jews."[124]

The research of these self-identified "professional Jews" focuses, in their
words, on "the ways in which Jews today craft identities, not as diasporic,
homeless, or exilic subjects but as people rooted in and tied to particular
places. These roots shape how new Jews identify themselves and view the
world and how new Jews also traverse many places as part of the process
of communal identity formation."[125] It is no criticism of these fine young
scholars to note that their new *Jews* bear an unmistakable resemblance (cell
phones and iPads aside) to countless generations of multiply rooted, multiply situated, multiply identified *Jews*.

In fact, the title of Aviv and Shneer's book has an antecedent, just a
generation before, in a small trade book published in the United States
in 1971: *The New Jews* (note the definite article, absent from Aviv and
Shneer's iteration) is a collection of essays by young Jewish men (most in
their twenties; no women are represented), many of whom went on to
rise to prominence as scholars in the emerging field of academic Jewish
studies.[126] This earlier volume brims with the voices of student radicalism
and deep discontent (and occasional purple prose) common to its era.
"Many of the contributors to this volume," writes coeditor James A.
Sleeper in his introduction, "have wallowed for a time in the angst and
alienation of our century, a time in which 'all their bones' have pro-
claimed the absurdity of life, not the Glory of God."[127] But many of these
same voices also exult in fresh, new encounters with ancient forms of
"Jewish spirituality" and with burgeoning, local "experimental religious
communities" like those of the *Havurah* movement, founded in Boston
and New York in 1968–1969, which soon gave birth to the wildly popular
Jewish Catalog series published between 1973 and 1980.[128] *The New Jews* also
includes a handful of essays that grapple with Israel and Zionism in the
aftermath of the 1967 Six Day War. These few pieces, like the others in
the volume, convey a sense of their authors' deep-rootedness in
American culture and commitments. At the same time, the authors of

the two expressly "Zionist" essays in the volume are alone in positioning themselves as inhabitants of "Diaspora," or "*galut*" (exile), to a "homeland" embodied by the State of Israel.

In declaring "the end of the Jewish Diaspora" a generation later, Aviv and Shneer situate themselves, by contrast, in an expressly "post-Zionist" (but, in their case, not at all anti-Israel) global landscape. The political and ideological distance traveled between *The New Jews* of 1971 and *New Jews* of 2005 is captured in Aviv and Shneer's observation, in the preface to their volume, that "we are frequently asked to declare our allegiance to Israel, a place that, although halfway around the world, for many seems to sit at the center of the Jewish universe." It is a centering (although not a universe) that Aviv and Shneer both question and reject:

> Politically, we want to question the centrality of Israel in Jewish geography, culture, and memory. And intellectually, we want to move beyond the term "diaspora" as a mode of explaining postmodern collective identity, since such a conceptualization reinforces notions of centers and peripheries. . . . Rather than refer to Jews as "in Israel" or "in [the] diaspora," we refer to *new Jews* as "global" and break down the inherent dichotomy that the Israel/diaspora metaphor maintains. In this post-Zionist, post-Soviet, post-American-melting-pot moment, we show that looking at Jews as global rather than diasporic/Israeli serves several purposes.[129]

These "several purposes" add up, in effect, to a single goal—namely, to disrupt homogenizing narratives of unified peoplehood that mystify and misrepresent both current, diverse practices of identification and the exercise of a variety of forms of agency by those whom the authors term "new *Jews*." But Aviv and Shneer also want to displace the trope of the "rootless," or deracinated, *Jew* so celebrated by French postwar philosophy because it "has overshadowed the ways in which many Jews are remaking their sense of home and establishing new kinds of roots, not just to particular pieces of land, but also to concepts, ideas, stories, and spaces."[130]

Although Aviv and Shneer understand their project to run counter to recent valorizations of diaspora by others, in many respects it, instead, instantiates a number of attributes and models proposed by earlier Jewish "diasporists," for whom "diaspora" names their own *deep rootedness* in "concepts, ideas, stories, and spaces" that are at once local and global, particular and universal. Chief among these earlier articulators of a critical vision of diaspora are Daniel Boyarin and Jonathan Boyarin, whose 1993 essay "Diaspora: Generation and the Ground of Jewish

Identity" remains a landmark, so to speak, in important, ongoing conversations.

The Boyarins "propose Diaspora as a theoretical and historical model" that serves both analytical/descriptive and programmatic ends.[131] Characterizing the genius of diaspora as the "dissociation of ethnicities and political hegemonies," they suggest that this dissociation not only was key to a traditional rabbinic self-understanding that sustained *Jews* for much of the past two millennia and continues to do so for millions today, but that it is also "the only social structure that even begins to make possible a maintenance of cultural identity in a world grown thoroughly and inextricably interdependent. Indeed, we would suggest that Diaspora . . . may be the most important contribution that Judaism has to make to the world."[132]

This formulation challenges a by-now-familiar narrative that holds that the greatest danger to *Jews* living outside a sovereign, hegemonic Jewish state is the sheer freedom to mix and mingle with non-*Jews*, which inevitably leads to cultural dissolution through assimilation. Again, the Boyarins propose a radically different reading of diaspora: "Diasporic cultural identity teaches us that cultures are not preserved by being protected from 'mixing' but probably can only continue to exist as a product of such mixing. Cultures, as well as identities, are constantly being remade. . . . In other words, diasporic identity is a disaggregated identity. Jewishness disrupts the very categories of identity."[133] This disruptive quality of "Jewishness," moreover, serves to highlight how all modes of identification are "mixed," interdependent, partial, and contingent, and stand always "in dialectical tension with one another."[134] The Boyarins go on to propose that diaspora, as an embodied, ethically engaged cultural practice, may be realized across a whole range of categories by which selves are constructed and identities performed. They imagine the crafting of diasporic practices of gender, of religion, of ethnicity and nationality. "It is this idea that we are calling diasporized identity."[135]

Melanie Kaye/Kantrowitz builds on these propositions and explores at greater length what a lived diasporism—and *Jews* constituted by its practices—might look like. In her book *The Colors of Jews: Racial Politics and Radical Diasporism*, she asks, why "*radical* Diasporism"? Her reply:

> Because this is no casual invitation to perpetually wander. The Diasporism I have in mind recognizes the persecution and danger that have made many long for a home and passport, yearn to leave the wandering behind. Inside this longing, Diasporism represents tension, resistance to both assimilation and nostalgia, to both corporate globalization that destroys peoples and cultures, and to nationalism, which promises

to preserve people and cultures but so often distorts them through the prisms of masculinism, racism, and militarism. Radical Diasporism, *sans* army, *sans* military heroes and victories, meshes well with feminism in valuing a strength and heroism available to those without armies; and it suits queerness, in rejecting the constraints of traditional gendered existence.[136]

For Kaye/Kantrowitz, as for the Boyarins, the radical potentialities of a new, more encompassing diasporism can become potent tools for resisting all manner of hegemonies and harmful constraints. They can also, as her title suggests, lead to greater recognition of—and respect for—the kaleidoscopic variety of colors, histories, self-understandings, and ways of being to be found among those who identify as *Jews*.

In their epilogue to *New Jews*, Aviv and Shneer observe that

all Jews share one thing and one thing alone—they identify as Jews, whatever that may mean. It is a postmodern—some might even say an empty—definition of Jewish identity, which makes the definition of Jewishness completely subjective and slippery. . . . It is the very slipperiness of Jewish identity that provides so much fertile potential for creativity, innovation, and adaptation in all the places Jews call home. By abandoning the confines of nationalistic and diasporic constraints for a more nuanced, flexible understanding of Jewish identity that embraces difference and differences as core virtues, we as Jews can become better global citizens.[137]

The "mixed" (or admixed) identity, multiple-rootedness, and subjective slipperiness of *Jew* are impressions that arise easily—even necessarily—in the "New World," and, in particular, from within a U.S. cultural context where the free self-determination of identity—both individual and collective—is a widely embraced principle. The "more nuanced, flexible understanding of Jewish identity" represented by Aviv and Shneer's "postdiasporic" new *Jews* resonates in a powerful way with what Shaul Magid has characterized as a growing "postethnic" American Jewishness or understanding of *Jew*. Magid locates his new *Jews* in what he calls "an increasingly postethnic world, a world where identities are mixed, where allegiances are more voluntary than inherited, more the result of consent than descent"; where "young men and women . . . own multiple narratives, family histories, and affiliations without a sense of disparity" in a way that "includes many who wish to live in multiple ethnic communities without seeing that choice as a contradiction."[138]

As a case in point, Magid quotes from an open letter by a founding coeditor of *Jewcy*, an online magazine that calls itself "a platform for ideas that matter to young Jews today." Joey Kurtzman, the author of the letter, writes:

> At *Jewcy* we've half-jokingly referred to ourselves as part of the first generation of Jewish-American mongrels. . . . The majority of *Jewcy*'s staff is the product of intermarriage.
>
> . . . Needless to say, we are of dubious halakhic Jewishness. This will be truer of our children than it is of us.
>
> Our cultural influences are more polluted than our bloodlines, and that is the important part of our mongrelization. We're evolving new ideas and new forms of religious expression informed by non-Jewish traditions. This is not because we poached from alien traditions, but because those traditions, too, are our patrimony.[139]

Multiethnics, mongrels, and "half-*Jews*"—the latter a term unknown to Halacha but familiar from the Nazi Nuremberg Laws—have become terms of proud self-identification (along with "BuJews," "Jewfis," and the like)[140] for a new and expanding contingent of Americans who, Magid observes, "want a voice *as Jews*" and are claiming that voice both within the material worlds of action and activism and in the virtually boundless world of the global Web and social media.[141] "The internet gives them a voice that circumvents any interference by institutional Judaism," suggests Magid.[142] This is true, to a point, although "institutional" power is very much in evidence on the Web, as well. For example, *Jewcy* is, itself, hosted and funded by the very mainstream online magazine *Tablet.*[143]

As Susannah Heschel has observed, such new *Jews* are, indeed, "creating new forms of Judaism—Reconstructionist, Renewal, feminist— stemming from their interrogation and rejection of religious regimes of chosenness, patriarchy, authority, imitation of the Christian, and the old-fashioned modern."[144] Nor are these new Judaisms exclusive to *Jews*—new or otherwise. In fact, quips Heschel, "cultural boundaries in America become so porous that Jewishness develops into a free-floating identity open to appropriation by anyone, including Jews."[145]

Heschel elaborates that, in postmodern America, "Jewishness becomes staged, blurring the distinction between Jews and Gentiles, and obfuscating the nature of Jewish identity."[146] Rather than attempt to clarify or define that "nature," Heschel observes that "such staging is not unprecedented; at the Passover seder, for example, the liturgy demands that *all Jews view themselves as if* they had come out of Egyptian slavery and re-create the experience for a week."[147] In describing this particular sacred storytelling ritual of origin and constitution of peoplehood as "precedent" for "staging Jewishness," Heschel invokes Jewish tradition in such a way as to "refract it through the lens of the new," in Magid's formulation. The very "nature of Jewish identity" in postmodern society, in Heschel's reading, then, is such that "anyone, including Jews," can perform it, and that performance can itself be constitutive of *Jew* or "Jewishness."

At the close of her essay, entitled "The Myth of Europe in America's Judaism," Heschel further deepens and complicates her association of *Jew*-as-identity with staged performance:

> In yet another kind of performance, when Jewish vaudeville acts appropriated blackface in the early twentieth century they signified their entry into white American society. Michael Rogin has shown how blackface functioned to identify Jews with white America—only if one was white was it necessary to adopt blackface. In a similar way, postmodernity leads American Jews to appropriate a "Jewface," a kind of *imitatio Iudei*, imitation of the Jewish.[148]

The analogy is intriguing. If *Jews* constructed and signaled "their entry into white American society" by performing the "we-are-not-that" of blackface, then, by analogy, the performance of "*Jew*face" signals *Jews'* full entry into American postmodernity via a similarly "we-are-not-that" gesture or mimicry of *Jew*.

Jonathan Freedman, in his *Klezmer America: Jewishness, Ethnicity, Modernity*, celebrates this postmodern turn as he, too, invokes both blackface and *Jew*face in his analysis. Freedman's invocation of blackface comes as he lauds actor Sasha Baron Cohen's "deadpan performance of a white Jew doing a version of blackface . . . without blacking up," and using "this guise [the character Ali G] to speak truth to power" as he "outrageously interviewed U.S. and world powermongers," after which he moved on to create the antisemitic character Borat, which he used "to force Americans to come to terms with their own weird feelings about Jews."[149] *Jewface*, in Freedman's account, turns out to be the title of an album of vintage recordings compiled by a collective of musicians dedicated to "resuscitating narratives of Jewishness from the past that incorporate 'stories that have yet to be told [of] hybrid identities, eclectic communities, racial dialogue, and pioneering . . . style.'" Freedman expresses a close kinship between his book *Klezmer America* and *Jewface* as two among many such contemporary projects of "recovery" of "heterogeneous narratives" that may "provide new histories or new perspectives," as well as "new opportunities for critical intervention."[150]

Heschel and Freedman offer related insights about postmodern understandings and performances of *Jew* and the potential of these to

provide new tools both for critical intervention into racist power structures and for appropriating *Jew* as a staged (but no less "traditional")
identity. In this, they share obvious elements with the accounts of new
Jews and of "mongrel," "diasporized," or "postdiasporic" identities outlined by the Boyarins, Kaye/Kantrowitz, Magid, and Aviv and Shneer.
Others, while not employing precisely these categories or characterizations, nonetheless add to the collective store of such "heterogeneous
narratives" that "provide new histories or new perspectives" on still more
new *Jews* in the New World. A few brief examples follow.

Can a Jewface Be Black?

In their edited anthology *Black Zion: African American Religious Encounters
with Judaism*, American scholars Yvonne Chireau and Nathaniel Deutsch
introduce their subject matter by posing the following questions:

> If a group of African Americans who were raised as Christians form a
> new community and declare themselves to be Jews, does this act make
> them Jewish? Must they first be converted by one of the "official"
> branches of Judaism? Are these branches any more valid than another
> group that claims Jewish origins? Moreover, what about a group of
> African Americans who [claim] that they are legitimately Jewish and
> that others who call themselves Jews (i.e., Orthodox, Conservative,
> etc.) are imposters or "so-called Jews"? Finally, what happens when a
> group of African Americans who identify with biblical Israel reject the
> label "Jews" as inaccurate, emigrate to the modern state of Israel, and
> establish a community? These scenarios, far from being heuristic, are
> part of the current reality in America and Israel.[151]

In addition to the *Jews* described above, Chireau and Deutsch's volume
engages with "those [African Americans] who identify as members of
the larger Jewish community. Some have a Jewish and an African
American parent while others have converted to Judaism [or are descendants of converts]; some belong to predominantly African American
congregations, others identify with the Orthodox movement."[152]
According to Chireau and Deutsch, not only the former groups, but
also these latter *Jews*, in particular, present a "striking challenge to the
American notion of what constitutes Jewish culture and ethnicity, and
they form part of a broader contemporary awakening within both
Jewish and non-Jewish communities to the wide variety of Jewish
experiences."[153]

   The literature on African American *Jews*, while not extensive, is growing, and it reveals a range of genealogics of *Jew* that are quite explicitly
"insurgent acts of cultural translation," of deeply rooted traditions

"refracted through the lens of the new" in an African American context. Most prominent among these deeply rooted traditions is, of course, the Exodus/Passover story cited above by Heschel as foundational to the constructing and "staging" of *Jews* and "Jewish identity":

> The roots of African American identification with, and transformation of, Israelite and Jewish traditions are to be found in the central narrative of the Hebrew Bible: a lowly people is chosen by God, suffers slavery and exile, and is ultimately redeemed and returned to its Promised Land. This story resonated profoundly with the African slaves and their descendants who cried by the rivers of their own Babylon—America— during the centuries of oppression and exile. Blacks have consistently offered their own liberatory exegesis of biblical traditions by emphasizing the chosenness of African Americans and the promise of redemption for their suffering.[154]

Elements of this biblical narrative are key—both explicitly and implicitly— in writings, sermons, and speeches by founders of the movements explored in *Black Zion*. But other shared narratives of suffering and empowerment are likewise resonant and generative for Black *Jews*.

In his book *Black Jews in Africa and the Americas*, Tudor Parfitt recalls:

> One of the most remarkable figures in the history of black Jewish movements in the United States was Arnold Josiah Ford. . . . Ford, who was fluent in Yiddish and knew Hebrew well, studied the Bible and Talmud with white Jewish teachers. In 1923 he accepted the position of rabbi at Beth B'nai Abraham synagogue in Harlem. . . . He was much influenced by the historical parallels between the blacks of America and the Jews and by the fact that under Christianity both Jew and black had been persecuted: "they suffered side by side," he wrote, "during the horrible years of the Christian Inquisition and the Christian slave trade in Africa, the West Indies and South America."[155]

Parfitt elsewhere reports that this recognition of African Americans and *Jews* as fellow travelers was mutual: "In the Yiddish and English-language Jewish press" of the early twentieth-century United States, "African Americans were often referred to as the 'Jews of America.'"[156] One immediately recognizes, in this statement, an antecedent to the more recent discourse about the new *Jews* of Europe. Yet, here, as well, an exclusive focus on shared narratives of victimization misses a great deal that animates the stories of African American *Jews* and disregards the profoundly significant ways in which becoming *Jew* (or "performing *Jew*face") is understood not as a flight from Blackness but as a declaration of African American or Black power.

Whereas many African American *Jews* speak of being regarded as "neither as authentically black as other blacks nor as authentically Jewish as other Jews," many founders of congregations of African American *Jews* took to heart the biblical accounts tying the "chosen people" to North Africa and claimed identification with and descent from those African biblical Israelites/Hebrews.[157] By such new/old genealogics, Black *Jews* are not only more deeply African than their Christian cousins, whose Christianity was the product of white missionaries and slaveholders, but they are also more authentically *Jews* than are the Ashkenazi and Sephardi children of Europe. In this way, the indigenous Black Jewishness of African American *Jews* was part and parcel of pan-Africanist and Black-nationalist sensibilities that arose in the United States in the early twentieth century and attracted further adherents through the Black Power movements of the 1960s and 1970s.

One contemporary Black *Jew*, Capers Funnye, chief rabbi of Beth Shalom B'nai Zaken Ethiopian Hebrew Congregation in Chicago, a member of the Chicago Board of Rabbis, and a graduate of both the Ethiopian Hebrew Rabbinical College and the Spertus Institute for Jewish Learning and Leadership (and a close cousin to First Lady Michelle Obama), came to be a *Jew* by way of the Black Power movements in which he was active while in college. According to Bernard J. Wolfson, "Funnye views Judaism as a powerful force for the liberation of the human spirit—and of black Americans. He argues that the black Jewish movements of the early twentieth century—his spiritual and intellectual forefathers—were in the vanguard of black self-realization and were the forerunners of black nationalism and black power."[158]

Many of these movements continue today, and some are currently strengthening connections across communities of *Jews* worldwide. Rabbi Funnye, for example, is also head of the Pan-African Jewish Alliance, an international organization with participation by Black *Jews* of Uganda, Zimbabwe, Nigeria, Ethiopia, Ghana, Kenya, and the United States "that seeks to unite historic and emerging African and African-American Jewish communities around the world. PAJA also seeks to integrate African and African-American Jews into the mainstream of the Jewish community."[159] The Alliance is a project under the umbrella of the larger Be'chol Lashon (for which Rabbi Funnye also serves as associate director), an initiative of the Institute for Jewish and Community Research, a nonprofit organization based in San Francisco. Be'chol Lashon's mission statement reads, in part:

Imagine a new global Judaism that transcends differences in geography, ethnicity, class, race, ritual practice, and beliefs. Discussions about "who-is-a-real-Jew" will be replaced with the rich, multi-dimensional character of the Jewish people. . . .

Be'chol Lashon (In Every Tongue) grows and strengthens the Jewish people through ethnic, cultural, and racial inclusiveness. We advocate for the diversity that has characterized the Jewish people throughout history, and through contemporary forces including intermarriage, conversion, and adoption. We foster an expanding Jewish community that embraces its differences.[160]

This statement, which can be read as a kind of mainstream new-*Jew* manifesto, resonates strongly with a number of themes discussed above, including those of global movement and historical diversity, difference as a core virtue, and wide-ranging inclusiveness. At the same time, however, it envisions a unified, singular entity called "the Jewish people."[161] In joining with and helping to shepherd this organization, as well as his own flock of Black Hebrew Israelite *Jews* in Chicago, along with other communities of Black *Jews* in New York and throughout Africa, Rabbi Funnye performs a postdiasporic, "mixed," "global" identity as a new *Jew*, with deep roots in many places and ideas. One of the newer of these ideas—now just over a century old—is that *Jew* can be a name for liberation and Black power, such that *Black* and *African American* become not merely adjectives modifying *Jew* but rather subject positions deeply interwoven with it in a primordial and transformative embrace.[162]

Crypto-Jews *or* "Jews on the Inside"

"Assimilation, even conversion, its peak of expression, can create its own kind of psychosocial heritage," observes Susannah Heschel in her essay cited above. She continues:

> The initial group of Jews who arrived in Peter Stuyvesant's New Amsterdam in 1654 were Marranos, Jews who had converted to Catholicism under pressure from Spanish authorities and who often continued to practice Judaism in secret, or at least to maintain a surreptitious sense of Jewish identity. Their experience as Marranos, which was far from assimilationist, gave them a sense of social and political entitlement.[163]

This sense of entitlement, according to Heschel, came, in part, from the fact that, "because they did not come from ghettos but were assimilated into Christian society, they were not about to take discrimination lying down." They were, in a significant sense, "strengthened by their experiences . . . as Christians on the outside, Jews on the inside."[164]

In the latter decades of the twentieth century, in the southwestern United States, a number of persons of Latin American Catholic descent began to share stories about unusual family rituals and practices that seemed to set them apart from the majority of their neighbors, with whom they otherwise shared much in common. Many such practices were seen to bear resemblance to traditional Jewish dietary, Sabbath, and related traditions, while others were more obscure and secretive. In fact, secrecy and concealment were often significant elements of the practices themselves, and of their transmission. In the years since these stories first became public, they have spawned a growing body of literature and scholarship, and a similarly growing population of individuals and communities (virtual and otherwise) constellated around the identity of "crypto-Jews"—literally, "secret" or "hidden Jews"—also known as Marranos, conversos, or anusim.

These new crypto-Jews have come to understand themselves to be descendants of the Sephardim who were forced to convert or be expelled from Spain and Portugal in the fifteenth and sixteenth centuries, and who were hounded by the Inquisition for centuries more, even in the New World to which untold numbers fled. This new self-identification is expressed in a variety of ways by different members of this population. Some describe their new identification as simply adding another layer to already multilayered identities. For others, the newly acquired or affirmed identity as Jews is more deeply transformative. Many of these latter continue to embrace the Christianity in which they were raised through a range of strategies such as membership in more Judaic-inflected Christian denominations, like the Seventh-Day Adventists, or through coming to a more historical and philosophical, while less Christological, understanding of Jesus and Christianity's origins among Jews.[165] Others come to identify as "messianic Jews." Still others take a path that leads to formal conversion to Judaism and to joining existing congregations and communities. These new Jews are found among the full range of denominations from secular-humanist to Orthodox, although, "because Sephardic Judaism has no Reform or Conservative dimension, a descendant who wishes to become part of the Spanish Jewish tradition will have no choice but to become Orthodox."[166]

In her 2002 ethnographic study of contemporary crypto-Jews, the sociologist Janet Liebman Jacobs describes how these individuals come to craft "Jewish cultural identities" that reflect the sociopolitics of race and class in the U.S. Southwest:

> In the last two decades, as crypto-Jewish descendants have explored and adopted a Jewish cultural identity, it is primarily within the context of

white European ethnicity that some individuals have come to understand their Sephardic ancestry. . . . The association of Jewishness with
whiteness has led, in some instances, to a reification of the doctrine of
"pure origins" among those descendants who equate Jewish ancestry
with Spanish colonial heritage.

In contrast to this European emphasis, however, a sizable number
of descendants have taken a more multicultural view of their Jewish
lineage. These respondents, who identify as mestiza/o or as mixed-race
Latinas/os, have voiced concerns about preoccupation with
European heritage and a white cultural bias within the contemporary
descendant movement. . . . Descendants from Texas and New Mexico
also express a strong connection to Chicana/o ancestry and to Native
American heritage, a multiethnic background in which they take a
great deal of pride. Many of these respondents participated in the civil
rights movements of the 1960s and 1970s and were heavily influenced
by the politics of Mexican American identity. . . . With the recovery of
Sephardic roots, some descendants have reframed their political values
within a multiethnic perspective that has been broadened to include
Jewish secularism as a[nother] moral basis for social activism.[167]

As Jacobs observes, for some, the appropriation of *Jew* as identity serves
as a kind of assertion of whiteness, not only within the Black/white
racial politics of the United States, but, more specifically, within the Latin
American racialist legacies of Iberian blood-purity systems (*limpieza de
sangre*) and their New World iterations as a *sistema de castas*, or race/caste
hierarchy.[168] The full irony of the genealogics by which the ideology of
limpieza de sangre—explicitly designed to *exclude* crypto-*Jews* or *conversos*
from power and social privilege—begat an ideology by which "crypto-
Jew" now signifies a kind of *pure* Iberian ancestry, thereby privileging and
empowering Latinas/os, seems largely lost on those for whom Sephardic
Jew = Spanish colonizer = access to white privilege.

Others, as Jacobs notes, share much more of a kinship with the self-
described "mongrel" *Jews* discussed above, for whom ideas like "blood
purity" or "cultural purity" are not merely misguided and outdated but
demonstrably destructive and irredeemably racist in practice. These
mestizas/os, or "mixed bloods," embrace a new genealogics by which
their newfound Jewish ancestry is incorporated into the multiple-
rootedness that already was, for them, a source of pride and of a politics
of solidarity. Having been raised Christian in a hegemonically Christian
society, they now understand themselves to have been, like their Marrano
forebears, "Jews on the inside." They are "not about to take discrimination lying down," as Heschel puts it, whether from "gringos" or others.

In this, they also share a kinship with many Black *Jews* or African American *Jews*. In their "recovery" of "heterogeneous narratives," in Freedman's words, these new *Jews* of all stripes and colors "provide new histories or new perspectives," as well as "new opportunities for critical intervention" into tired old narratives and social hierarchies.

But this particular "project of recovery" is not without committed critics and detractors. Folklorist Judith S. Neulander, for example, has worked stringently to "debunk" these "new histories" and to discredit such new *Jews* and those she calls "their academic enablers." Neulander argues that much of the evidence that leads to crypto-*Jewish* identification "can be explained either by the presence of Ashkenazi Jews in twentieth-century New Mexico . . . or by the influence of Seventh-Day Adventism, which exerted a powerful force in New Mexico at the turn of the century and borrowed liberally from Judaism's customs and tropes."[169] It is one thing to identify as descendants of Abraham, Isaac, and Jacob, it seems (not to mention as descendants of a sovereign Judaea), but quite another to identify as descendants of Sephardic *conversos*. Neulander cites "Hispano racism" and "real" *Jews*' pride and credulity as primary determinants of crypto-*Jews*' acceptance: "To a significant extent, local Hispano acceptance reflects the traditional mode of asserting overvalued, white ancestral descent in the multiracial Spanish-Americas. . . . At the same time, widespread Jewish acceptance seems to reflect a beleaguered people's need to believe itself indomitable, as evidenced by a miraculous crypto-Jewish survival."[170]

Whereas establishing "historical truth" regarding distant ancestry often matters a great deal to both those who claim and those who dispute the identifications of crypto-*Jews*, my own interest here, as throughout this chapter, remains in the claims, themselves, and in what—and how— *Jew* comes to mean in these contexts. In Freedman's assessment, "the appearance of self-described Crypto-Jews, whatever the truth or falsehood of their claims, is of signal importance because it provides a compelling example of the ways in which Jewishness intersects with other cultural formations in ways that are richly transformative of both."[171] For Freedman, the claims and counterclaims surrounding crypto-*Jews* provide not only new, "heterogeneous"—even "transformative"—narratives about *Jews*, but they provide, as well, opportunities for critical insights into how

> individual [and collective] subjects can construct new narratives out of the materials that history has bequeathed them—sometimes playfully, sometimes in deadly earnest, always, constantly, testing the limits of authoritative markings of identity, origin, and cultural and social meaning. . . . The cultural claims of Southwestern Crypto-Jews . . . can

remind us how rich have been the stories we make out of the cascadings of diaspora and how productively syncretism complicates our conceptual models of difference and ethnicity.[172]

The cherished stories and varied practices of America's new crypto-*Jews* invite us to imagine, in the words of the Boyarins, how cultures of *Jews* have always been, and will continue to be, preserved through "diasporized identities" that are "products of mixing" and "are constantly being remade."

"Today, We Are All Jews by Choice"

In *American Post-Judaism: Identity and Renewal in a Postethnic Society*, Shaul Magid writes, "For the first time in modern history, many Gentiles, for a variety of reasons, actually *want* to become Jews."[173] And many choose to do so. These new *Jews*, according to Magid,

> do not all feel bound to the Jewish people, nor do they [all] come to Judaism, or Jewishness, with a strong commitment to Jewish belief and practice to the exclusion of all else. However, they do come . . . because there is something about it [Judaism], or about Jews, that is compelling. Many do not want to sever their ties with their families or their past in an absolute way. And many come with significant spiritual gifts they attained elsewhere.[174]

Magid's assertions appear clearly borne out by the rise of Black *Jews* and crypto-*Jews* in the past and present century, and he aptly names the multiple-rootedness and attachment to those multiple roots that many such new *Jews* express. But Magid does not have these particular communities in mind; his observations encompass, more broadly, many of those who choose to become *Jews* in the current era. "Increasing numbers of converts to Judaism in America," he notes, "want to refer to themselves ritually as 'son/daughter' of their biological parents and not the halakhic 'son of Abraham and Sarah.' They want to retain [their existing] . . . cultural narratives, and even rituals and ceremonies. . . . The notion of severing one's ties to a part of one's past seems unnecessary if not offensive."[175] In this respect, converts, as new *Jews*, mirror the growing number of those from so-called intermarried families who identify strongly as *Jews* from birth while also sharing traditions, formative cultural narratives, and aspects of self-understanding with close family members—parents, grandparents, spouses, children, and others—who do not all identify as *Jews*. Soon, it seems, such *Jews* as these will constitute the majority of those who identify and are identified as *Jews* in the

United States. As a result, the meanings of *Jew* are being further expanded and transformed.

In 2013, the Pew Research Center, a widely respected U.S. demographic and public-policy "think tank," published *A Portrait of Jewish Americans: Findings from a Pew Research Center Survey of U.S. Jews.*[176] The study is a fascinating cultural artifact, not only for the data it produced and the findings it reports, but as much so for the methods, definitions, frameworks, and questions it employs. To begin with, the study was carried out by the "Religion and Public Life Project" of the Pew Center, thus situating the study of *Jews* within the framework of American "religions." The lack of a clear "fit" between the research framework ("religions") and the research subjects (*Jews*)—in fact, the lack of a secure "fit" for *Jew* within any of a number of ascribed social-scientific categories or definitions (see chapter 1 of the present volume)—is in evidence throughout the study and its published findings. This is nowhere more the case than in the study's description of how eligible research subjects—that is, *Jews*—were identified:

> Because there is no scholarly consensus on who exactly qualifies as Jewish, and no clear demarcation of where the line dividing Jews and non-Jews lies, this study takes a broad approach in determining eligibility. The full interview was offered to anyone who described themselves as Jewish or partially Jewish by religion, to anyone who identified themselves as Jewish or partially Jewish *aside* from religion, and to anyone who was raised Jewish or partially Jewish or had a Jewish parent—even if they do not think of themselves as Jewish.[177]

In my discussion of sociopolitical and theological definitions of *Jew* in chapter 1, I noted the peculiar categories "*Jew* by religion" and "*Jew* of no religion" employed by the Pew researchers in their study, which are reflected, as well, in this description of research subjects. In the context of the present exploration of new *Jews*, however, it is worth remarking on the study's evidence for a proliferation of new categorizations of *Jew* ("by religion," "of no religion," "aside from religion," "partially Jewish," "raised Jewish," "raised partially Jewish"), as well as its confirmation of the strikingly "slippery" nature of *Jew* as a mode of identification. With regard to Magid's observations, the prominent descriptor "partially Jewish" and the study's findings on family demographics and attitudes toward "belief" and "religious practice" are particularly noteworthy.

The Pew survey finds, for example, that of those who self-identify as *Jews* in the United States, close to 60 percent of those who married in the past ten years, and 44 percent overall, are married to a spouse who does not self-identify as a *Jew*. Of these, 45 percent are "raising their children

Jewish by religion" or "raising their children partly Jewish by religion."[178] No statistics are offered regarding those in the above category who are raising their children "Jewish aside from religion."[179] This seems a particularly odd omission given the finding that, whereas 46 percent of American adults who identify as *Jews* consider that identification "very important" to them, "religion" is "very important" to only 26 percent of them.[180] Confining themselves to a conventionally limited, "religious" definition of *Jew*, the researchers report that "the percentage of U.S. adults *who say they are Jewish when asked about their religion* has declined by about half since the late 1950s and currently is a little less than 2%"—this in a society in which "*religious* disaffiliation" is rising and reported at similar rates among *Jews* and non-*Jews*.[181] The growing "trend toward secularism," with its complex relationship to American religiosity, has been observed and remarked upon by sociologists since the mid-twentieth century. Will Herberg's *Protestant, Catholic, Jew* remains the landmark study of this dynamic in that era.[182]

Magid, whose book was written before publication of the Pew study, cites a 1990 National Jewish Population Survey (NJPS) finding that "many children of intermarried couples in America who identify as Jews (and are therefore considered as such by the Reform movement, the largest denomination in America) *also* identify with the ethnicity of their Gentile parent. That is, they identified, for example, as part Irish-Catholic (which constitutes an ethnicity) and also Jewish."[183] Such *Jews* in "mixed" families, as described by Magid, Pew, and the NJPS, embrace a wide variety of beliefs, practices, narratives of ethnicity or ancestry, and family configurations. Some of these are quite common, conventional, and familiar; others are uncommon or new.

Susan Katz Miller, who identifies as a *Jew* and has recently come to identify "religiously" as "Jewish/interfaith," describes a typical family Passover observance as follows:

> Each year my extended clan gathers for a huge Passover seder in Florida. My eighty-eight-year-old father presides over the ritual meal, leading us through the prayers and songs of religious freedom. The family at the table includes believers, seekers, and secularists, Jews, Catholics, Protestants, Buddhists, and those who claim interfaith identity. A Jewish nephew who is about to become a bar mitzvah and a Catholic nephew who just received First Communion compete with my interfaith son to find the traditional hidden matzoh. We are a joyous, motley crew, intent on celebrating together.[184]

Miller's account, while far from the norm, is also far from unusual in the United States today. Less common is the choice that she and her husband have made to raise their children in a small but growing "interfaith" movement in which both Jewish and Christian clergy collaborate with parents to educate children in both traditions and to support welcoming, nurturing communities and dialogue groups for "mixed" families. Online networks, resources, and advocacy groups such as the Half-Jewish Network, Interfaith Community, and Interfaithfamily also help to sustain a kind of "mediated kinship" or virtual community among this growing population.[185]

Miller extols the unanticipated "joy, and not simply compromise," that her family members have found in sharing their multiple traditions together, and she writes that she feels "exhilarated by this new fluidity, empowered by the transition away from restrictive either/or identity labels and into the inevitable and more expansive both/and future."[186] Other *Jews* in this "brave new world" of fluid, mixed, and slippery identities, however, have not come through unscathed. One of them, Chav Doherty, a transgender *Jew* whose family became (Orthodox) *Jews* when he was a young girl, riffs on the multiple meanings of "mosaic" in describing how his embodied differences have led him to feel broken, as well as whole:

> Although the term *identity* generally connotes self-consistency and coherence, the way I have lived my identity suggests a more complicated picture. I embody differences commonly regarded as distinct and contradictory: male and female, Jewish and non-Jewish, queer and straight. These differences have, at times, bent me up and torn me apart. Like a literal mosaic, my identity is composed of pieces broken and arranged to form a new whole. It includes shards of distinct identification. The glue that holds them together is my lived experience.[187]

Doherty's narrative conveys the often-painful challenges of living in "cultures, as well as identities, [that] are constantly being remade" and of embodying a "diasporic identity [that] is a disaggregated identity."[188] But one may perceive, as well, how Doherty has harnessed the "radical diasporism" of the *Jew* he calls a "mosaic man" to "reject the constraints of traditional gendered existence" and other either/or choices, so as to construct "a *new whole*," a sense of integrity, and an act of *tikkun olam* ("repair of the world") out of what would otherwise be disparate "shards of distinct identification."[189]

New Lenses, New Challenges

The foregoing small collection of "heterogeneous narratives" and "new histories"; of age-old traditions and understandings "refracted through the lens of the new"; and of identities performed sometimes joyfully, sometimes painfully, but almost always in earnest, provides the briefest glimpse of some of the new *Jews* brought forth amid the fluxes and forces at play in the modern and postmodern New World. Some of these *Jews* inhabit the borderlands of conventional dichotomies like us/them, diaspora/homeland, and *Jew*/Gentile, whereas others seek to move beyond such boundaries altogether. Some of these *Jews* embody multiple or mixed identifications and spring from varied roots sunk into the soils of many continents. All stand as testament to the deep attachments, apparent contradictions, and inexhaustible variety currently encompassed by *Jew*: "All of us, we're trying to unearth 'who we are.' We're going to have to define it for ourselves. That's a process that takes self-realization, dialogue, and self-reflection. For me, it's not just about what I believe. It's where I'm from. It's in my blood, in my genes. It's beyond choosing, by me. It's in God's hands."[190] Such conflicting and conflicted assertions as these represent the sense of both volition and lack of volition widely expressed by those who identify as *Jews*. "Self-realization" and self-determination contend with science and mythos, "blood," "genes," and "God" in constituting *Jews*. We must define *Jew* "for ourselves," and yet, it lies "beyond [our] choosing." The words might be those of any number of *Jews* described above. But, as it happens, the speaker is Father William Sánchez, a Catholic priest in New Mexico who "discovered he is a *Jew*" through DNA testing.

Father Sánchez's ruminations not only demonstrate the ambivalence and ambiguity that attend postmodernity's slippery hold on identities, but also reveal a decidedly premodern sense of a sacred, mystical power of affirmation and determination that is attributed to genetic ways of knowing. This kind of knowing promises to press beyond narrative and belief, to see behind the curtains of time and tradition. It is not merely his priestly vocation that leads Father Sánchez, a crypto-*Jew*, to see the hidden hand of God in the obscure "testimony" of DNA.

Laurie Zoloth, a bioethicist, theologian, and Orthodox *Jew*, remarks on the culturally conditioned resonance between the language of DNA and that of the Jewish God:

> Genetic knowledge is hidden knowledge. The language of the genetic code is difficult, based on a limited set of base pairs and expressed as code. Like Hebrew, it is both the sign, meaning the actual language of the people, and the symbol of their difficult, ancient, unknowableness. Hebrew is *lashon kodesh*, the holy tongue, God's language, and these very things are what is said about DNA base pairs. Both are ambiguous (in biologic terms, they have redundancy) and need interpretive

settings to do the work of creation of the self. The theme[s] of a hidden
soul, a hidden self, and a codal key are familiar ones.[191]

With the rise of the genomic *Jew*, we have entered a truly new age of
high-tech and sophisticated self-perception, but one already rife with
antique notions of bloods and essences, fates and destinies, souls and
selves, the *Jew* "inward" and the *Jew* "outward." Postmodern insights and
uncertainties (such as the indeterminacy of the self) are seemingly dis-
sipated by the unimpeachable facts of biological science. Yet a closer look
reveals that genomic *Jews*—like all other *Jews*—raise far more questions
than they are able to answer.

For example, "if Jewish mothers lead to Jewish belonging, but Jewish
fathers do not, then what is biology or Jewish blood?" asks Jessica
Mozersky in her book *Risky Genes: Genetics, Breast Cancer, and Jewish
Identity*. She goes on to point out that the longstanding and still widely
embraced matrilineal principle for determining who is a *Jew* "would not
meet a biogenetic definition about genetic inheritance as a child inherits
equal amounts of genetic material from both parents. So this is not a
biological understanding of belonging that fits with biomedicine or science or genetics; rather, it is a biological understanding that reiterates
the social."[192] The reverse is likewise the case: to those for whom the
halachic matrilineal principle or act of conversion defines a *Jew*, the bio-
genetically determined genomic *Jew* is indeterminate—that is to say,
irrelevant.

For those who look to genetics to provide meaning about who they
understand themselves (or others) to be, as *Jews*, there is much usable
material available—more and more of it every day. But such meaning-
making is an exercise of *choice*, a volitional, creative, and interpretive
undertaking. In the absence of the desire and the will—and of nonbio-
logical, cultural definitions and determinants—genetics neither makes
nor unmakes *Jews*.

In his essay "Conversos, Marranos, and Crypto-Latinos: The Jewish
Question in the American Southwest (and What It Can Tell Us about
Race and Ethnicity)," Freedman relates that, "in search of something
more tangible than family narratives or ambiguous cultural artifacts,
participants on both sides of the Crypto-Jewish debate . . . turned to idi-
oms of race—to the language, in this case, of genetic determinism."[193]
After having assessed the claims and genetic evidence on both sides and
found these to be "oddly beside the point," Freedman concludes:

> If nothing else they [the claims and genetic evidence] remind us of how
> perdurable a racialist understanding of identity remains and how
> essential Jewishness remains to that understanding. The lesson here is

that the turn to the genetic to explain matters that are cultural in nature and meaning can only remind us of the importance of a perspective which insists on culture and history as consequential in terms of human identity or group affiliation.[194]

Parfitt offers a related assessment of a similar turn to genetics to "determine the Jewishness" of one group of Black African *Jews*, the Lemba. "The 'Jewishness' of the Lemba," according to Parfitt, "may be seen as a twenty-first-century genetic construction."[195] This "genetic construction," built on a high frequency of the legendary Cohen Modal Haplotype on Y chromosomes among Lemba men, in turn triggered a vast mobilization of cultural and economic capital, by means of which

> the Lemba leadership was increasingly drawn into a wide range of Jewish and other networks in South Africa and the United States that were closed to them before. Indeed, now it can be stated with a considerable degree of certainty that the genetic findings will have an overwhelming impact upon the future narratives of the Lemba community, upon their sense of where they belong, and indeed upon the way in which the community is regarded by other people.[196]

Genetic testing here, as elsewhere, becomes an engine of what is ultimately a sociopolitical, cultural, and economic transformation by which new *Jews* are brought into being as persons "who have always been" *Jews*.

Zoloth observes how this process necessitates still other transformations: "The Lemba claim Jewishness through genetics, not through practice (which is Christian, in large part), and this claim reorganizes what claims need to be valid. On some level, the story that is the oral tradition is 'authenticated' by the neutral form that genetics provides."[197] She elaborates: "The way to know identity in the twenty-first century is to know the genetic self—the inner helix that names us as unique, each one by one. Hence, the Lemba can be 'really Jews' because they 'really' have the correct genes of identity."[198] But this peculiarly twenty-first-century way of asking and answering the question "*Jews?*" only leads Zoloth to further, more complex, questions about meaning and relation and about a new genealogics of genetic kinship among *Jews*:

> What is the Jewish community's connection to the Lemba, the cousins they seem to turn out genetically to be? Kinship implies duty; hence, what is our new duty toward the other who is our new kin? And in what sense are Ashkenazi Jews more "like" the Lemba than they are "like" the Celts? How is it that their fates are (to put it figuratively) intertwined? This question turns out to be harder to unpack in a world in

which social grouping around what is understood as race turns out to be so intensely connected to identity, standing, and health.[199]

Additional hard questions arise as a result of growing bodies of knowledge about genetic links to disease and, in particular, to genetically transmitted diseases or predispositions found at higher-than-average rates—or even seemingly exclusively—among Ashkenazi or Sephardi populations. These developments have led to a new twist on the old trope of *Jew* as unhealthy, degenerate spreader of disease, which has now entered the genomic age, arousing new fears of an old stigmatization. In the introduction to their 2015 edited anthology *Jews and Genes: The Genetic Future in Contemporary Jewish Thought*, ethicists Elliot N. Dorff and Laurie Zoloth respond to these fears by assuring their readers that "Ashkenazic Jews are *not* a diseased population; in even the most prevalent of these diseases, only 3 percent of Ashkenazic Jews are carriers, which means that 97 percent are not."[200] At the same time, they strongly endorse genetic-disease testing of all Ashkenazi *Jews*. Indeed, genetic-disease vigilance and action has become institutionalized across a vast range of Jewish networks that include synagogues, schools, community centers, hospitals, periodicals, and dating websites, while geneticists like Harry Ostrer have envisioned "a personalized medicine for the Jewish people based on genomics."[201]

To be identified genetically as a *Jew*, then, is often to become part of an extensive regime of genetic testing and medical interventions, and the target of a variety of related marketing campaigns. In this way, *Jew* has come to name a new kind of medical condition. In an essay entitled "What Is a Jew? The Meaning of Genetic Disease for Jewish Identity," Rebecca Alpert offers a brief genealogical account of how this (pathologized) new *Jew* came to be, and of some of its implications. She suggests that, rather than signifying a particularly disease-prone population, this medicalized *Jew* represents, instead, a kind of "canary in the mine" (or, as Faye Ginsburg has punningly put it, a "canary in the Gemeinschaft"), signaling a fast-advancing era in which, no doubt, "we will learn about the susceptibilities of other communities," so that medicalization of identity may soon become an equal-opportunity enterprise.[202]

These same developments in genetic medicine have opened yet another avenue to the emergence of still more genomic *Jews*—namely, those who "discover that they are *Jews*" when they or a near relative contract(s) one of the growing class of "Jewish genetic diseases." "I may not have known I was Jewish, but I carried the gene," says filmmaker Stephen Frears in a 2001 interview with the *Jewish Journal*.[203] Shortly before his son was born with a genetic disease—familial dysautonomia, strongly associated with Ashkenazi populations—Frears learned, through a chance comment, that his mother had been a *Jew*. Had the revelation not come by word of mouth, it would have been definitively heralded by the child's affliction. Frears now identifies as a *Jew* by virtue of a single mutated "Jewish gene." Many (other) crypto-*Jews* have trodden a similar path.

Had Frears known of his genetic risk, he might have taken preventative measures to ameliorate it. His mother's silence and secrecy—or perhaps merely her free choice not to self-identify or think of herself as a *Jew*—deprived him, in a sense, of that knowledge of risk that could have informed his choices and thereby radically altered his subsequent quality of life and that of his family. But this way of thinking, warns Zoloth, "creates a vexing problem. It arises when identity becomes predicative, prognosticative. It implies the future choices that self will make—that is, that ontology implies morality in that it defines commitments and relationships and thus morality as well."[204] Ginsburg, whose daughter, Sam, suffers from this same disease, invokes related concerns when she emphasizes the ways in which "the new genetics of the late twentieth and early twenty-first centuries exists in the shadow of the last century's eugenics, haunting the present like a 'ghost in the machine.' . . . 'Those who see in genetic manipulation, alteration or selection the potential for the elimination of genetically transmitted diseases . . . confront a history that they claim not to be their own.'"[205]

The new genomic *Jew*, then, in its many permutations and guises, has far-reaching sociocultural implications and presents profound ethical challenges that are barely beginning to be discerned and articulated. For all the technological sophistication of its production, this *Jew* represents a mode of (self-)identification that is no less "subjective" and "slippery," no less culturally constructed, than all the others explored in this chapter and throughout this book. It is easy to forget this, given the nearly divine determinative power so often accorded scientific systems of knowledge-generation and meaning-making. The fact that the genetic/genomic *Jew* is an amalgam of peculiarly circumscribed and contrived (albeit useful) collections of research subjects and data is nicely brought home by the query of one U.S.-born reader of the genomic studies discussed earlier in the present chapter. This ethnically "mongrel" scholar asks, "What if scientists sampled a random set of contemporary Jews, many of whom may not have two Jewish parents let alone four Jewish grandparents? What would 'Abraham's Children in the Genome Era' . . . look like then?"[206]

The answer seems fairly clear. We would look like the full "motley crew" of new *Jews* explored throughout this chapter—and then some.

As products of numerous ancestries and migrations, multiple and diverse lineages, joined and divided roots, mixed and guarded cultures, shared and discrete practices, complex and interwoven narratives, and an almost infinite number of aspirations and self-understandings, *Jews* no longer look like the other, the not-self, that *Jews* so long remained. In the "genome era," *Jews* look like the peoples of all the lands, nations, and families of the earth.

Notes

1. See, e.g., Oz Almog, *The Sabra: The Creation of the New Jew*, trans. Haim Watzman (Berkeley: University of California Press, 2000), 76–78. Gil Anidjar refers to "the anti-Semitism of Zionism, which, seeking the End of Exile, *shlilat ha-galut*, strives to bring to its conclusion the alleged ahistoric (non)existence of the 'exilic' Jew, be he the Oriental, *Mizrahi*, Jew or the no less Oriental Eastern Jew, *Ostjude*" (Gil Anidjar, *Semites: Race, Religion, Literature* [Stanford: Stanford University Press, 2008], 33).

2. Zhou Xun, *Chinese Perceptions of the 'Jews' and Judaism: A History of the Youtai* (Richmond, UK: Curzon Press, 2001), 4. The book is based on the author's doctoral dissertation at the University of London. Cf. Clarissa Sebag-Montefiore, "The Chinese Believe That the Jews Control America. Is That a Good Thing?: Prof. Xu Xin's Institute of Jewish and Israel Studies at Nanjing University seeks to establish Chinese scholarship on Jews," *Tablet* (March 27, 2014), http://www.tabletmag.com/jewish-arts-and-culture/books/167289/nanjing-jewish-studies.

3. David Nirenberg, *Anti-Judaism: The Western Tradition* (New York: Norton, 2013), 2.

4. Tal Ilan has recently demonstrated a pronounced decline in the appearance of the term *Ioudaios* as a self-designation between the Ptolemaic and Roman periods, as evidenced on surviving papyri and ostraca from that time. Roman backlash following the Jewish revolts in first-century CE Judaea and early second-century CE Egypt, according to Ilan, most likely accounts for the apparent increased reluctance to self-identify as a *Ioudaios*. (Tal Ilan, "The New *CPJ*: Documents and Concepts" [paper delivered at the Annual Meeting of the Society of Biblical Literature, Atlanta, Georgia, November 2015]. My thanks to the author for sharing the unpublished manuscript of this talk with me.)

5. Excerpts from the *Alliance* document may be found on the organization's website at http://www.aiu.org.

6. Paula Fredriksen, *Augustine and the Jews* (New York: Doubleday, 2008), 308.

7. Augustine, *De Doctrina Christiana*, trans. J. F. Shaw, in *A Select Library of the Nicene and Post-Nicene Fathers of the Christian Church*, ed. Philip Schaff (Buffalo: Christian Literature Company, 1887), 3.5.

8. The English translations are from Mary Hunt, *The French Revolution and Human Rights: A Brief Documentary History* (New York: St. Martin's Press, 1996), 86–88.

9. Ibid., 88.

10. Gary Kates, "Five Jews into Frenchmen: Nationality and Representation in Revolutionary France," in *The French Revolution and the Birth of Modernity*, ed. Ferenc Fehér (Berkeley: University of California Press, 1990), 109.

11. Édouard Drumont, an anti-Enlightenment, anti-Jewish, French nationalist, wrote during the Dreyfus affair and on the centenary of the Revolution that "the centenary of 1789 is the centenary of the Jew" (quoted in Pierre Birnbaum, *The Idea of France* [New York: Hill and Wang, 2001], 114).

12. See, e.g., Anidjar, *Semites*.

13. Zygmunt Bauman, "Allosemitism: Premodern, Modern, Postmodern," in *Modernity, Culture and 'the Jew,'* ed. Bryan Cheyette and Laura Marcus (Stanford: Stanford University Press, 1998), 143–144.

14. See, e.g., Esref Günaydın, *Yahudi Kürtler: Babil'in Kayıp Çocukları* (Istanbul: Karakutu Yayınları, 2003); Yalçın Küçük, *Tekeliyet*, vol. 2 (Istanbul: Ithaki Yayinlar, 2003); Ahmet Uçar, "Hahamlarin Torunları Barzaniler," *Tarih ve Düşünce*, no. 34 (December 2002): 16–24; Ahmet Uçar, "Barzanilerin Yahudiliğiyle ilgili bir Osmanlı Belgesi," *Tarih ve Düşünce*, no. 36 (February 2003); all cited by Mesut Yeğen, "'Jewish-Kurds' or the New Frontiers of Turkishness," *Patterns of Prejudice* 40, no. 1 (2007): 1–20. The term, in these cases, was not applied to self-identified Kurdish *Jews* or Jewish Kurds, most of whom have immigrated to Israel, Europe, or the United States.

15. "Turkish Expert Resigns: Scholar Steps Down after Comparing Turks to Jews," *Spiegel Online International*, July 16, 2008, http://www.spiegel.de/international/germany/turkish-expert-resigns-scholar-steps-down-after-comparing-turks-to-jews-a-566190.html.

16. Ceyda Çağlayan, "Academic Faces Sacking for Describing Turks as the New Jews," *Hürriyet Daily News*, June 28, 2008, http://www.hurriyetdailynews.com/academic-faces-sacking-for-describing-turks-as-the-new-jews.aspx?pageID=438&n=academic-faces-sacking-for-describing-turks-as-the-new-jews-2008-06-28.

17. "Turkish Expert Resigns."

18. Çağlayan, "Academic Faces Sacking."

19. John Biguenet, "I Am Not a Jew," in *The Torturer's Apprentice* (New York: Harper-Collins, 2001), 50.

20. Ibid., 50–51.

21. Http://jewishjumpstart.org.

22. Quoted in Suzanne Kurtz, "Young Jews Urged to Become Stakeholders in Judaism," *Washington Jewish Week*, June 2, 2010, http://www.washingtonjewishweek.com. On "Judaism" versus "Jewishness," see, e.g., Daniel Boyarin, *Judaism* (New Brunswick, NJ: Rutgers University Press, forthcoming).

23. See, e.g., Alain Finkielkraut, *The Imaginary Jew*, trans. Kevin O'Neill and David Suchoff (Lincoln: University of Nebraska Press, 1994); and Sarah Hammerschlag, *The Figural Jew* (Chicago: University of Chicago Press, 2010).

24. *Annie Hall*, directed by Woody Allen (1977; Santa Monica, CA: MGM Home Entertainment, 2005), DVD.

25. Stephen Sharot, "Judaism and Jewish Ethnicity: Changing Interrelationships and Differentiations in the Diaspora and Israel," in *Jewish Survival: The Identity Problem at the Close of the Twentieth Century*, ed. Ernest Krausz and Gitta Tulea (New Brunswick, NJ: Transaction Publishers, 1998), 99. Reform is, by far, the largest denomination of Judaism in the United States.

26. This quotation comes from a "Sponsored Link" message by Google regarding "Offensive Search Results" that, for a time, appeared on the search engine's results page when one searched the term "Jew." The link to the full note was provided in a short statement that read, "We're disturbed about these results as well. Please read our note here. http://www.google.com/explanation.html." (At the time of this writing, this is no longer a functioning web address.) For a transcript of the note in full, see Arnold Zwicky, "The Chosen People," *Language Log* (blog), February 19, 2007, http://itre.cis.upenn.edu/~myl/languagelog/archives/004216.html.

27. See, e.g., Hyam Maccoby, *Judas Iscariot and the Myth of Jewish Evil* (New York: Free Press, 1992).

28. *Oxford English Dictionary Online*, December 2015, s.v. "Jew | jew, v.," http://www.oed.com/view/Entry/101211?rskey=P06IqG&result=2.

29. David Biale, ed., *Cultures of the Jews: A New History* (New York: Schocken, 2002).

30. Andrew Bush, *Jewish Studies: A Theoretical Introduction* (New Brunswick, NJ: Rutgers University Press, 2011), 89.

31. Many thanks to Stefanie Hoss and Katharina Galor for consulting with me on current German conversational usage.

32. On these associations, see Amy-Jill Levine, "A Jewess, More and/or Less," in *Judaism Since Gender*, ed. Miriam Peskowitz and Laura Levitt (New York: Routledge, 1997).

33. See, e.g., "Jewesses with Attitude," a blog project of the online *Jewish Women's Archive* (http://www.jwa.org/blog). The *Archive* also features "The American Jewess Project," which digitizes issues of the magazine *The American Jewess*, which was published monthly from 1895 to 1899 (http://www.jwa.org/research/americanjewess). See also *Heeb* magazine's now defunct raunchy "Gratuitous Jewess" feature (http://www.heebmagazine.com/category/gratuitous-jewess).

CHAPTER 1 — TERMS OF DEBATE

Epigraphs for this chapter are from the following: Richard Rodriguez, "An American Writer," in *The Invention of Ethnicity*, ed. Werner Sollors (New York: Oxford University Press, 1989), 8–9; Gil Anidjar, *Semites: Race, Religion, Literature* (Stanford: Stanford University Press, 2008), 21; Shaye J. D. Cohen, *Beginnings of Jewishness: Boundaries, Varieties, Uncertainties* (Berkeley: University of California Press, 1999), 10. Cohen dedicates this book to his children with the anxious wish: "May their Jewishness always be secure."

1. Quoted in Max Weinreich, *History of the Yiddish Language* (Chicago: University of Chicago Press, 1980), 296–297; Weinreich's translation.

2. Note that *Jew* in this juridical construal appears to be an explicitly male identity.

3. Cf. Daniel Boyarin's observation that "Christian identification of Judaism as a religion has had ongoing and complex effects on Jewish self-definition . . . from Late Antiquity and until modernity but never, until modernity, has it issued in a notion of Judaism as a 'faith'" ("Rethinking Jewish Christianity," *Jewish Quarterly Review* 99, no. 1 [2009]: 36).

4. Joseph Blenkinsopp, *Judaism: The First Phase: The Place of Ezra and Nehemiah in the Origins of Judaism* (Grand Rapids, MI: Eerdmans, 2009), 23.

5. Genesis 26:34.

6. See the biblical books of Ezra and Nehemiah.

7. For an excellent scholarly forum addressing many aspects of these *Jew*/Judaean questions, see Timothy Michael Law and Charles Halton, eds., *Jew and Judean: A Marginalia Forum on Politics and Historiography in the Translation of Ancient Texts* (Los Angeles: Marginalia Review of Books, 2014), https://dl.orangedox.com/yTWsrMw DFZF3fqx2kt/Jew%20and%20Judean.pdf.

8. Morton Smith, *Studies in Historical Method, Ancient Israel, Ancient Judaism*, vol. 1 of *Studies in the Cult of Yahweh*, ed. Shaye J. D. Cohen (Leiden: Brill, 1996), 264.

9. Cohen, *Beginnings*, 70.

10. Steve Mason, "Jews, Judaeans, Judaizing, Judaism," *Journal for the Study of Judaism* 38 (2007): 457.

11. See the extensive discussion of this emerging consensus and related scholarship in Cynthia Baker, "A Jew by Any Other Name?," *Journal of Ancient Judaism* 2 (2011): 151–178.

12. On "Hellene," see below.

13. Thomas Wilson and John Bagwell, *A Complete Christian Dictionary Wherein the Significations and Several Acceptations of All the Words Mentioned in the Holy Scriptures of the Old and New Testament*, 7th ed. (London: E. Cotes, 1661), 326. Interestingly, an entry for the word *Jew* did not even appear in editions of this dictionary prior to the seventh, greatly revised and supplemented, edition.

14. Judith Butler, *Gender Trouble: Feminism and the Subversion of Identity* (New York: Routledge, 1990), 133–134.

15. Frederick William Danker, ed., *Greek-English Lexicon of the New Testament and Other Early Christian Literature*, 3rd ed. (Chicago: University of Chicago Press, 2000). The volume is a revised translation of Walter Bauer, *Griechisch-deutsches Wörterbuch zu den Schriften des Neuen Testaments und der Frühchristlichen Literatur*, 6th ed. (Berlin: Walter de Gruyter, 1988).

16. Danker, *Greek-English Lexicon*, 478.

17. If the *Ioudaioi* of John are "'Judeans' *for the most part*" (emphasis added), one wonders what the remaining part are. For an excellent discussion of the term in the Gospel of John, see Adele Reinhartz, "The Gospel of John: How the 'Jews' Became Part of the Plot," in *Jesus, Judaism, and Christian Anti-Judaism: Reading the New Testament after the Holocaust*, ed. Paula Fredriksen and Adele Reinhartz (London: Westminster John Knox, 2002).

18. Danker, *Greek-English Lexicon*, 479.

19. Mason, "Jews, Judaeans," 458. Cf. Cohen: "I remain a positivist: I study the past in order to make positive statements about what I believe happened or did not happen. I study not only the historical traditions about an event but also the event itself" (*Beginnings*, 347).

20. Donald S. Lopez Jr., "Belief," in *Critical Terms for Religious Studies*, ed. Mark C. Taylor (Chicago: University of Chicago Press, 1998), 33.

21. Cohen, *Beginnings*, 3, emphasis added.

22. Ibid., 340.

23. Blenkinsopp, *Judaism*, 26. Blenkinsopp translates the verse in question as follows: "In those days, from each of the nations with their own languages ten men will take hold of the hem (of the garment) of a Jewish man ('*îš yĕhûdî*), saying, 'Let us go with you, for we have heard that God is with you.'"

24. Cohen, *Beginnings*, 78–79.

25. Among other key Pauline texts. For a particularly fine example of interpretation and critique of traditional misreadings and misappropriations of Romans 2:28–29, see Daniel Boyarin, *A Radical Jew: Paul and the Politics of Identity* (Berkeley: University of California Press, 1994), 78–97 and 209–210.

26. Cohen, *Beginnings*, 105.

27. Ibid., 109.

28. I discuss such "genetic identities" at length in chapter 3.

29. Cohen, *Beginnings*, 136.

30. See, e.g., Mary Gordon, "The Nationality of Slaves under the Early Roman Empire," *Journal of Roman Studies* 14 (1924); Moses Finely, *Ancient Slavery and Modern Ideology* (London: Chatto & Windus, 1980); Claude Meillassoux, *The Anthropology of Slavery: The Womb of Iron and Gold* (Chicago: University of Chicago Press, 1991); and Catherine Hezser, *Jewish Slavery in Antiquity* (New York: Oxford University Press, 2005), esp. chap. 1, "The Denationalization of Slaves."

31. Ross Kraemer, *Unreliable Witnesses: Religion, Gender, and History in the Greco-Roman Mediterranean* (New York: Oxford University Press, 2011), 198–199.

32. Cohen, *Beginnings*, 168.

33. Ibid., 170.

34. Ibid. Cf. 156 in the same book, where Cohen concedes that a Gentile woman's marriage to a *Jew* was "de facto an act of conversion" but insists that such a wife most likely would still regard herself and be regarded by others as a Gentile, although her children would be Jewish. Cohen's basis for such presumptions is not stated. All of this ultimately changes with the later rabbinic innovation that holds that the status of the offspring of intermarriage follows that of the mother. Such a child's status most likely continued to be determined by that of the father (regardless of rabbinic injunctions), for several centuries into the Common Era.

35. Daniel R. Schwartz, "Doing like Jews or Becoming a Jew? Josephus on Women Converts to Judaism," in *Jewish Identity in the Greco-Roman World*, ed. J. Frey, D. Schwartz, and S. Gripentrog (Leiden: Brill, 2007), 108.

36. Ibid., 93–98.

37. Ruth 1:16–17 (New Revised Standard Version).

38. Kraemer, *Unreliable*, 194.

39. Ibid.

40. This last part is implied by Kraemer, although left unstated (ibid.).

41. Cohen, *Beginnings*, 122n36.

42. Seth Schwartz, "How Many Judaisms Were There?," *Journal of Ancient Judaism* 2, no. 2 (2011): 233.

43. On the question of "feminine" versus "masculine" language, it is striking that Seth Schwartz describes Ruth as leaving her *father's* house and accepting the God of *Elimelech's family*, whereas the book itself speaks of the young widows returning each to her *mother's* house (1:8) and of Ruth pledging herself to the God of *Naomi* (1:16).

44. The name Judith, however, is the feminine of the ethnonym *Jew*, a fact that goes unremarked and unelaborated in the book itself, which speaks of the heroine's people consistently as "Israelites."

45. Schwartz, "Doing like Jews," 99.

46. Deuteronomy 23:3 in the Septuagint (LXX)/Christian version.

47. See the discussion of this distinction in the context of ancient Jewish multi-ethnicity in Cynthia Baker, "From Every Nation under Heaven: Jewish Ethnicities in the Greco-Roman World," in *Prejudice and Christian Beginnings*, ed. Elisabeth Schüssler Fiorenza and Laura Nasrallah (Minneapolis: Fortress Press, 2009).

48. See, most recently, Carlin A. Barton and Daniel Boyarin, *Imagine No Religion: How Modern Abstractions Hide Ancient Realities* (New York: Fordham University Press, 2016). I regret that this study—which promises extensive examination of the terms *religio*, *thréskeia*, and *eusebeia*—will appear after the present volume goes to press.

49. Jonathan Hall, *Hellenicity* (Chicago: University of Chicago Press, 2002), 17. See also Jonathan Hall, *Ethnic Identity in Greek Antiquity* (Cambridge: Cambridge University Press, 2000), 34–42.

50. See especially Denise K. Buell, *Why This New Race: Ethnic Reasoning in Early Christianity* (New York: Columbia University Press, 2005).

51. On this, see Baker, "From Every Nation."

52. Quoted from Seneca's *De Superstitione* by Augustine in *City of God* 6.11, emphasis added.

53. On the invention of Hellenes and barbarians, see Hall, *Hellenicity*, 8.

54. The quoted phrase is from Mason, "Jews, Judaeans," 483.

55. Philo, *On the Migration of Abraham* 89-93; for Paul, see Galatians, throughout.

56. Isokrates, *Panegyricus* 50. Scholars debate how narrowly or broadly Isokrates intended his rhetorically potent analysis to apply.

57. See, e.g., Dale Martin, "Paul and the Judaism/Hellenism Dichotomy: Toward a Social History of the Question," in *Paul beyond the Judaism/Hellenism Divide*, ed. Troels Engberg-Pedersen (Louisville: Westminster John Knox, 2001), 30.

58. See the discussion of Denise Buell on "Hellene" in Christian usage, below.

59. See Baker, "From Every Nation," 63-78. In note 40 of that essay, the citation of "2 Maccabees" should read "I Maccabees" in reference to the Spartan connection.

60. I Maccabees 12:1-23. Hall would call the narrative strategy of II Maccabees "oppositional" and that of I Maccabees "aggregative"; see Hall, *Ethnic Identity*, 47-51. See also Buell's adaptation of these categories to her analysis of early Christian racial rhetoric in "Race and Universalism in Early Christianity," *Journal of Early Christian Studies* 10, no. 4 (2002): 441-445. Buell rightly critiques Hall for positing a historical progression from "aggregative" to "oppositional" mechanisms rather than recognizing that both are mobilized throughout history in varying contexts.

61. Philo, *On the Life of Moses* 2.44.

62. On Paul's metaphors of grafting and adoption, see Caroline Johnson Hodge, *If Sons, Then Heirs: A Study of Kinship and Ethnicity in the Letters of Paul* (Oxford: Oxford University Press, 2007), esp. 141-147.

63. Buell, *Why*, 139-140.

64. Ibid., 152-153. See also Greg Woolf, *Becoming Roman: The Origins of Provincial Civilization in Gaul* (Cambridge: Cambridge University Press, 1998); James B. Rives, *Religion in the Roman Empire* (Oxford: Blackwell, 2007); and Steven J. Friesen, *Twice Neokoros: Ephesus, Asia and the Cult of the Flavian Imperial Family* (Leiden: Brill, 1993).

65. See Rives, *Religion*, 148-157.

66. Buell, *Why*, 152-153.

67. Andrew Jacobs, *Remains of the Jews: The Holy Land and Christian Empire in Late Antiquity* (Stanford: Stanford University Press, 2003), 26.

68. On Eusebius's narrative of the degeneration of these "peoples" from "astral polytheism" to "lower" and "later" forms of idolatry, see Aaron P. Johnson, *Ethnicity and*

Argument in Eusebius' Praeparatio Evangelica (New York: Oxford University Press, 2006), 55–100.

69. Jacobs, *Remains*, 26–27.

70. Eusebius, *Demonstratio Evangelica* 1.2, cited and translated by Daniel Boyarin, *Border Lines: The Partition of Judaeo-Christianity* (Philadelphia: University of Pennsylvania Press, 2006), 205.

71. Eusebius, *Praeparatio Evangelica* 1.5 and throughout; *Demonstratio Evangelica* 2.1 and throughout.

72. Daniel Boyarin, "The Christian Invention of Judaism," *Representations* 85, no. 1 (2004): 21.

73. See Mason, "Jews, Judaeans," 473–474. See also Boyarin's discussion of *superstitio* and *religio* in "Christian Invention," 32–33.

74. Johnson, *Ethnicity*, 94, emphasis added. On *Hebrew* versus *Jew* versus *Israel*, see below.

75. Jacobs, *Remains*, 45, quoting *Panarion* 8.3. The Tower of Babel as origin of the world's misguided *ethnē* is a motif developed by Origen in *Contra Celsum*, Book V, and discussed by Buell, "Race and Universalism," 450–453. Epiphanius's gloss on this biblical story is notably different from Origen's, as are his operative categories.

76. Boyarin, *Border Lines*, 206; cf. Jacobs, *Remains*, 44–55; Mason, "Jews, Judaeans," 475.

77. Boyarin cites Seth Schwartz for the language of "disembedding" to describe the perceived dynamic here. Schwartz continues to employ this word and concept while referring to his use of it as strategic and "provocative" rather than simply descriptive ("How Many Judaisms," 236). Cf. Mason, who describes Tertullian's "decoupling of the Judaean people from its land and legitimacy, therefore from what had made it *different in kind* from Christian belief" ("Jews, Judaeans," 473, emphasis in original).

78. Buell, *Why*, throughout. See also Denise Buell, "Early Christian Universalism and Racism," in *The Origins of Racism in the West*, ed. Miriam Eliav-Feldon et al. (Cambridge: Cambridge University Press, 2009).

79. Buell, *Why*, 139.

80. Mason, "Jews, Judaeans," 504–505.

81. Jacobs, *Remains*, 27. Early iterations of this narrative are already found in the New Testament. See, e.g., Acts 17:26–30, where "[God] made from one every race of humans to live on all the face of the earth, having determined allotted periods and the boundaries of their habitations, that they would search for God and perhaps grope after him and [eventually] find him. . . . The times of ignorance God overlooked, but now God commands all humans everywhere to repent." See discussion of this passage in Buell, "Early Christian Universalism," 125–128.

82. Mason, "Jews, Judaeans," 457.

83. *Oxford English Dictionary Online*, s.v. "religion," http://www.oed.com.lprx/view/ Entry/161944?redirectedFrom=religion#eid.

84. The *Oxford English Dictionary Online*, s.v. "ethnic" (http://www.oed.com.lprx/ view/Entry/64786?redirectedFrom=Ethnic#eid), cites the first occurrence of this usage in English in 1851: "That ethnic stock which embraced all existing European races." On modern nationalism and the study of ancient "ethnicity," see Johannes Siapkas, *Heterological Ethnicity: Conceptualizing Identities in Ancient Greece* (Uppsala, Sweden: Uppsala University Press, 2003). For a discussion of the relationship between the terms "ethnicity" and "race," see Denise Buell, "Rethinking the Relevance of Race for Early Christian Self-Definition," *Harvard Theological Review* 94, no. 4 (2001): 450n3. On this, see also Baker, "From Every Nation," 75–76.

85. Joseph Morgan, *Complete History of Algiers* (London: J. Bettenham, 1728), quoted in *Oxford English Dictionary Online*, s.v. "ethnic."

86. W. D. Whitney, "On the So-Called Science of Religion," *Princeton Review* 57, no. 1 (1881): 451, cited by Jonathan Z. Smith, "Religion, Religions, Religious," in *Critical Terms for Religious Studies*, ed. Mark C. Taylor (Chicago: University of Chicago Press, 1998), 277.

87. Smith, "Religion," 278–279.

88. "For the Church," cautions Daniel Boyarin at the close of his *Border Lines*, "Judaism is a religion, but for the Jews . . . only occasionally, ambivalently, and strategically is it so" (224).

89. On the mid-twentieth-century emergence of "identity" as a social-scientific category, see Philip Gleason, "Identifying Identity: A Semantic History," *Journal of American History* 69, no. 4 (1983): 910–931; and Talal Asad, *Formations of the Secular: Christianity, Islam, Modernity* (Stanford: Stanford University Press, 2003), esp. 161. *Identity* is another word, like *religion*, that has no equivalent in ancient Greek, Latin, Hebrew, or Aramaic.

90. Sander Gilman, *The Jew's Body* (New York: Routledge, 1991), 6.

91. Anidjar, *Semites*, 28.

92. Gershom Gorenberg, "A Jew of No Religion," *American Prospect*, October 19, 2011, http://prospect.org/article/jew-no-religion. Gorenberg cites Charles Liebman, *The Ambivalent American Jew* (Philadelphia: Jewish Publication Society, 1973), for his observations about European versus American classifications.

93. See Ralph Slovenko, "Brother Daniel and Jewish Identity," *Saint Louis University Law Journal* 9 (1964): 1–28; Marc Galanter, "A Dissent on Brother Daniel," *Commentary* 36, no. 1 (July 1963): 10–17; and Nechama Tec, *In the Lion's Den: The Life of Oswald Rufeisen* (New York: Oxford University Press, 1990).

94. From Israel's Ministry of Foreign Affairs website: http://www.mfa.gov.il/mfa/ mfa-archive/19501959/pages/law%20of%20return%205710-1950.aspx.

95. In October 2013, the Israeli Supreme Court rejected an appeal on a case brought by Israelis seeking to have their state-issued identification cards register their "ethnicity" not as "Jewish" but as "Israeli." According to a story about the decision in the *Times of Israel*, "The petition was led by Professor Uzzi Ornan, a Jerusalem-born 90-year-old linguist and social activist. When the state was formed in 1948 he refused to be registered as Jewish, claiming he had no religion and was of 'Hebrew' ethnicity. The request was accepted" (Aaron Kalman, "Supreme Court Rules against 'Israeli' Ethnicity on ID," *Times of Israel*, October 3, 2013, http://www.timesofisrael.com/supreme-court-rules-israeli-ethnicity-doesnt-exist/). On "no religion," see Gorenberg, "A Jew."

96. Pew Research Center, "Sidebar: Who Is a Jew?" *Pew Forum: A Portrait of Jewish Americans*, October 1, 2013, http://www.pewforum.org/2013/10/01/sidebar-who-is-a-jew/.

97. Pew Research Center, "A Portrait of Jewish Americans," *Pew Forum: A Portrait of Jewish Americans*, October 1, 2013, http://www.pewforum.org/2013/10/01/jewish-american-beliefs-attitudes-culture-survey/.

98. Scholarship on these matters is, however, voluminous and widely available. I return to the Pew study, briefly, in chapter 3.

99. Zvi Gitelman, ed., *Religion or Ethnicity? Jewish Identities in Evolution* (New Brunswick, NJ: Rutgers University Press, 2009).

CHAPTER 2 — STATE OF THE (JEW[ISH]) QUESTION

Epigraphs for this chapter are from the following: Paul Celan, "Conversation in the Mountains," in *Paul Celan: Selections*, ed. and with an introduction by Pierre Joris (Berkeley: University of California Press, 2005), 149; Judith Butler, *Bodies That Matter: On the Discursive Limits of "Sex"* (New York: Routledge, 1993), 228; William Shakespeare, *Othello*, act 4, scene 2.

1. Adapted from Woody Allen and Marshall Brickman, screenplay for *Annie Hall* (1977).

2. The phrase in question translates to "Are you a *Jew?*" From Franz Kafka, *Letters to Milena*, trans. Phillip Boehm (New York: Schocken Books, 1990), 46.

3. The exchange between Woody Allen's Annie Hall and Alvy Singer, recounted in the Introduction, resonates strongly with Kafka's description here.

4. Jacques Derrida, *Judeities: Questions for Jacques Derrida*, ed. Bettina Bergo, Joseph Cohen, and Raphael Zagury-Orly, trans. Bettina Bergo and Michael B. Smith (New York: Fordham University Press, 2007), 10–11.

5. Derrida's musings echo, for example, those of Rahel Levin (who later converted to Christianity and became Antonie Friederike Varnhagen von Ense), who wrote in 1795: "I have a strange fancy: it is as if some supramundane being, just as I was thrust into this world, plunged these words with a dagger into my heart: 'Yes, have sensibility, see the world as few see it, be great and noble, nor can I take from you the faculty of eternally

thinking. But I add one thing more: be a Jewess!' And now my life is a slow bleeding to death." From Barbara Hahn, "Rahel Levin Varnhagen," in *Jewish Women: A Comprehensive Historical Encyclopedia*, at the *Jewish Women's Archive*, http://jwa.org/encyclopedia/article/varnhagen-rahel-levin. On Varnhagen, see also Hannah Arendt, *Rahel Varnhagen: The Life of a Jewess*, ed. Liliane Weissberg, trans. Richard and Clara Winston (Baltimore: Johns Hopkins University Press, 1997).

6. See Miriam Bodian, "'Men of the Nation': The Shaping of Converso Identity in Early Modern Europe," *Past and Present* 143 (May 1994): 48–76; and Renée Levine Melammed, *A Question of Identity: Iberian Conversos in Historical Perspective* (London: Oxford University Press, 2004), 61–67. "Men of the Nation" has an interesting resonance with the more recently coined phrase "Members of the Tribe," or "MOT."

7. *We Jews: Who Are We and What Should We Do?* is the title of a perplexing book by the well-known rabbi Adin Steinsaltz (San Francisco: Jossey-Bass, 2005). For more on its author's perspective, see below.

8. On Haskalah, see Olga Litvak, *Haskalah: The Romantic Movement in Judaism* (New Brunswick, NJ: Rutgers University Press, 2012).

9. The first quote is from Cynthia Baker, "When Jews Were Women," *History of Religions* 45, no. 2 (November 2005): 115, wherein Michel Foucault's analysis is applied to a reading of the term *Jew* in its scarce appearances in the ancient rabbinic collection known as the Mishnah. The second quote is from Judith Butler, *The Psychic Life of Power: Theories in Subjection* (Stanford: Stanford University Press, 1997), 83. See also Michel Foucault, *Discipline and Punish: The Birth of the Prison*, trans. Alan Sheridan (New York: Random House, 1979).

10. Jean Améry, *At the Mind's Limits: Contemplations by a Survivor on Auschwitz and Its Realities*, trans. Sidney Rosenfeld and Stella Rosenfeld (New York: Random House, 1990), 90–91, emphasis added. Other survivors' accounts reveal a variety of forms of resistance and revolt, some like Améry's but also many others that are far subtler and less overt.

11. Citing Primo Levi's and Giorgio Agamben's focus on the *"Muselmänner,"* those "silenced" death-camp inmates and survivors "who were so extenuated by exhaustion and starvation that they were beyond resistance of even the most minimal kind," Andrew Bush suggests that "it is possible to hear a voice that is not a voice, to recuperate a humanity below the threshold of resistance," and thereby to recognize in that silenced voice a kind of subject (Andrew Bush, *Jewish Studies: A Theoretical Introduction* [New Brunswick, NJ: Rutgers University Press, 2011], 53–54).

12. Kafka, *Letters to Milena*, 217–218. Alternate translations are inserted in square brackets.

13. The term *Yiddish* (translation: "Jewish") is applied to a language family, with many local dialects, that developed from about the tenth century onward in what became Central/Eastern Europe. Yiddish came to be spoken by communities throughout

Europe, the United States, Israel, Latin America, and elsewhere. Although somewhat dated, a good starting place to gain a sense of the history and breadth of this linguistic culture is Max Weinreich, *History of the Yiddish Language* (Chicago: University of Chicago Press, 1980; or New Haven, CT: Yale University Press, 2008). See also Joshua Fishman, ed., *Never Say Die! A Thousand Years of Yiddish in Jewish Life and Letters* (New York: Mouton de Gruyter, 1981). Yiddish is by no means the only historically "Jewish language," and its exploration here is not meant to imply the irrelevance or insignificance of others. Scholarship on these other languages is growing but remains less readily accessible to nonspecialists than does scholarship on Yiddish.

14. Leo Rosten, *The Joys of Yinglish* (New York: Penguin, 1989), 511; Leo Rosten, *The Joys of Yiddish* (New York: McGraw-Hill, 1968).

15. On this, see John Efron, "When Is a Yid Not a Jew? The Strange Case of Supporter Identity at Tottenham Hotspur," in *Emancipation through Muscles: Jews and Sports in Europe*, ed. Michael Brenner and Gideon Reuveni (Lincoln: University of Nebraska Press, 2006).

16. Ibid., 238.

17. The example appears in Michael Wex, *Just Say Nu* (New York: Harper, 2007), 93, parenthetical in the original.

18. Naomi Seidman, *Faithful Renderings: Jewish-Christian Difference and the Politics of Translation* (Chicago: University of Chicago Press, 2006), 1.

19. Ibid., 1–2. The "great Frenchman" cited in Hillel Seidman's speech to the policeman is identified by Naomi Seidman in a footnote as most likely Henri de Bornier (1825–1901).

20. Ibid., 4.

21. Ibid., 4–5, quoting James C. Scott, *Domination and the Arts of Resistance: Hidden Transcripts* (New Haven, CT: Yale University Press, 1990).

22. Seidman, *Faithful*, 3, quoting Weinreich, *History of the Yiddish Language*.

23. Seidman, *Faithful*, 4.

24. Seidman, whose focus is on translation, observes that "translation more particularly appears as a negotiation of an unavoidably asymmetrical *double*-situatedness. As such, it both complicates and is informed by issues of identity" (*Faithful*, 9). The phrase also resonates with W.E.B. Du Bois's statements about "double consciousness" in *The Souls of Black Folk* (New York: Dover, 1903), 2–3.

25. Seidman, *Faithful*, 4. On "Yiddishland," see Gérard Silvain and Henri Minezele, *Yiddishland* (Corte Madera, CA: Gingko Press, 1999); and Jeffrey Shandler, *Adventures in Yiddishland: Postvernacular Language and Culture* (Berkeley: University of California Press, 2006).

26. Seidman, *Faithful*, 10.

27. Yudel Mark, "The Yiddish Language: Its Cultural Impact," in Fishman, *Never Say Die!*, 124.

28. In fact, the *New Oxford American Dictionary* that came standard issue on my computer provides as the "informal" definition of *Christian*: "having or showing qualities associated with Christians, esp. those of decency, kindness, and fairness."

29. *Goyisher mazl*: "Gentile luck"; *goyisher kopf*: non-*yidisher*, not astute, naive, displaying an unselfconscious sense of (Gentile) entitlement. The well-known phrase *mazel tov*—literally, "good luck" or "good fortune"—functions more like the English *congratulations*: an exclamation of delight rather than a wish for a positive outcome.

30. See, for example, Weinreich, *History*, 247–314; Naomi Seidman, *A Marriage Made in Heaven: The Sexual Politics of Hebrew and Yiddish* (Berkeley: University of California Press, 1997), throughout; Benjamin Harshav (who prefers "polylingualism"), *The Meaning of Yiddish* (Berkeley: University of California Press, 1990), 9–40; and Dovid Katz (who prefers "trilingualism"), *Words on Fire: The Unfinished Story of Yiddish* (New York: Basic Books, 2004), 45–77.

31. Weinreich, *History*, 247.

32. Sander Gilman, *Jewish Self-Hatred: Anti-Semitism and the Hidden Language of the Jews* (Baltimore: Johns Hopkins University Press, 1990), 68–69.

33. Ibid., 71–72.

34. Ibid., 81.

35. Michael Meyer, *The Origins of the Modern Jew: Jewish Identity and European Culture in Germany, 1749–1824* (Detroit: Wayne State University Press, 1967), 9.

36. The translation is my own; the sentence is found on the third page of the original German manuscript of Mendelssohn's letter to Lavater.

37. Moses Mendelssohn, *Jerusalem: or On Religious Power and Judaism*, trans. Allan Arkush (Hanover, NH: University Press of New England, 1983), 13. The quote is from the volume's introduction, written by Alexander Altmann.

38. Bush, *Jewish Studies*, 15, emphasis added.

39. Weinreich, *History*, 276. For an excellent analysis of the inherent "hybridity" and "double bind" evident in Mendelssohn's and other German-Jewish translation projects, see Seidman, *Faithful*, 162–177.

40. Meyer, *Origins*, 27–28; Altmann, introduction to Mendelssohn, *Jerusalem*, 13.

41. Gilman, *Jewish Self-Hatred*, 91–98.

42. Ibid., 102.

43. Weinreich, *History*, 247.

44. Seidman, *Marriage*, 1.

45. Ibid., 6.

46. Weinreich, *History*, 323.

47. Wex, *Just Say Nu*, 94.

48. Weinreich, *History*, 274.

49. Daniel Boyarin, *Unheroic Conduct: The Rise of Heterosexuality and the Invention of the Jewish Man* (Berkeley: University of California Press, 1997), 152. Cf. Seidman, *Marriage*, 16–31.

50. Seidman, *Marriage*, 18.

51. Seidman, *Faithful*, 235–236. The latter phrase summarizes a long and detailed discussion comparing Elie Wiesel's earlier, Yiddish, Holocaust memoir, published under the title *Un di velt hot geshvign* (*And the World Kept Silent*) to his well-known French version, *Nuit* (*Night*).

52. Michael Berkowitz, *Zionist Culture and West European Jewry before the First World War* (Cambridge: Cambridge University Press, 1993), 19, emphasis added. Quoted by Seidman, *Marriage*, 116.

53. Daniel Boyarin, in a chapter entitled "The Colonial Drag: Zionism, Gender, and Mimicry," remarks on how, "over and over again, Zionist writers of the 1940s wrote in near-fascist terms of the 'beautiful death' of the Warsaw rebels and the 'ugly death' of the martyrs of the camps" (*Unheroic*, 291–293).

54. Paul Breines, *Tough Jews: Political Fantasies and the Moral Dilemma of American Jewry* (New York: Basic Books, 1990), 142–147. Cf. Seidman, *Marriage*, 116; Gilman, *Jewish Self-Hatred*, 291; Boyarin, *Unheroic*, 76–77.

55. Quoted by Amos Elon, who calls it "a piece of anti-Semitic horror propaganda," in his *Herzl* (New York: Holt, Rinehart, and Winston, 1975), 251–252. Gilman quotes it in *Jewish Self-Hatred*, where he suggests that Herzl's invocation of *Mauschel* "is not aimed at Yiddish-speaking Jews . . . [but merely] represents the antithesis of his romanticized image of his own identity" (239).

56. Quoted by Amnon Rubenstein in his book (translated from the Israeli Hebrew publication *Me-Hertsel 'ad Gush emunim ya-hazarah*) *The Zionist Dream Revisited: From Herzl to Gush Emunim and Back* (New York: Schocken Books, 1984), 4. Also quoted in Breines, *Tough Jews*, 165–166. Cf. Seidman's observations about Jabotinsky's "misogynist revulsion" for Yiddish-inflected Hebrew in *Marriage*, 113. Note the humorously ironic resonance between Jabotinsky's final sentence and the story that opens the present volume.

57. Boyarin, *Unheroic*, 68.

58. Ibid., xxi.

59. Ibid.

60. Seidman, *Marriage*, 136.

61. Emma Morgenstern, "This Polish Grad Student Wants to Help Bring Yiddish Back to Life in Poland," *PRI's The World*, March 24, 2014, http://www.pri.org/

stories / 2014–03–24 / polish-grad-student-wants-help-bring-yiddish-culture-back-life-poland.

62. Dudi Goldman, "Nu? Arab Students' New Shtick: Kibitzing in Yiddish," *Al Monitor*, October 15, 2012, http:// www.al-monitor.com / pulse / culture / 2012 / 10 / the-surprising-students-of-the-c.html.

63. Vita Bekker, "Arab Students in Israel Are Turning to Yiddish," *The National*, July 12, 2013, http:// www.thenational.ae / news / world / middle-east / arab-students-in-israel-are-turning-to-yiddish.

64. Bush, *Jewish Studies*, 20.

65. Ibid., 67.

66. "The Questionnaire: Why Did You Go into Jewish Studies?" *AJS Perspectives: The Magazine of the Association for Jewish Studies* (Spring 2012): 54–58. The writers of these statements are, respectively, Attina Grossman, Alan Mintz, Deborah Green, Alan Mintz, Anita Norich, Seth Schwartz, Froma I. Zeitlin, and Na'ama Rokem.

67. See, e.g., "AJS Directory of Endowed Chairs in Jewish Studies," http:// www.ajsnet.org / chairs.php.

68. Moshe Idel, foreword to *Inventing the Jew: Antisemitic Stereotypes in Romanian and Other Central European Cultures*, by Andrei Oisteanu (Lincoln: University of Nebraska Press, 2009), ix.

69. Steven F. Kruger, *The Spectral Jew: Conversion and Embodiment in Medieval Europe* (Minneapolis: University of Minnesota Press, 2006), xvii.

70. Bryan Cheyette, *Constructions of "the Jew" in English Literature and Society: Racial Representations, 1875–1945* (Cambridge: Cambridge University Press, 1993), 8–9.

71. Mitchell B. Hart, *The Healthy Jew: The Symbiosis of Judaism and Modern Medicine* (Cambridge: Cambridge University Press, 2007), 25.

72. On the latter, see, e.g., Sander Gilman, *Multiculturalism and the Jews* (New York: Routledge, 2006).

73. Sander Gilman, *The Jew's Body* (New York: Routledge, 1991), 3–6.

74. Hart, *The Healthy Jew*, 23–24.

75. Ibid., 24.

76. Ibid., 24–25.

77. Ibid., 25–26.

78. Ibid., 26.

79. Ibid.

80. Gilman, *The Jew's Body*, 7–8.

81. Ibid., 8.

82. Seidman, *Faithful*, 278, emphasis added.

83. Ibid.

84. Juliet Steyn, *The Jew: Assumptions of Identity* (London: Cassell, 1999), 1.

85. Ibid., emphasis in the original.

86. Ibid., 5, emphasis in the original.

87. Jay Geller, *The Other Jewish Question: Identifying the Jew and Making Sense of Modernity* (New York: Fordham University Press, 2011), 2, emphasis in the original; Rogers Brubaker, *Ethnicity without Groups* (Cambridge, MA: Harvard University Press, 2004), 41, 44.

88. Steyn, *The Jew*, 13, emphasis in the original.

89. Jonathan Z. Smith, "What a Difference a Difference Makes," in *"To See Ourselves as Others See Us": Christians, Jews, "Others" in Late Antiquity,* ed. Jacob Neusner and Ernest S. Frerichs (Chico, CA: Scholars Press, 1985), 5.

90. Steyn, *The Jew*, 18, emphasis in the original.

91. Ibid.

92. Clement Greenberg, "Self-Hatred and Jewish Chauvinism: Some Reflections on 'Positive Jewishness,'" *Commentary,* November 1950, 434, emphasis in the original.

93. The phrase "denial of right" is drawn from Derrida's reflections at the beginning of the present chapter.

94. Steyn, *The Jew*, 141.

95. David Suchoff, introduction to *The Imaginary Jew*, by Alain Finkielkraut, trans. Kevin O'Neill and David Suchoff (Lincoln: University of Nebraska Press, 1994), vii.

96. Finkielkraut, *The Imaginary Jew*, 176.

97. Ibid., 33.

98. Ibid., 34.

99. Ibid., 18.

100. Steyn, *The Jew*, 13.

101. Finkielkraut, *The Imaginary Jew*, 34.

102. Ibid.

103. Cited in Daniel Boyarin and Jonathan Boyarin, "Diaspora: Generation and the Ground of Jewish Identity," *Critical Inquiry* 19, no. 4 (Summer 1993): 698.

104. Finkielkraut, *The Imaginary Jew*, 34, 18.

105. Ibid., 18.

106. Alain Badiou, *Polemics*, trans. Steve Corcoran (London: Verso, 2006), 159; cf. Judith Butler, *Giving an Account of Oneself* (New York: Fordham University Press, 2003), 92–96.

107. Badiou, *Polemics*, 160.

108. Ibid., 170, 247, 230–247, respectively.

109. Finkielkraut, *The Imaginary Jew*, 34; Badiou, *Polemics*, 214.

110. See Finkielkraut, *The Imaginary Jew*, 33.

111. Ibid., 14–15.

112. These words are spoken by a character, "a Jewish mathematician," in Badiou's novel *Calme bloc ici-bas*, excerpted in Badiou, *Polemics*, 186.

113. Jean-Paul Sartre, *Anti-Semite and Jew*, trans. George J. Becker (New York: Schocken Books, 1948).

114. Finkielkraut, *The Imaginary Jew*, 33–34.

115. Zygmunt Bauman, "Allosemitism: Premodern, Modern, Postmodern," in *Modernity, Culture and 'the Jew,'* ed. Bryan Cheyette and Laura Marcus (Cambridge: Polity Press, 1998), 147.

116. Jean-François Lyotard, *Heidegger and "the jews,"* trans. Andrea Michel and Mark S. Roberts (Minneapolis: University of Minnesota Press, 1990), 3. The translators of the English-language volume, in keeping with English conventions, capitalize each of the letters I have placed in square brackets in the quotation. I have substituted lowercase letters where Lyotard employed them in the French-language original for reasons that I hope will become clear below.

117. The statement is Jean-Claude Milner's (*L'arrogance du présent: Regards sur une décennie: 1965–1975* [Paris: Grasset, 2009], 212), quoted and affirmed by Slavoj Žižek in a critique of Zionism entitled "The Jew Is within You, but You, You Are in the Jew," in Udi Aloni with Slavoj Žižek, Alain Badiou, and Judith Butler, *What Does a Jew Want? On Binationalism and Other Specters* (New York: Columbia University Press, 2011), 168.

118. Finkielkraut, *The Imaginary Jew*, 34.

119. Jonathan Boyarin, invited response to Sarah Hammerschlag's *The Figural Jew: Politics and Identity in Postwar French Thought*, http://divinity.uchicago.edu/martycenter/publications/webforum/102010/Boyarin%20Response%20to%20Hammerschlag.pdf. Boyarin's remarks are a condensation of "Diaspora: Generation and the Ground of Jewish Identity," 693–725, a longer and more developed engagement with Lyotard's formulation that he coauthored with his brother Daniel Boyarin.

120. Geoffrey Bennington, "Lyotard and 'the Jews,' " in Cheyette and Marcus, *Modernity, Culture and "the Jew,"* 194.

121. Alain Finkielkraut, "The Glamourous Appeal of the Common Noun," in his *In the Name of Humanity*, trans. Judith Friedlander (New York: Columbia University Press, 2000), 39. The quote continues, "such was the humanistic charm of Stalin in 1945," referencing not *Jews*, in this case, but an imagined Soviet collective subject.

122. Max Silverman, "Re-figuring 'the Jew' in France," in Cheyette and Marcus, *Modernity, Culture and "the Jew,"* 205.

123. Butler, *Bodies That Matter*, 230.

124. Derrida, *Judeities*, 18.

125. *Yehi 'or* is a transliteration of the Hebrew "Let there be light" (Gen. 1:3); *dos pintele yud* is a transliteration of the Yiddish "the dear / little point of [the tenth letter of the Hebrew alphabet] *yud*," and a play on *pintele yid* (the "Jewish spark," or "essential Jewishness"). The divine name *yhwh* first appears in Genesis 2; a story of its revelation to Moses is narrated in Exodus 3.

126. Derrida, *Judeities*, 10, italics in the original translation. I have substituted "names / nouns" where the translators have settled on one or the other word to translate the indeterminate French *"noms."*

127. Boyarin and Boyarin, "Diaspora," 697.

128. Finkielkraut, *The Imaginary Jew*, 32.

129. Derrida, *Judeities*, 5.

130. Sarah Hammerschlag, *The Figural Jew: Politics and Identity in Postwar French Thought* (Chicago: University of Chicago Press, 2010), 5–10.

131. Ibid., 18.

132. Ibid., 21.

133. Jonathan Boyarin, invited response to Sarah Hammerschlag's *The Figural Jew*; see note 119, above.

134. Hammerschlag, *The Figural Jew*, 10.

135. Ibid., 266.

136. Finkielkraut, *The Imaginary Jew*, 32–33, emphasis in the original.

137. Ibid., 175.

138. Ibid., 18.

139. Steinsaltz, *We Jews*, 5.

140. Art Spiegelman, *MetaMaus: A Look Inside a Modern Classic, Maus* (New York: Pantheon, 2011), 148–149.

141. Art Spiegelman, "Art on Art" (digital voice recording of the author), in *The Complete Maus Files*, DVD accompanying Spiegelman, *MetaMaus*.

142. "Time Flies" is the subtitle of the second chapter of the second volume of *Maus*—a title underlined by a visual pun of swarming flies born from a mountain of rotting mouse corpses that hold up the drafting desk of the now wildly successful author of *Maus I* (Art Spiegelman, *Maus II* [New York: Pantheon, 1991], 41).

143. Spiegelman, *MetaMaus*, 8–9.

144. Ibid., 301; Spiegelman, *Maus II*, 5.

145. Joshua Furst, "How a Schlumpy Kid Named Art Spiegelman Changed Pop Culture," *Jewish Daily Forward*, November 21, 2013, http://www.forward.com/articles/187977/how-a-schlumpy-kid-named-art-spiegelman-changed-po/?p=all.

146. Butler, *Bodies That Matter*, 230.

147. Améry, *Mind's Limits*, 82.

148. Ibid., 83.

149. Ibid., 83–84.

150. Ibid., 84.

151. Indeed, it is uncertain that Steinsaltz, an Orthodox rabbi, would even recognize Améry as a *Jew* due to the "mixed" parentage of Améry's mother, whereas Israel's Law of Return would recognize him as one.

152. Rebecca Goldstein, *Mazel* (New York: Viking, 1995), 224.

153. Judith Butler, *Parting Ways: Jewishness and the Critique of Zionism* (New York: Columbia University Press, 2012), 15.

154. Ibid., 19–20.

155. Finkielkraut, *The Imaginary Jew*, 162–163.

156. Jonathan Boyarin and Daniel Boyarin, *Powers of Diaspora* (Minneapolis: University of Minnesota Press, 2002), 4–5.

157. Alisa S. Lebow, *First Person Jewish* (Minneapolis: University of Minnesota Press, 2008), xvi.

158. Ibid.

159. Ibid., xvi–xvii.

160. Ibid., xix.

161. Ibid., xxvii, quoting Faye Ginsburg, emphasis in the original.

162. This orientation is evidenced in the lively and worldwide Jewish Film Festival circuit.

163. Lebow, *First Person*, 93–94.

164. Ibid., 108–109.

165. The film was released in 1998; Lebow's "autocritique" of it, in 2008.

166. Finkielkraut, *The Imaginary Jew*, 178–179.

167. Butler, *Parting Ways*, 6–7.

CHAPTER 3 — IN A NEW KEY: NEW *JEWS*

Epigraphs for this chapter are from the following: Faye Ginsberg, "The Canary in the Gemeinschaft? Disability, Film, and the Jewish Question," in *Deus in Machina: Religion, Technology, and the Things in Between*, ed. Jeremy Stolow (New York: Fordham University Press, 2013), 160; filmmaker Stephen Frears to interviewer Naomi Pfefferman, regarding his son born with a genetic disease, familial dysautonomia, associated with Ashkenazi populations, in Naomi Pfefferman, "Hidden Heritage Inspires Director," *Jewish Journal*, September 27, 2001, http://www.jewishjournal.com/arts/article/hidden_heritage_inspires_director_20010928/; Shireen M. Mazari, "Are Muslims Europe's New Jews?," *Pakistanpal's Blog*, July 17, 2009, http://www.pakistanpal.wordpress.com/tag/europe-new-jews/.

1. Oz Almog, *The Sabra: The Creation of the New Jew*, trans. Haim Watzman (Berkeley: University of California Press, 2000), 4.

2. Haim Watzman, "Translator's Note," in ibid., xv.

3. Homi K. Bhabha, *The Location of Culture* (London and New York: Routledge, 1994), 8, 10, 2, respectively.

4. See, e.g., Michael F. Hammer et al., "Extended Y Chromosome Haplotyes Resolve Multiple and Unique Lineages of the Jewish Priesthood," *Human Genetics* 126 (August 2009): 707–717.

5. See, e.g., Keith Wailoo and Stephen Pemberton, "Eradicating a 'Jewish Gene': Promise and Pitfalls in the Fight against Tay-Sachs Disease," chap. 1 in *The Troubled Dream of Genetic Medicine: Ethnicity and Innovation in Tay-Sachs, Cystic Fibrosis, and Sickle Cell Disease* (Baltimore: Johns Hopkins University Press, 2008); and Jessica Mozersky, *Risky Genes: Genetics, Breast Cancer, and Jewish Identity* (New York: Routledge, 2013).

6. On the new *Jews* resulting from communist campaigns, see, e.g., Jonathan Dekel-Chen, "'New' Jews of the Agricultural Kind: A Case of Soviet Interwar Propaganda," *Russian Review* 66, no. 3 (July 2007): 424–450; and David Shneer, *Yiddish and the Creation of Soviet Jewish Culture 1918–1930* (Cambridge: Cambridge University Press, 2004).

7. Zionist Organization Statement on Palestine at the Paris Peace Conference, February 3, 1919, from *Jewish Virtual Library*, http://www.jewishvirtuallibrary.org/jsource/History/zoparis.html.

8. Vladimir Jabotinsky, "A Letter on Autonomism," *Evreiskaya zhizn* no. 6 (June 1904), as translated in *Israel among the Nations: Selection of Zionist Texts*, ed. Zvi Zohar (Jerusalem: World Zionist Organization, Organization Department, Research Section, 1966), 110–111.

9. Ibid., 117.

10. Jabotinsky's face, for example, adorned the hundred-shekel bill from 1978 to 1984, and, according to a 2007 Israeli newspaper article, more street signs, parks, and squares throughout Israel bear Jabotinsky's name than that of any other figure (Ofer Petersburg, "Jabotinsky Most Popular Street Name in Israel," *Ynetnews*, November 28, 2007, http://www.ynetnews.com/articles/0,7340,L-3476622,00.html).

11. See Raphael Falk, "Zionism and the Biology of the Jews," *Science in Context* 11, no. 3–4 (January 1998): 587–607; Raphael Falk, "Zionism, Race, and Eugenics," in *Jewish Tradition and the Challenge of Darwinism*, ed. Geoffry Cantor and Marc Swetlitz

(Chicago: University of Chicago Press, 2006); and Raphael Falk, *Zionut Vehabiologia shel Hayehudim* (Tel Aviv: Ressling, 2006). Cf. Nadia Abu El-Haj, *The Genealogical Science: The Search for Jewish Origins and the Politics of Epistemology* (Chicago: University of Chicago Press, 2012).

12. Quoted in Mitchell B. Hart, *Social Science and the Politics of Modern Jewish Identity* (Stanford: Stanford University Press, 2000), 29.

13. Ibid., 29–30.

14. Ibid., 31.

15. The quoted phrases are Bhabha's, cited above.

16. On further such "midrashic" gestures, see Cynthia M. Baker, "Nationalist Narratives and Biblical Memory," in *Celebrate Her for the Fruit of Her Hands: Essays in Honor of Carol Meyers*, ed. Susan Ackerman, Charles E. Carter, and Beth Alpert Nakhai (Winona Lake, IN: Eisenbrauns, 2015).

17. David appears as a reluctant but deeply committed young leader of the young nation in Herzl's novel *Altneuland* (Leipzig: Hermann Seemann Nachfolger, 1902); Jabotinsky's Samson is the eponymous protagonist in his novel *Samson Nasorei* (Berlin: Slovo, 1927). On Nordau's Bar Kochba gymnastic club, see Gideon Reuveni, "Sports and the Militarization of Jewish Society," in *Emancipation through Muscles: Jews and Sports in Europe*, ed. Michael Brenner and Gideon Reuveni (Lincoln: University of Nebraska Press, 2006), 47.

18. George L. Mosse, "Max Nordau, Liberalism, and the New Jew," *Journal of Contemporary History* 27, no. 4 (October 1992): 576–577.

19. Vladimir Jabotinsky, *The Road to Zionist Revisionism: Essays from Resviyet 1923–1924* [Hebrew], ed. Y. Nedava (Tel Aviv: Jabotinsky Institute, 1984), 106–109, 115–119; English translation from *Jewish Virtual Library*, https://www.jewishvirtuallibrary.org/jsource/Zionism/ironwall.html.

20. Ibid.

21. Yitzhak Conforti, "'The New Jew' in the Zionist Movement: Ideology and Historiography," *Australian Journal of Jewish Studies* 25 (2011): 103.

22. Ibid., 103, quoting from Yitzhak Ben-Zvi, *Shear Yeshuv* [Hebrew], ed. M. Ish-Shalom (Jerusalem: Yad Ben-Zvi, 1965), 9; and Yitzhak Ben-Zvi, *The Land of Israel and the Jewish Settlements at the Time of the Ottoman Empire* [Hebrew] (Jerusalem: Bialik Institute, 1955), 15, emphasis added.

23. Conforti, "'The New Jew,'" 104.

24. *"Altneuland"* is, of course, a reference to the Zionist visionary novel penned by Theodore Herzl. For a schematic review of contending versions of the new Jew among Zionist thinkers, see Conforti, "'The New Jew.'" Cf. Amnon Rubenstein, *The Zionist Myth Revisited: From Herzl to Gush Emunim and Back* (New York: Schocken, 1984), 7.

25. See, e.g., Gad Barzilai, "Who Is a Jew?: Categories, Boundaries, Communities, and Citizenship Law in Israel," in *Boundaries of Jewish Identity*, ed. Susan A. Glenn and Naomi B. Sokoloff (Seattle: University of Washington Press, 2010).

26. Falk, "Zionism, Race, and Eugenics," 156.

27. Robert Tissot, "Population Genetics," online document for Human Genetics course at the University of Illinois, Chicago, https://www.uic.edu/classes/bms/bms655/lesson13.html.

28. Duana Fullwiley, "The Molecularization of Race: U.S. Health Institutions, Pharmacogenetics Practice, and Public Science after the Genome," in *Revisiting Race in a Genomic Age*, ed. Barbara A. Koenig, Sandra Soo-Jin Lee, and Sarah S. Richardson (New Brunswick, NJ: Rutgers University Press, 2008).

29. Jonathan Kahn, "Patenting Race in a Genomic Age," in *Revisiting Race*, ed. Koenig, Lee, and Richardson, throughout.

30. Gil Atzmon et al., "Abraham's Children in the Genome Era: Major Jewish Diaspora Populations Comprise Distinct Genetic Clusters with Shared Middle Eastern Ancestry," *American Journal of Human Genetics* 86 (June 2010): 850.

31. Sander L. Gilman, "Foreword," in *Race, Color, Identity: Rethinking Discourses about "Jews" in the Twenty-First Century*, ed. Efraim Sicher (New York: Berghahn Books, 2013), xv.

32. Harry Ostrer, *Legacy: A Genetic History of the Jewish People* (New York: Oxford University Press, 2012), xiii.

33. Doron Behar et al., "The Genome-Wide Structure of the Jewish People," *Nature* 466 (July 2010): 238–242.

34. Anna Need et al., "A Genome-Wide Genetic Signature of Jewish Ancestry Perfectly Separates Individuals with and without Full Jewish Ancestry in a Large Random Sample of European Americans," *Genome Biology* 10 (January 2, 2009): R7, doi: 10.1186/gb-2009–10–1–r7, emphasis added.

35. Sander Gilman, "The New Genetics and the Old Eugenics: The Ghost in the Machine: Guest Editor's Introduction," *Patterns of Prejudice* 36, no. 1 (2002): 3–4.

36. Gilman, "Foreword," in Sicher, *Race, Color, Identity*, xvi.

37. Petter Hellström, "Genetic Diaspora, Genetic Return," *Studies in History and Philosophy of Biological and Biomedical Sciences* 44 (2013): 442.

38. The World Wide Web address provided in multiple publications for the Jewish Hapmap Project, http://pediatrics.med.nyu.edu/genetics/research/jewish-hapmap-project, appears to be nonfunctional as of March 2016. *Hapmap* is short for "haplotype map."

39. Ostrer, *Legacy*, 33.

40. Ibid., 220.

41. On the problem of disparate understandings of "ancestry" in genetics, see Charmaine D. Royal et al., "Inferring Genetic Ancestry: Opportunities, Challenges, and Implications," *American Journal of Human Genetics* 86 (May 2010): 661–673.

42. Atzmon et al., "Abraham's Children."

43. Ibid., 850.

44. Ibid., 858.

45. Moshe Rosman, *How Jewish Is Jewish History?* (Oxford: Littman Library of Jewish Civilization, 2007), 47.

46. Atzmon et al., "Abraham's Children," 851.

47. Ibid., 855.

48. Ibid., 857.

49. Ibid.

50. There is, for example, no clear evidence for widespread Jewish proselytism in antiquity.

51. Atzmon et al., "Abraham's Children," 851, emphasis added.

52. Ibid., 857.

53. Ibid.

54. Doron Behar et al., "Multiple Origins of Ashkenazi Levites: Y Chromosomes Evidence for Both Near Eastern and European Ancestries," *American Journal of Human Genetics* 73 (2003): 768–779.

55. Marta D. Costa et al., "A Substantial Prehistoric European Ancestry amongst Ashkenazi Maternal Lineages," *Nature Communications* 4.2543 (October 8, 2013), doi: 10.1038/ncomms3543.

56. Several books summarize and popularize many of the highest-profile studies in this field. Besides Ostrer's book, these include David B. Goldstein, *Jacob's Legacy: A Genetic View of Jewish History* (New Haven, CT: Yale University Press, 2008); Jon Entine, *Abraham's Children: Race, Identity, and the DNA of the Chosen People* (New York: Grand Central Publishing, 2007); and Rabbi Yaakov Kleiman, *DNA and Tradition: The Genetic Link to the Ancient Hebrews* (Jerusalem: Devora Publishing, 2004), which includes a preface recommending "this masterful book" by geneticist Karl Skorecki, director of the Rappaport Research Institute at the Technion-Israel Institute of Technology.

57. Sam Vaknin (pen name), "Europe's New Jews," *Ezine Articles*, April 23, 2005, http://ezinearticles.com/?Europes-New-Jews&id=30310. This piece has been reproduced on multiple websites since its first publication.

58. Mazari, "Are Muslims."

59. Ibid. Mazari's words echo a sentiment voiced by Abdel Azeem Hamad, editor of the Egyptian daily *al-Shorouk*, and reprinted around the world via the Associated Press.

60. Ibid.

61. Ibid.

62. Ibid.

63. Ibid., emphasis added.

64. Steffen Winter, "The Marwa Al-Sherbini Case: Investigators Believe Killer 'Hated Non-Europeans' and Muslims," *Spiegel Online International*, September 2, 2009, http://www.spiegel.de/international/germany/the-marwa-al-sherbini-case-investigators-believe-killer-hated-non-europeans-and-muslims-a-646292.html.

65. Odile Quintin, "Opening Speech" to a roundtable meeting on "Manifestations of Islamophobia in Europe" (Brussels, Belgium, February 6, 2003), in *The Fight against Anti-Semitism and Islamophobia: Bringing Communities Together: A Summary of Three Round Table Meetings Initiated by Commissioner Anna Diamantopoulou* (Brussels/Vienna: European Commission, 2003), 57.

66. Odile Quintin, "Opening Speech" to a roundtable meeting on "Manifestations of Anti-Semitism in Europe" (Brussels, Belgium, December 5, 2002), in *The Fight against Anti-Semitism and Islamophobia*, 12, emphasis added.

67. David Cesarani, "Muslims the 'New Jews'? Not by a Long Way," *Jewish Chronicle Online*, January 17, 2008, http://www.thejc.com/comment/comment/muslims-new-jews%E2%80%99-not-a-long-way.

68. Ibid.

69. James Kirchick, "Meet the New Jews, Same as the Old Jews: Why 'Islamophobia' in Europe Cannot Be Equated with Anti-Semitism, Either in Nature or Degree," *Tablet*, August 28, 2014, http://www.tabletmag.com/jewish-news-and-politics/182608/islamophobia-anti-semitism.

70. Ibid.

71. Ibid.

72. Maleiha Malik, "Muslims Are Now Getting the Same Treatment Jews Had a Century Ago," *Guardian*, February 1, 2007, http://www.theguardian.com/commentisfree/2007/feb/02/comment.religion1.

73. Ibid.

74. Kirchick, "Meet the New Jews."

75. Ibid.

76. Diana Pinto, "Israel Poses a Serious Dilemma for Europe's Jews," *Haaretz*, February 13, 2014, http://www.haaretz.com/opinion/israel-poses-a-serious-dilemma-for-europe-s-jews.premium-1.503489.

77. Diana Pinto, "Are There Jewish Answers to Europe's Questions?" *European Judaism* 39, no. 2 (Autumn 2006): 50.

78. Matti Bunzl, *Anti-Semitism and Islamophobia: Hatreds Old and New in Europe* (Chicago: Prickly Paradigm Press, 2007), 14.

79. Ibid., emphasis in the original.

80. Ibid., 14–15.

81. Quoted from a speech at the Assemblée Nationale, in Natasha Lehrer, "The Threat to France's Jews," *Guardian*, January 15, 2015, http://www.theguardian.com/news/2015/jan/15/-sp-threat-to-france-jews.

82. Valls's speech clearly resonates with that delivered by Hillel Seidman to the gendarme at the Gare de l'Est in postwar Paris, recounted by Naomi Seidman in her *Faithful Renderings: Jewish-Christian Difference and the Politics of Translation* (Chicago: University of Chicago Press, 2006), 1–2, discussed in chapter 2.

83. Efraim Sicher, "Jews, Muslims, European Identities: Multiculturalism and Anti-Semitism in Britain," in Sicher, *Race, Color, Identity*, 290.

84. Bhabha, *Location of Culture*, 2, 8.

85. Esra Özyürek, "The Politics of Cultural Unification, Secularism, and the Place of Islam in the New Europe," *American Ethnologist* 32, no. 4 (November 2005): 512.

86. Bunzl, *Anti-Semitism and Islamophobia*, 12.

87. Ibid., 13. Cf. Talal Asad, *Formations of the Secular: Christianity, Islam, Modernity* (Stanford: Stanford University Press, 2003), esp. chap. 5, "Muslims as a 'Religious Minority' in Europe."

88. Bunzl, *Anti-Semitism and Islamophobia*, 13.

89. Ibid., 14.

90. Özyürek, "The Politics of Cultural Unification," offers a particularly cogent critique of the term.

91. Dominic Boyer, "Welcome to the New Europe," *American Ethnologist* 32, no. 4 (November 2005): 523.

92. Yascha Mounk, "Europe's Jewish Problem: The Misunderstood Rise of European Anti-Semitism," *Foreign Affairs*, September 17, 2014, https://www.foreignaffairs.com/articles/western-europe/2014-09-17/europes-jewish-problem.

93. Ibid.

94. Paul A. Silverstein, "Comment on Bunzl," in Bunzl, *Anti-Semitism and Islamophobia*, 64–65.

95. Mazari, "Are Muslims."

96. Stephan J. Kramer, "In Solidarity with All Muslims," *Qantara*, July 13, 2009, http://en.qantara.de/content/stephan-j-kramer-on-the-murder-of-marwa-al-sherbini-in-solidarity-with-all-muslims.

97. Ibid.

98. Mounk, "Europe's Jewish Problem."

99. Silverstein, "Comment on Bunzl," 64–65.

100. Jonathan Boyarin observes that "'Anti-Semitism' becomes unbearably oxymoronic when used as a label for a phenomenon found, according to [many users of the phrase 'new anti-Semitism'] . . . primarily among Muslims" (Jonathan Boyarin, "Discerning the Ghosts and the Interests of the Living," *American Ethnologist* 32, no. 4 [November 2005]: 516). On Jewish/Muslim dynamics in France, in particular, see Maud S. Mandel, *Muslims and Jews in France: History of a Conflict* (Princeton, NJ: Prineton University Press, 2014).

101. Silverstein, "Comment on Bunzl," 66–67.

102. Cesarani, "Muslims the 'New Jews'?"

103. Ibid.

104. Silverstein, "Comment on Bunzl," 67.

105. Pinto, "Are There Jewish Answers," 55, emphasis added.

106. Ibid., 53.

107. Ibid., 55.

108. Ibid., 50.

109. Pinto, "Israel Poses a Serious Dilemma."

110. Ibid.

111. Ibid.

112. Pinto, "Are There Jewish Answers," 51.

113. Reports of criticism by local or national Jewish leaders in Europe may be found in virtually every major press report of such calls by Israeli prime ministers. See, e.g., John Hall and Dan Bloom, "'I Will Not Let People Believe That Jews No Longer Have a Place in Europe': Hollande's Fury after Netanyahu Makes Plea for 'Mass Emigration' to Israel in Wake of Anti-Semitic Terror Attacks," *DailyMail*, February 16, 2015, http://www.dailymail.co.uk/news/article-2955293/French-PM-slams-Israel-s-call-Jews-leave-amid-fears-terror-attack-tells-France-wounded-you.html; and "French Jews 'Must Move to Israel,'" *BBC News*, July 18, 2004, http://news.bbc.co.uk/2/hi/middle_east/3904943.stm.

114. Caryn Aviv and David Shneer, *New Jews: The End of the Jewish Diaspora* (New York: New York University Press, 2005), 64.

115. Diana Pinto, "I'm a European Jew—and No, I'm Not Leaving," *New Republic*, March 26, 2015, https://newrepublic.com/article/121388/why-jews-arent-leaving-europe-contra-atlantics-jeffrey-goldberg.

116. Pinto, "Are There Jewish Answers," 50.

117. Ibid., 51–52.

118. Pinto, "Israel Poses a Serious Dilemma."

119. Ibid., emphasis added.

120. Gemma Mullin et al., "'The Chief Rabbi's Son, Shop Worker Saving for His Marriage, Teacher and Pensioner: Faces of Kosher Deli Hostages Killed by Jew-Hating Jihadist—One of Whom Was Executed When He Grabbed One of Terrorist's Guns and It JAMMED," *DailyMail*, January 9, 2015, http://www.dailymail.co.uk/news/article-2903950/First-chilling-image-shows-murdered-hostage-dramatic-standoff-ends-deaths-terrorist-four-captives.html; "France Attacks: 'Hero' Lassana Bathily Gets Citizenship," *BBC News*, January 20, 2015, http://www.bbc.com/news/world-europe-30905262; and Dimi Reider, "Netanyahu's Invitation to French Jews Was Awkward. For Many Reasons," *Reuters*, January 14, 2015, http://blogs.reuters.com/great-debate/2015/01/14/netanyahus-invitation-to-french-jews-was-awkward-for-many-reasons/.

121. Lauren Frayer, "After 522 Years, Spain Seeks to Make Amends for Expulsion of Jews," *National Public Radio*, December 25, 2014, http://www.npr.org/sections/parallels/2014/12/25/371866778/after-522-years-spain-seeks-to-make-amends-for-expulsion-of-jews.

122. Cnaan Liphshiz, "Citizenship for Sephardic Jews 'Corrects Historical Wrong': Jewish Dreamers and Fortune Seekers First in Line for Portuguese Citizenship under a 2013 Law," *Times of Israel*, April 12, 2015, http://www.timesofisrael.com/citizenship-for-sephardic-jews-corrects-historical-wrong/. Cf. Philip Roth, *Operation Shylock: A Confession* (New York: Simon and Schuster, 1993).

123. Shaul Magid, *American Post-Judaism: Identity and Renewal in a Postethnic Society* (Bloomington: Indiana University Press, 2013), 33.

124. Aviv and Shneer, *New Jews*, xvi, emphasis in the original.

125. Ibid., xiii, 18–19.

126. James A. Sleeper and Alan L. Mintz, eds., *The New Jews* (New York: Random House, 1971).

127. Ibid., 5.

128. Ibid., 24; Richard Siegel, Michael Strassfeld, and Sharon Strassfeld, eds., *The Jewish Catalog* (New York: Jewish Publication Society, 1973). Two subsequent volumes, *The Second Jewish Catalog* and *The Third Jewish Catalog*, edited by the Strassfelds, were also published by JPS in 1976 and 1980, respectively.

129. Aviv and Shneer, *New Jews*, 1, emphasis added.

130. Ibid., 20.

131. Daniel Boyarin and Jonathan Boyarin, "Diaspora: Generation and the Ground of Jewish Identity," *Critical Inquiry* 19, no. 4 (Summer 1993): 711.

132. Ibid., 723. See also Daniel Boyarin, *A Traveling Homeland: The Babylonian Talmud as Diaspora* (Philadelphia: University of Pennsylvania Press, 2015).

133. Boyarin and Boyarin, "Diaspora: Generation," 721.

134. Ibid.

135. Ibid.

136. Melanie Kaye/Kantrowitz, *The Colors of Jews: Racial Politics and Radical Diasporism* (Bloomington: Indiana University Press, 2007), xii.

137. Aviv and Shneer, *New Jews*, 175.

138. Magid, *American Post-Judaism*, 5, 21.

139. Quoted in ibid., 31.

140. The terms designate Buddhist Jews and Jewish Sufis, respectively. On the former, see, e.g., Rodger Kamenetz, *The Jew in the Lotus* (San Francisco: Harper One, 2007).

141. Magid, *American Post-Judaism*, 31.

142. Ibid.

143. See http://www.tabletmag.com.

144. Susannah Heschel, "The Myth of Europe in America's Judaism," in *Writing a Modern Jewish History: Essays in Honor of Salo W. Baron*, ed. Barbara Kirshenblatt-Gimblett (New York: The Jewish Museum and Yale University Press, 2006), 103.

145. Ibid.

146. Ibid.

147. Ibid., emphasis added.

148. Ibid., 104.

149. Jonathan Freedman, *Klezmer America: Jewishness, Ethnicity, Modernity* (New York: Columbia University Press, 2008), 326.

150. Ibid., 325. Freedman is quoting from the liner notes to the album *Jewface* (Idelsohn Society, 2006).

151. Yvonne Chireau and Nathaniel Deutsch, eds., *Black Zion: African American Religious Encounters with Judaism* (New York: Oxford University Press, 2000), 6–7.

152. Ibid., 7.

153. Ibid.

154. Ibid., 8.

155. Tudor Parfitt, *Black Jews in Africa and the Americas* (Cambridge, MA: Harvard University Press, 2013), 91–92.

156. Ibid., 77.

157. Bernard J. Wolfson, "African American Jews: Dispelling Myths, Bridging the Divide," in *Black Zion*, ed. Chireau and Deutsch, 41. Such biblical traditions include, for example, the Hebrews' going forth from North Africa (Egypt); Moses's own wife's (and therefore his descendants') being black; King Solomon's close alliance with the Queen of Sheba (a place that came to be identified as Ethiopia); and the flight to North Africa by refugees from the Babylonian conquest of Judaea.

158. Ibid., 51.

159. See http://www.bechollashon.org/projects/paja.php.

160. See http://www.bechollashon.org/about/mission.php.

161. This gesture is of a piece with other assertions of unity that run throughout Institute for Jewish and Community Research publications, accompanied by the frequent labeling of criticism of Israel's actions or policies, or any anti-Israel protest, as "anti-Jewish"—that is, as antisemitism. On the concept of "Jewish Peoplehood," see Noam Pianko, *Jewish Peoplehood: An American Innovation* (New Brunswick, NJ: Rutgers University Press, 2015).

162. "I was a Black Jew before I was a Jew Jew," says Funnye (quoted in Wolfson, "African American Jews," 46).

163. Heschel, "The Myth," 91.

164. Ibid., 92, 104.

165. See Janet Liebman Jacobs, *Hidden Heritage: The Legacy of the Crypto-Jews* (Berkeley: University of California Press, 2002), 83–99.

166. Ibid., 105–106.

167. Ibid., 145–146.

168. On this, see Maria Elena Martínez, *Genealogical Fictions: Limpieza de Sangre, Religion, and Gender in Colonial Mexico* (Stanford: Stanford University Press, 2008).

169. Jonathan Freedman, "Conversos, Marranos, and Crypto-Latinos: The Jewish Question in the American Southwest (and What It Can Tell Us about Race and Ethnicity)," in *Boundaries*, ed. Glenn and Sokoloff, 192. Freedman here cites Judith S. Neulander's anthropological fieldwork among American Southwestern crypto-*Jews* and, in particular, her article "The New Mexican Crypto-Jewish Canon: Choosing to Be 'Chosen' in Millennial Tradition," *Jewish Folklore and Ethnology Review* 18 (1994): 19–58.

170. Judith S. Neulander, review of *To the End of the Earth: A History of the Crypto-Jews of New Mexico*, by Stanley M. Hordes, *Shofar: An Interdisciplinary Journal of Jewish Studies* 25, no. 2 (January 2007): 179.

171. Freedman, "Conversos," 196–197.

172. Ibid., 199.

173. Magid, *American Post-Judaism*, 56.

174. Ibid.

175. Ibid., 49–50.

176. Pew Research Center, *A Portrait of Jewish Americans: Findings from a Pew Research Center Survey of U.S. Jews* (Washington, DC: Pew Research Center's Religion & Public Life Project, 2013).

177. Ibid., 120, emphasis in the original.

178. Ibid., 9.

179. Ibid.

180. Ibid., 15.

181. Ibid., 7–8, emphasis added.

182. Will Herberg, *Protestant, Catholic, Jew* (New York: Doubleday, 1955). Herberg explores the "paradox" presented by American religiosity expressed in tandem with a strong "trend toward secularism" (13). In plotting generational movement between (second-generation) ethnic assimilation and (third-generation) religious reclamation on the part of immigrant groups in the United States, Herberg observes that "among the Jews alone [the] religious community bore the same name as the old ethnic group and was virtually coterminous with it. The young Jew for whom the Jewish immigrant-ethnic group had lost all meaning, because he was an American and not a foreigner, could still think of himself as a Jew" (202).

183. Magid, *American Post-Judaism*, 30–31, emphasis in the original.

184. Susan Katz Miller, *Being Both: Embracing Two Religions in One Interfaith Family* (Boston: Beacon Press, 2013), ix.

185. The Half-Jewish Network: https://half-jewish.net; Interfaith Community: http://www.interfaithcommunity.org; Interfaithfamily: http://www.interfaithfamily.com.

186. Miller, *Being Both*, 225, x.

187. Chav Doherty, "The *Trayf* Jew," in *Balancing on the Mechitza: Transgender in Jewish Community*, ed. Noach Dzmura (Berkeley, CA: North Atlantic Books, 2010), 20–21.

188. Boyrarin and Boyarin, "Diaspora: Generation," 721.

189. Doherty, who studied the Jewish mystical traditions from which the messianic concept of *tikkun olam* arises, invokes this hope in the final paragraph of his essay ("The *Trayf* Jew," 22).

190. William Sánchez, quoted in Entine, *Abraham's Children*, 29.

191. Laurie Zoloth, "Yearning for the Long-Lost Home: The Lemba and the Jewish Narrative of Genetic Return," in *Jews and Genes: The Genetic Future in Contemporary Jewish Thought*, ed. Elliot N. Dorff and Laurie Zoloth (New York: Jewish Publication Society, 2015), 174.

192. Mozersky, *Risky Genes*, 77–78.

193. Freedman, "Conversos," 195.

194. Ibid., 197.

195. Parfitt, *Black Jews*, 169.

196. Ibid., 164.

197. Zoloth, "Yearning," 167.

198. Ibid., 177.

199. Ibid., 176.

200. Introduction to Dorff and Zoloth, *Jews and Genes*, xv, emphasis in the original.

201. Harry Ostrer and Karl Skorecki, "The Population Genetics of the Jewish People," *Human Genetics* 132 (2013): 125.

202. Rebecca Alpert, "What Is a Jew? The Meaning of Genetic Disease for Jewish Identity," in Dorff and Zoloth, *Jews and Genes*, 155. See also Ginsburg, "The Canary."

203. Pfefferman, "Hidden Heritage."

204. Zoloth, "Yearning," 177–178.

205. Ginsburg, "The Canary," 161. Ginsburg here cites and quotes Sander Gilman, "The New Genetics and the Old Eugenics."

206. Abu El-Haj, *The Genealogical Science*, 243–244.

Index

About the Author

CYNTHIA M. BAKER (M.T.S. Harvard, Ph.D. Duke) is the author of numerous works on Jews and history, including *Rebuilding the House of Israel: Architectures of Gender in Jewish Antiquity*, "When Jews Were Women," and "A Jew by Any Other Name?" She is a professor and chair of Religious Studies at Bates College.